THE DISPOSSESSED: LIFE AND DEATH IN NATIVE CANADA

Geoffrey York was the Winnipeg Bureau-Chief for *The Globe and Mail* where he covered native issues from 1983-1990. He now works for the *Globe & Mail* in Ottawa. His article on the repatriation of adopted Indian children was nominated for a National Newspaper Award. Geoffrey York is the author of *The High Price of Health: A Patient's Guide to the Hazards of Medical Politics*.

Tomson Highway is a Cree Indian from Brochet, Manitoba. He is the author of the highly acclaimed plays *The Rez Sisters*, which was nominated for a Governor General's award, and *Dry Lips Oughta Move to Kapushasing*. He has received two Dora Mavor Moore Awards and is the Artistic Director of Native Earth Performing Arts, a native theatre company based in Toronto.

The Dispossessed

The Dispossessed

Life and Death in Native Canada

Geoffrey York

V

VINTAGE U. K.

VINTAGE U. K.
20 Vauxhall Bridge Rd
London 5W1V 2SA

FIRST EDITION

Canadian Cataloguing in Publication Data

York, Geoffrey, 1960-
   The dispossessed

1st paperback ed.
Includes bibliographical references.
ISBN 0-09-982540-6

1. Indians of North America – Canada – Social
conditions.   2. Indians, Treatment of – Canada.
I. Title.

E78.C2Y67 1990   305'.897'071   C90-094603-2

Jacket design by Robin Uchida

Printed and bound in Canada by Gagné Ltée
for Vintage U. K.

First published by
Lester & Orpen Dennys 1989
Vintage U.K. edition 1990

Contents

Foreword

It's been seven lifetimes since Europeans first arrived on the shores of North America. Our ancestors, of course, had already lived here for many thousands of years. But as early as that very first encounter, extraordinary events began to occur among us. That initial meeting touched off a shock wave that was felt by Indian people right across the continent. And is still felt to this day.

The events and conditions documented in this book are all too true. Hardly a day goes by that the average Canadian does not read or hear about them in the media: poverty on the reserves, invasion of hunting and trapping grounds by corporate interests, inequities in education and justice.

It does not mean, however, that these circumstances have to continue, because they won't. And they won't, precisely because we are witnessing the emergence of a generation of Indian people clearly more vocal, more articulate, and more aggressively unwilling to continue playing victim.

This generation is fluent in the English language for one thing, but, even more important, it is armed with university degrees and diplomas. We now have chiefs with degrees in the arts and in the sciences, we have Indian lawyers, we have Indian businessmen and businesswomen who can negotiate the complexities of the modern corporation and of free enterprise, and we have artists—writers not least among them— who are just now beginning to make their presence felt in the national and international arenas. And these are people who come from the very heart of the Indian reserves this book speaks of.

I myself come from the Brochet Reserve in northwestern Manitoba, one of the province's most remote and certainly one that has not been left unscarred by the forces of social and spiritual destruction. Like many of those whose lives are described in this volume, I went through the entire Indian residential school system—nine years at the Guy Hill Indian Residential School near The Pas, Manitoba—and the entire white foster home cycle, through three years of high school in Winnipeg, where I was one of two Indians in a middle-class high school of approximately two thousand mostly Anglo-Saxon students. And after having survived that, I went on to receive the benefit of a first-class university education.

I was one of the lucky ones. My parents are strong, beautiful people, as are my numerous brothers and sisters. And they all, except for three, speak nothing but Cree and, in the case of my parents, Chipewyan. The white people whom I happened to meet and associate with along the way were, almost without exception, tremendously supportive and encouraging. With their help, I am now, like many Indians of my generation, able to go back to help my people—equipped, this time, with the wisdom of Homer and Faulkner and Shakespeare and Bach and Beethoven and Rembrandt and McLuhan and many other thinkers, artists, and philosophers of the white world, but equipped, as well, with the wisdom and the vision of Big Bear and Black Elk and Chief Seattle and Tom Fiddler and Joe Highway and the medicine people, the visionaries of my ancestry—and the Cree language in all its power and beauty.

At all times I have had the Trickster sitting beside me. In Cree we call him/her *Weesageechak*—the being who inhabits that area of our dream world, our subconscious, where we connect with the Great Spirit, with God. As with every mythology the world over, she/he—in Cree, there is no gender—is the central hero figure, that essential link, who exists to teach us about the nature and the meaning of existence on the planet Earth. It is just unfortunate that his/her first meeting, seven lifetimes ago, with the central hero figure from that other mythology—Christian mythology—was so shocking and resulted in so many unpleasant occurrences.

But we of this generation are fixing that. Ever so little by little, we are picking the Trickster, that ancient clown, up from under that legendary beer table on Main Street in Winnipeg or Hastings Street in Vancouver, and will soon have her standing firmly up on his own two feet so she can make us laugh and dance again. Because, contrary to the viewpoint presented by that other hero figure, what she says foremost is that we are here to have one hell of a good time.

It's an exciting time to be alive, seven lifetimes after that first meeting. I look forward to every minute of it.

Tomson Highway
Toronto, Ontario
May 1989

Introduction

As we sat in Albert Julian's kitchen, watching the solitary flight of a bald eagle over the luminescent blue waters of Bras d'Or Lake on Cape Breton Island, I listened to the story of the Micmacs of Malagawatch— the people who once lived on the wooded peninsula across the lake. Albert Julian's aunt was one of them. She is buried on the peninsula in an unmarked grave.

No one lives at Malagawatch today. In the early 1940s, in an effort to cut administrative costs, the Canadian government moved all the residents of that thriving community to Eskasoni, an isolated reserve southwest of Sydney. The houses at Malagawatch were emptied and burned down, and within a few years the place was a silent forest. Although government officials knew that Eskasoni could support only twenty families, more than two thousand Micmacs are now crowded into the reserve, jammed between the lake and the hills. Farming is impossible because nobody has enough land, and other economic activities are limited because of Eskasoni's isolation.

Albert Julian still lives on the reserve today. As administrator of the band, he doles out the welfare cheques that are the legacy of the federal government's destructive policy.

When I visited him, he took me to see Malagawatch—now an empty peninsula with an almost mystical presence. Its original residents and their descendants return each summer to remember their deserted home.

A few months before my conversation with Albert Julian, I had talked with Ruby Dunstan, the fiery chief of the Lytton band in the Fraser Canyon of British Columbia's interior. Her office is just a stone's throw from the cliffs overlooking the confluence of the Thompson and Fraser rivers. She was talking about the sheer terror of her years in an Indian residential school from 1948 to 1953. Like dozens of others across Canada, the school was operated by missionaries who tried to suppress Indian culture.

Ruby Dunstan's parents were told they would be jailed if they refused to force their child to attend. At the school, the Indian children were whipped if they tried to speak their own language, their clothing was taken away and replaced by uniforms, and they were not permitted to see their own parents, except under strict regulations. "You were told you shouldn't be an Indian, but you knew damn well that you'd always been an Indian, you couldn't change," Dunstan recalled.

A couple of years earlier, I had watched a beaver roasting over a crude wood stove in northern Quebec. It was soon to be a meal for a Cree family living in a one-room shack in the Quebec wilderness. Like all the houses of the Cree of Chibougamau, their overcrowded shack was a fire trap. Rain and snow blew through holes in the walls and the wooden floor and foundations were rotting. Many of the neighbouring houses were covered with makeshift roofs of plastic sheets that could collapse at any moment. Children were falling ill from the polluted lake water that they were forced to drink because there was no running water.

Preoccupied with their daily survival, the Chibougamau Cree did not dwell on the events of the 1950s and the 1960s—the years of exodus and transience that had shaped their fragile existence today. Time after time, they were dislodged by governments and mining companies, until they were scattered in six remote campsites, squatters on their own land. There they were ignored while the federal and provincial governments argued over the question of whether a reserve should be created for them.

The stories of the people of Malagawatch and Lytton and Chibougamau are unique in their own ways, but each is an example of the physical and cultural dislocations that have devastated native communities across Canada. In the second half of the twentieth century—hundreds of years after the arrival of Europeans in North America—white society is continuing to devise new ways to strip aboriginal people of their land, their culture, their spiritual beliefs, and their way of life.

Strangely, most Canadians are better acquainted with the history of native people in the eighteenth and nineteenth centuries than they are with the unsavoury realities of recent years. Canadians know that the early settlers and governments took land from the Indians, but it is easy to feel detached from those events of long ago. It is more difficult to deny responsibility for the misguided policies of the twentieth century. And so the ugly events of recent history are buried behind a wall of illusion—the illusion that progressive thinking and improved attitudes have brought fair treatment to Canada's native people.

Occasionally, a twentieth-century tragedy—a Grassy Narrows or a Lubicon Lake— is revealed and debated. Yet it is treated as an isolated event, a curious aberration, a temporary lapse in the judgement of the administrators and leaders of our civilized society. There is rarely any understanding of the sheer number of similar events taking place in aboriginal communities across the country. And few Canadians realize the connections between all of these stories—the recurring pattern of the disintegration of entire communities as a direct consequence of assaults made by the institutions of modern Canadian society.

In this book I try to show those connections. Hundreds of native communities are still enduring the malignant effects of institutions that seem benign to non-native Canadians: the churches, religious boarding schools, provincial and federal schools, child welfare agencies, courts, government departments, hydro corporations, and resource developers. The social conditions on modern-day reserves are a legacy of the decisions and policies of the most powerful institutions of the nineteenth and twentieth centuries. Many of those policies—and the attitudes that shaped them—still exist today.

There are about 450,000 status Indians in Canada, about two-thirds of whom live on Indian reserves. They are the members of 596 registered Indian bands. In addition, there are perhaps 500,000 non-status Indians and people of Métis origin. Together the Métis and Indians represent about 4 percent of the national population—the fourth-largest ethnic group in the country.

In this book I do not attempt to portray the issues facing the Inuit, nor do I try to describe the unique history of the Métis people. However, thousands of Métis are living side-by-side with Indians in northern native communities and most are grappling with identical problems in the courts, housing, health, the child welfare system, and the economic system. For that reason, the Métis are included in several of the chapters in this book. To exclude them would be to create an artificial dividing line where none really exists.

This book is a collection of stories from Indian and Métis communities across Canada. Each story is intended simply as an introduction to the major issues facing aboriginal people today. The focus is on ordinary people and their leaders and how they are coping with the legacy of Canadian policies that have led to physical and cultural dislocation.

Perhaps the most remarkable element in these accounts is the vitality of native culture—a culture which has survived persecution, endured centuries of hardship, and eventually produced solutions to the problems imposed on aboriginal people by Canadian society. These solutions, too, are part of the story in each community. The events that take place in native communities are often portrayed as grim tragedies to be lamented and written off. The truth of these stories is different. Ultimately, they are stories of hope and an indomitable spirit.

Geoffrey York
Winnipeg, Manitoba
August 1989

CHAPTER ONE

Shamattawa: The Gasoline Plague

You begin to understand the overwhelming isolation of Shamattawa when you try to telephone someone on the reserve. It can take several days to reach the Cree Indian band's administrative office. You ask the Winnipeg operator to connect you to Shamattawa 6020, and she calls another operator, who tries to complete the call. After a few seconds, she says: "Sorry, NC"—which means there are no circuits available for this remote community in a desolate corner of northeastern Manitoba.

The operators try again and again over the next few hours or days, and eventually they find a circuit available. It is something like a Westerner's attempt to telephone a civil servant in a tiny country in Africa or the Middle East. But this is not the Third World. This is Canada.

There is something else that troubles the outsider in those first hesitant contacts with Shamattawa. Something is missing. There is none of the familiar routine of a receptionist or secretary answering your call. Instead of these comfortable office rituals, the telephone at Shamattawa is answered by a child who quickly hangs up. Or it is answered by an unidentified person who apparently cannot hear your voice. They, too, hang up. Or the telephone rings endlessly and is not answered at all.

*

It is the fall of 1987 and a small airplane from the northern Manitoba mining town of Thompson is flying to Shamattawa. For an hour, it travels above forests and lakes where there is no sign of human life, then touches down on a bumpy airstrip.

The reserve's ninety houses are scattered at the confluence of two powerful rivers, Gods River and the Echoing River, overlooking an austere and barren wilderness. In the early fall, a sharp Arctic wind blows down from the north, and at night the remote sound of geese honking can be heard far overhead. The northern lights are an awesome spectacle in Shamattawa. It is one of the few inhabited places in the world where the aurora borealis is pure and unsullied by the artificial lights of civilization. Scientists have travelled to Shamattawa to study the nightly miracle of those strange mystical curtains of celestial light hovering above the ramshackle dwellings of the reserve.

The houses, strewn randomly in an area of several square kilometres, are each the size of a suburban garage. Most are tattered and weatherbeaten; very few have glass windows. After years of rock throwing by bored teenagers, many of the windows are covered with plastic sheets or wooden planks. In the winter, there is frost on the inside of the walls. Packs of dogs roam through the reserve, and garbage blows through the scrub between the houses. A few children are wandering around. Despite the bitter wind and the freezing temperatures, most of them are wearing just a shirt or a thin polyester jacket.

The unemployment rate at Shamattawa exceeds 80 percent. Of the band's population of about seven hundred people, more than one-third are essentially homeless—sharing the overcrowded homes of friends or relatives, or living in shacks or decaying houses that desperately need replacement. The people of Shamattawa get their water in buckets from the river, and their homes are heated by wood stoves constructed from old oil drums. The stoves are constant fire hazards, sometimes sparking fatal blazes. To gather wood to heat their homes, the Cree Indians travel as far as fifteen kilometres, towing the fuel back by snowmobile or floating it down the river to the reserve in large rafts. Each year, as the trees disappear, the hunt for firewood becomes more difficult.

Because of the cost of transportation, food is extremely expensive. A litre of milk costs $2.08—more than double the price in Winnipeg. A loaf of bread goes for $1.79, and a 284-millilitre can of soup is $1.24. Gasoline is about $1.80 a litre. A young boy's cotton and polyester jacket is priced at $73.98. The Hudson's Bay store, where most of these items are purchased, still dominates the reserve in its centuries-old role as the chief trading post—but now the Cree cash their social assistance cheques there in exchange for bags of groceries.

For years, bizarre stories of violence and tragedy have trickled out of Shamattawa, condensed into the cold sentences of the daily police reports. A pair of juveniles was arrested for the shooting deaths of two adults, one of whom was the father of one of the juveniles. A twelve-year-old girl was charged with the attempted murder of an infant who was immersed in water, kicked, whipped, and abandoned in the bush. A woman was charged with arson after her infant daughter suffered burns to 85 percent of her body in a house fire. Teachers and nurses have fled from Shamattawa, afraid of further outbreaks of violence. In the newspapers of southern Manitoba, Shamattawa has been branded as the most dangerous community in the province.

Some of the mysteries of Shamattawa can be explained by a quick tour of the reserve. The telephones, it turns out, are ancient devices controlled by a curious cranking mechanism. They operate on a party-line system, so that they are easily clogged by one or two calls. It sometimes takes two hours for a resident to contact an outside office. Only the RCMP and the nursing station have the luxury of modern telephones. Yet the crank-operated telephones are actually a sign of improvement for the reserve. Until the early 1980s, Shamattawa was forced to use radio phones to contact the outside world. If the weather was bad, the radios were useless.

The other mysteries of Shamattawa are harder to solve. The outsider watches a game of floor hockey at a brand-new school gymnasium. For three hours, without a single break, the Indian teenagers rush silently and tirelessly up and down the gymnasium floor. There is no elbowing or slashing or fighting—not a single act of violence in three hours. There is not even a referee. The hockey game at Shamattawa is much cleaner and more sportsmanlike than high school games in the big cities of southern Canada. The people of Shamattawa are not a violent people. By instinct and by disposition, they are peaceful. And yet there are horrifying crimes of violence on the reserve. Why? The answers are not easy or simple. The clues lie deeper, at the heart of the Indian condition in Canada after centuries of discrimination and colonialism.

For hundreds of years, the Shamattawa Cree were an important band, controlling about 50,000 square kilometres of northeastern Manitoba. They roamed throughout their territory, hunting and fishing as the seasons changed. In the nineteenth century, they trapped and traded their furs at a Hudson's Bay Company post at York Factory.

The Cree of Shamattawa were ignored by the federal government for decades. Unlike many other Indian bands, they were so isolated that they were no obstacle to the advance of white settlement and industry. There was no need to shunt them onto a reserve to keep them out of the way. But in 1908, the federal government decided to confirm its legal control of northern Manitoba. Treaty commissioners were sent into the region to persuade the Indians to sign an "adhesion" to Treaty Number Five, which had originally been signed by several other Prairie Indian bands in 1875. (The previous four treaties had been signed in northwestern Ontario and the southern regions of the Prairies from 1871 to 1874.)

Under the terms of the treaty, the Shamattawa Cree surrendered all rights to their traditional land. In exchange, they were given an annual payment of $5 per person and were offered the same benefits as those given to the southern bands—farming equipment and cattle (which were useless in the northern wilderness), schools, and money for the purchase of ammunition and twine. They were also promised a reserve, equal to 160 acres for every family of five. Similar terms were included in every other Prairie treaty.

For the administrative convenience of the federal commissioners, the Shamattawa Cree were lumped in with two unrelated bands. Their treaty was signed at York Factory in August of 1910, but no land was allocated for several decades. It was not until 1947 that the government recognized the Shamattawa Cree as a separate band. And it was not until 1978 that the Shamattawa reserve was legally established.

The band members continued their nomadic life of hunting and trapping until the 1940s. Then, as they were gradually drawn into the bureaucratic world of compulsory education and welfare payments, they were required to settle at a fixed location. A federal school was built, and the children were required to attend. To avoid the breakup of their families, and to ensure they received their social assistance cheques, the Shamattawa Cree were forced to settle at the site where they live today. Soon, as fur prices in Europe dropped drastically, their trapping fell into decline and they became dependent on government assistance. Their traditional culture was broken and replaced by a new one.

Only about one-quarter of the 2,300 Indian reserves in Canada were created by treaties. Most reserves—particularly in British Columbia and the Maritimes—were simply set aside by legislation or Cabinet order as an allocation of land for Indians. Under the Indian Act, reserves are not legally owned by the six hundred bands that inhabit them. Even the reserves created by treaty are legally owned by the federal government, which retains tremendous powers to expropriate or sell the land.

The people of Shamattawa managed to avoid the restrictions of life on a reserve until the 1940s—much later than most Canadian Indian bands, who were pushed onto reserves in the second half of the nineteenth century. But regardless of when it occurred, the transition to life on the reserve was traumatic and dislocating for most bands. They were effectively stripped of the power to control their own lives. Even today, the bylaws and spending decisions of the elected chiefs and councillors can be vetoed by the federal government whenever the Indian Affairs minister decides that a particular bylaw or decision is inappropriate.

The chief of the Shamattawa band is Judah Miles, a respected elder who heads an elected council. Although the chief and council are technically the senior authorities on the reserve, the Indian Act curtails their powers in key areas. They have trouble raising money for business ventures, for example, because they are not permitted to mortgage their land. And before they can purchase land, they need approval from Ottawa.

By controlling the flow of money to the reserve, the Department of Indian Affairs[1] can influence many of the most important decisions

---

[1] The Department of Indian Affairs was created in 1880 to govern the lives of Canada's aboriginal people. In later years, the department became a branch of several different departments. But in 1966, a separate department—now known as Indian and Northern Affairs—was again established.

on the reserve. Economic development, education, housing, programs to fight alcohol abuse—all depend on budget approvals from the department's offices in Ottawa or the regions. Judah Miles and his council, like the elected councils at most other Indian reserves across Canada, are left without much effective power. Their main job is the administration of the monthly welfare cheques.

The public buildings at Shamattawa are segregated into two separate areas. The school, the nursing station, and the RCMP office are grouped together at one end of the reserve, not far from the airport. These are tidy new buildings, built by the federal government at a cost of millions of dollars. The other public buildings—the band administrative office, a drop-in centre, and a small band-owned convenience store—stand near the Hudson's Bay store on the riverbank, surrounded by the homes of the Indians.

The white residents of Shamattawa include the Hudson's Bay managers, the RCMP officers, the Anglican missionary, the teachers, and the nurses. All of them are housed in their own compounds, isolated from the grim daily reality of Indian life on the reserve. The whites are the only residents who enjoy the comforts of running water, indoor plumbing, and modern heating. Without these benefits, few whites would agree to live on an Indian reserve, and it would be impossible to recruit teachers and nurses. So the white compounds have become an inevitable sight in every Indian community.

Because of Shamattawa's reputation for crime and violence, many teachers and nurses are reluctant to accept jobs at the reserve. Those who do agree to move to Shamattawa tend to be young men and women with cheerful, optimistic personalities. Most of them remain at Shamattawa for a year or two. Then their ideals and their good intentions begin to fade away, and they move on.

Despite the friendly behaviour of the white residents, they are still perceived as symbols of the authority of outside institutions. For decades, Indian leaders have resented the dominance of white agencies in their communities. The situation of Shamattawa in 1987 is typical of most reserves in Canada. The nurses are hired by the federal Health and Welfare Department. The police officers are assigned by the Royal Canadian Mounted Police. The teachers are hired by the Indian Affairs Department. And the Hudson's Bay managers are assigned by their head office. All of them are crucial decision makers in the community, yet they are controlled by outsiders.

Beyond the walls of the white compounds, Shamattawa is a tightly knit community. In their battles with crime and addiction, the Cree tend to rise or fall together. Almost all of the Cree on the reserve are closely or distantly related to each other. Two surnames—Miles and Redhead—predominate among the band members.

The Shamattawa band office and the nearby drop-in centre are battered structures, resembling barracks, with boarded-up windows. There are no locks on the doors. In fact, there are not even any doorknobs—a loop of wire holds the door shut. There is nothing to indicate that this building is one of the focal points of the community. The only sign on the exterior of the office is a small "1981" tacked above the door to indicate the date of construction.

Inside the band office, there are muddy floors and a collection of desks and chairs. Here, once a month, the people of Shamattawa wait patiently for their social assistance cheques from the federal government—$100 each for food and $27.20 for clothing, plus a similar amount for each child in the family. At the back of the building is a meeting room. Along the top of the walls are a series of drawings and small posters in crayon and pencil, most of which were produced by the school children of the reserve. Many of the drawings have anti-alcohol messages. One portrays a prone man flat-out on a snowbank, with a bottle next to him and a caption reading: "Stay sober, live longer."

About half a kilometre from the band office is the home of Bertie Miles. There are two families living in his small shack—a typical living arrangement for hundreds of people at Shamattawa. For many months, thirteen people from three families had shared the house. Bertie Miles is thirty years old and unemployed. Married for the past thirteen years, he has six children ranging in age from two months to twelve years old, yet he has never had a house of his own.

His children sleep together on mattresses or the couch. The house is heated erratically by a 150-litre gasoline container that has been converted into a stove. Plastic sheets are tacked over the empty windows, and the sheets are flapping violently in the freezing wind. One of the holes in the sheets is plugged with a jacket, and a baby's pyjama is stuffed into another. To prepare for the winter, Miles will have to purchase more plastic sheeting from the Hudson's Bay store, at a cost of $4.39 per metre, to cover the windows and the holes. There are huge rolls of plastic sheeting at the store, but almost everyone needs some. "Sometimes it runs out and you can't buy it," says Miles.

"The house is no good," he goes on. "It's cold in the winter. It's hardly ever warm in the bedroom. It gets cold quickly at night. We can't keep the stove going when we're sleeping. When it rains, it leaks through the windows and it drips in the bedroom."

The flimsy houses are easy to break into, and thieves often intrude. Usually they are looking for gasoline.

Gasoline is the lifeblood of Shamattawa. It is the lifeblood of any northern Indian reserve. Without it, the Cree cannot run their skidoos or their motorboats. Without these vehicles, they cannot collect firewood to heat their homes, nor can they hunt or fish or trap to supplement their social assistance cheques.

But gasoline is also the deadliest poison at Shamattawa. Children and teenagers sniff it to gain a quick escape, a cheap and immediate high—a few minutes of euphoria in a land of poverty and misery. It gives them a sense of power. Their fears and inhibitions disappear, and they begin to hallucinate. Their attraction to gasoline becomes irresistible. The children of Shamattawa teach each other how to inhale it. At night, they break into snowmobile gas-tanks to steal more of the precious substance, until finally it dominates their existence.

In the daylight outside the shacks, children are clutching plastic bags containing grimy rags, soaked in gasoline. They amble casually through the brush, between the houses, carrying their bags. A young girl playfully waves a rag in a dog's face. Some of the children are just five or six years old.

At the federal school on the reserve, the teachers can tell if their students have been sniffing. "They're very hard to control," says George Redhead, a band employee who is leading the battle against gas sniffing. "They don't sit still. They're restless. Their eyes are red and glassy. It affects everything in their body—physically, mentally—the nervous system, the brain, hearing, seeing. Even their appetite. They don't eat much if they're a sniffer. It affects every part of them."

Maggie Miles, a Shamattawa band official who specializes in education, watches the children in their classes at school. "We can tell which ones do a lot of sniffing," she says. "They come in the afternoon and they're drowsy. You can tell from the odour on their clothes. After several days of sniffing, they get shaky and they can't cope with anything. They're not there. They just shake and they can't concentrate on anything. Sometimes they're just wandering around the school. Some students have been sniffing for years."

In the summer, George Redhead has to keep a close eye on his small Honda all-terrain vehicle to make sure the children don't break into it. "If I leave my Honda outside after 9:30 at night and my lights are out, they're here right away, taking the gas. Some of them are chronic sniffers. They want to sniff all the time. It's like a drug. They need it in their system."

Medical experts have concluded that gasoline sniffing is one of the most dangerous addictions in the world. It is so addictive that a single inhalation can be enough to hook a child. The hydrocarbons in the gasoline have the same effect as drugs like LSD, producing euphoria and a state of altered consciousness. Gasoline sniffers often become convinced that they are invincible.

Once inhaled, gasoline harms the kidneys and liver, and inflicts permanent damage on the nervous system and the brain, especially those parts of the brain that control visual coordination, motor skills, and memory. It impairs the cognitive abilities that would normally permit children to learn. In the early stages of its use as an inhalant, gasoline reduces inhibitions and thus can help to trigger violence. Chronic sniffers become dull and clumsy, shake uncontrollably, and sometimes have difficulty walking. They often become anemic and suffer weakness in their arms and legs. The emotional and psychological consequences of gasoline sniffing are just as severe: it produces feelings of paranoia, isolation, and indifference toward oneself and others.

Gas sniffing is a serious problem at scores of native communities across the country. At the Cree community of South Indian Lake in northern Manitoba, the bodies of two children are buried in graves behind a ramshackle house. They were gas sniffers, and their graves were intended to be a warning to others in the community. But the warning is ignored. Teachers at South Indian Lake still discover child sniffers passed out on the floor of the school washroom.

Over the past twenty years, many Canadian Indian children have died from the devastating physical effects of inhalant abuse. Others have been crippled or have become permanently retarded. Pregnant women who sniff gasoline have delivered babies with serious birth defects.

Epidemics of gasoline sniffing were first noticed in the Indian communities of northern Manitoba in the early 1970s. But the problem has been recorded in most of Canada's provinces. In 1975, a survey of Ojibway Indians at Poplar Hill in Ontario found that 22 percent were chronic gasoline sniffers. High lead levels were discovered in their blood. At about the same time, a survey of Cree and Inuit youths at Great Whale River in northern Quebec revealed that 62 percent had sniffed gasoline at least once in the previous six months. Gasoline sniffing has also been reported among Indian and Métis children in inner-city Winnipeg, and it has been reported at several Alberta Indian reserves, including one where children as young as nine years old were sniffing.

In 1986 a detailed study commissioned by an association of twenty-five northern Manitoba bands, found that 70 percent of all Indian children in northern Manitoba had sniffed gasoline. About 1,400 of these children were in "serious trouble" and needed treatment for their addiction.

The researchers described the life of a seventeen-year-old native boy who had started sniffing when he was nine. He slept most of the day, got up to sniff gasoline, and then went back to bed. He ate no regular meals and was poorly nourished. His parents were unemployed alcoholics. He did not respond to questions, did not talk, kept to himself, and said only "I don't know" when people asked him anything.

Researchers, including those who conducted the northern Manitoba study, have found that gasoline sniffing can trigger extreme violence—a clue to the horror stories that have come out of Shamattawa and other reserves. "On one of the reserves, during the winter months," the Manitoba researchers wrote, "four teens broke into a small house while under the influence of sniffing. They brutally beat and raped a fragile and deaf seventy-two-year-old grandmother, breaking ribs. At the end of the ordeal, one half of her face was caved in through repeated blows."

Police and court officials in northwestern Ontario have heard the same kinds of stories. In the early 1980s, they estimated that gasoline sniffing was linked to 60 to 70 percent of the crime committed by juveniles in the reserves north of Kenora.

It is mostly the children and the teenagers who sniff gasoline, but adults are also among the abusers. The study in northern Manitoba found at least four reserves where parents were sniffing with their children. Shamattawa was one of the four. Some parents have used gasoline to sedate their infant children.

Gasoline is not the only substance that is inhaled. The children of Shamattawa have discovered that the same intoxicating effects are produced by glue, nail-polish remover, wood filler, aerosol sprays, typewriter correction fluid, and felt-tip markers. Once hooked, the sniffers will try anything. Teenagers who travel to Thompson for medical appointments return to Shamattawa with large stocks of nail-polish remover, which they sell to their friends for $15 a bottle. For a while, some of the children succeeded in getting nail-polish remover from department store mail-order catalogues. The caps from the bottles litter the ground near their homes.

Children on other reserves have made the same discoveries. At one reserve in northern Manitoba during a cold winter month, an eight-year-old Indian boy was found dead, his body frozen and tangled in a barbed-wire fence. The only clue to his death was a white coating of typewriter correction fluid in his nostrils. The autopsy concluded that the boy was a victim of "sudden sniffing death syndrome"—a common cause of death on the reserves today. The heartbeat of a sniffer becomes irregular because of the chemicals in the inhalants. Then, when he tries to run or fight, adrenalin rushes through his body and his heartbeat becomes even more irregular and uncontrollable. His heart fails and he dies.

To combat the sniffing problem, the Hudson's Bay store at Shamattawa has refused to sell any potential inhalants. It has also stopped selling potatoes, raisins, yeast, and anything else that can be fermented into alcohol. But since gasoline is an essential product for the community's vehicles, it cannot be banned.

The people of Shamattawa are doing what they can to fight the gas-sniffing plague. They tried to impose a 10:00 P.M. curfew, but it proved impossible to enforce. In an attempt to discourage the sniffers, they established a gas patrol that operates until 2:00 A.M., five nights a week. However, its power is limited. The patrollers write down the names of the children who are caught sniffing and, once a week, they prepare a report on the patrol's activities. Then, in a sort of meaningless ritual, the list of sniffers is delivered to the band office and the nursing station. In reality, the gas patrol is virtually helpless, since gasoline sniffing is not illegal. The police cannot arrest the sniffers. And the doctors know, from experience, that compulsory medical treatment cannot cure the plague.

On a cold night in late September 1987, the two-man patrol sets out from the drop-in centre. There is a bitter wind and the first snow of the winter is coming down hard. About fifty people are playing bingo in the drop-in centre as the patrollers depart. The patrollers—Raymond Napoakesik, eighteen, and Ellis Redhead, twenty-one—are taciturn, jean-clad youths who carry flashlights and long wooden sticks covered with black tape to keep the dogs at bay. They have been hired by George Redhead because of their reliability and their abstinence from alcohol. It is 9:00 P.M. and already they have spotted ten sniffers, whose names they have recorded carefully in a small crumpled notebook which Ellis carries in his pocket.

They walk silently through the pitch-black night, their flashlights switched off. Just a few minutes after leaving the drop-in centre, they hear the loud voices of a drinking party in a nearby house. Raymond and Ellis walk toward the house and soon they hear the soft voices of children outside.

Raymond switches on his flashlight and there is a sudden flurry of running. Children scatter in all directions. Raymond races after them and grabs the arm of a young boy, while Ellis stays beside a girl who did not try to flee. Both of the children have been sniffing rags. Raymond picks up a black rag from the ground where he has caught the boy. It is reeking with gas fumes.

Raymond and Ellis question the boy sharply in Cree. They learn that his parents are drinking tonight, so there is no point in taking him home. "We can't do anything," Raymond says. They question the girl. Her parents aren't drinking, so they accompany her back to her home. They wait for her parents to open the door and let her in, then they leave without speaking a word.

The gas patrol continues toward the main road of the reserve. Within a few minutes, they hear music coming from a storage shed. Inside, there is a group of young men. At least one of them is sniffing gas. Raymond searches through the shed. "What do you want?" says one of the men. "Stop sniffing," Raymond mutters. "No way," the man says. The patrollers walk away. Eventually they return to the drop-in centre, known officially as the Leonard Miles Memorial Centre, to warm up and check their notes.

For a decade, the Shamattawa gas patrol has carefully compiled statistics on the number of sniffers caught during their nightly rounds. In the past five years, that number has been increasing. In October 1982, for example, 91 sniffing incidents were recorded by the patrol. Five years later, 258 incidents were reported in the period from August 28 to September 24, 1987. The number of incidents per day increased from a maximum of 19 to a maximum of 39 in the same five-year period.

George Redhead is the supervisor of the gas patrol and the coordinator of the Leonard Miles Memorial Centre. For years, he has been doing his best to fight the curse of gas sniffing. He tries to introduce recreational programs and social activities to keep the children out of trouble. The number of sniffers fluctuates, but the problem never disappears. He estimates that 60 to 65 percent of the Shamattawa children are sniffers—some as young as four years old. "They see their brothers and sisters doing it," he explains.

"I've seen children who are sniffing in the morning. On Saturday or Sunday morning, after their parents have been drinking, they're sniffing. The parents know. And the grandparents know. The parents aren't prohibiting their kids from sniffing. Maybe they don't think it's dangerous."

In the summer of 1974, a young medical student who was working in Shamattawa noticed that some of the Cree children were suffering tremors and delirium. Suspecting that the children were displaying the bizarre symptoms of lead poisoning, he arranged for two young boys to be evacuated to a Winnipeg hospital for treatment. It was soon confirmed that they were suffering from lead poisoning caused by their chronic gasoline sniffing.

A survey revealed that about half of Shamattawa's 350 children and young adults were sniffing gasoline regularly. Thousands of dollars' worth of gasoline was being stolen from the Hudson's Bay store each year to fuel the self-destructive habit.

In 1976, fifty children and young adults were sent to Winnipeg for treatment. Several children died—among them, seventeen-year-old Leonard Miles, whose name was given to the drop-in centre as a futile reminder of the dangers of sniffing.

Daniel Redhead was another of the fifty sniffers who were transported to Winnipeg in 1976. He was detoxified in hospital but began sniffing again when he returned to Shamattawa. After a second detoxification in Winnipeg, he finally stopped sniffing. Today, after a training course, he works as a counsellor on the reserve, trying to help children stop inhaling gasoline. He is the only trained counsellor for chemical addictions and alcoholism at Shamattawa.

Daniel Redhead's work is financed by the federal government's Native Alcohol and Drug Abuse Program (NADAP)—the main government program designed to help Indian addicts. It is grossly underfunded. The federal government has been aware of the inhalant-abuse problem for the past fifteen years, yet there is still a shortage of trained counsellors at Indian reserves across Canada. Studies have estimated that at least three or four trained workers are needed at most reserves, yet the typical reserve has only one or two counsellors. In 1987, the Shamattawa Cree pleaded for another counsellor to help Daniel Redhead, but their request was denied.

"There's a lot for me to do," he says. "There are seven hundred people here. We need more workers. We need more solvent-abuse counsellors. There's a lot of pressure on me, working alone in the community. I can't solve the problem overnight. It takes years. I do the best I can, but I need more training."

The federal government feels no political pressure for greater action on the sniffing problem. Hidden in remote northern reserves, far from the public eye, the gasoline addicts are easy to ignore. There are no high-profile charity organizations fighting on their behalf. "It's not fancy or glamorous," says Dr. Luis Fornazzari, a neurologist at the Addiction Research Foundation in Toronto and an expert on inhalant abuse. "It's a minority problem. You don't get votes from solvent abusers. No famous actors die from solvent abuse."

For years, Canadian health experts tried to cure the sniffers by using classic medical treatments or traditional alcohol-addiction programs.

They tested for lead in the blood of the sniffers, they sent them to hospital for detoxification, and they enrolled them in alcohol treatment programs. But these approaches were doomed to failure. There is anecdotal evidence, from stories told by the abusers, that inhalants are as addictive as hard drugs. "They feel it is the strongest craving," Dr. Fornazzari says.

Moreover, chemicals from the inhalants remain in the brain much longer than the chemicals from alcohol. They are still measurable ten days after the last inhalation. According to Dr. Fornazzari, it can take three or four weeks of recovery before an abuser begins to understand his addiction. For this reason, traditional alcohol treatment programs or hospital detoxifications are inadequate for chronic sniffers. "They need a longer treatment program," Dr. Fornazzari says. "They don't do well in traditional treatment centres. They don't feel confident in these programs. They quit early. They need specialized therapies."

The Indian bands of northern Manitoba have proposed the construction of a treatment centre at the Cross Lake reserve to provide specialized therapy for young inhalant abusers. The centre, which would be unique in Canada, would provide several months of treatment and counselling for each sniffer.

During their first month in the treatment centre, high levels of inhalants would still be present in the brains of the young addicts, so counselling would not be effective. Instead they would simply receive good nutrition and be encouraged to participate in recreational programs during this period to build their strength and avoid boredom. After the first month, they would begin talking to counsellors and role models such as reformed sniffers. Special classes would help them develop a sense of cultural pride and identity. Doctors and nurses would monitor their condition, but the emphasis would be on non-medical solutions.

Dr. Milton Tenenbein, director of the poison control centre at the Health Sciences Centre in Winnipeg, agrees that a specialized treatment centre must be created to provide therapy to the children who are addicted to inhalants. He supports the concept of long-term treatment. "Two or three weeks wouldn't be worth a nickel," Dr. Tenenbein says.

The Cross Lake proposal was submitted to the federal Health and Welfare Department in 1987, but it has been held up by a shortage of federal funds and the absence of any federal policy on solvent abuse.

In medical terminology, gasoline sniffing is now considered to be endemic in northern Manitoba. Dr. Tenenbein believes that government action is long overdue. "This has been studied to death. These children aren't receiving treatment at all."

Why did gasoline sniffing take control of the children of Shamattawa? Inhalant abuse has been reported by medical researchers around the world. It has been recorded among Indians in the southern United States and among the aborigines of Australia, the Maoris of New Zealand, and the children of unemployed Hispanic migrant workers and illegal aliens in Texas. And in almost every case, there is one unifying factor: the young addicts are poverty-stricken members of a community that has been overwhelmed by a more powerful outside culture. They are victims of cultural invasion or dislocation. The economic influence of the outsiders has forced an ethnic group to move to a foreign place, or it has surrounded and besieged the indigenous culture, destroying the traditional economy and social harmony. In each case, members of the minority group are stripped of their identity and their traditional way of life, and they descend into a pattern of self-destructive behaviour. Inhalants are simply the cheapest and most accessible of the weapons of self-destruction.

Beginning in the 1940s, when they were moved onto the site of their future reserve, the Cree of Shamattawa suffered the trauma of a sudden dislocation. Their traditional culture was virtually destroyed and replaced by a new culture of dependency, and they lost the ability to control their fate. Foreign institutions took control of their education, their justice system, their economy, and their way of life. With the arrival of satellite television, the cultural invasion has been completed. Now the children of Shamattawa are immersed in the images of a faraway urban paradise. They see commercials for cars, clothing, and toys they could never afford. They are trapped between the vision of a wealthy urban culture and the reality of an isolated community with a high unemployment rate.

A similar story has unfolded among the aborigines who live on the small island of Elcho in the remote north of Australia. Gasoline sniffing became a serious problem among the island's aborigine children in the mid-1960s. At one point, chronic sniffers were quarantined in an uninhabited chain of islands for a month, but the plague continued. The aborigines of Elcho Island, known as the Murngin people, have suffered the same cultural dislocation as the Indians of Canada.

"The Murngin are in the throes of rapid and radical social change," the *British Journal of Medical Psychology* reported in 1970. "Several thousand years of European social evolution have been telescoped into a quarter of a century. The traditional society was based on nomadic hunting and fishing.... The Murngin have been asked to transform themselves into townsmen with a harvesting orientation based on planning, prediction and technology."

For centuries, the children of Elcho Island were educated by their relatives. "Today the Western educational system has intruded, cutting across the responsibilities of the aboriginal adults and placing a barrier between man and boy," the medical journal noted. "The aboriginal adolescent is doubly excluded. On the one hand he is blocked from sharing in the benefits of European society by educational deficiencies and by the fear of breaking step; on the other, he is ambivalent about many of the old ways. Some he has forgotten altogether." Gasoline sniffing is a result of the "disorientation" of the Murngin adolescents, the medical journal concluded. "Adolescents reflect the conflicts of a people."

Although the aboriginal children of Elcho Island are aware of the dangers of gasoline inhalation, they keep sniffing. "They are suffused by a free-floating hostility, the outcome perhaps of the combined effects of territorial disruption, overcrowding, sociocultural change... the conviction of powerlessness in the face of incomprehensible forces.... This diffuse hostility has no specific object and appears to be turned inwards in the form of self-destructiveness...."

In the Northern Territory of Australia today, an estimated 20 percent of aboriginal children are sniffing gasoline. The problem is equally serious among Indian children in the United States. In one study it was found that 75 percent of the boys in a poverty-stricken Pueblo Indian village in New Mexico had sniffed gasoline at least once. "It makes you feel like walking on air," a nine-year-old Pueblo boy told the researchers.

A study of more than 10,000 Indian children in the United States found a dramatic increase in inhalant abuse from 1975 to 1983. About 40 percent of American Indian youths had tried inhalants by the age of eighteen, and the average Indian youth had begun taking inhalants at the age of eleven and a half. Gasoline was the most common of the inhalants, although glue and aerosol sprays were also widely used. Inhalant abuse was much more widespread among Indian youths than among non-Indians.

Dr. Fornazzari and Dr. Tenenbein both believe that cultural dislocation is the common denominator among the gasoline sniffers in Canada and other countries. To illustrate the point, Dr. Tenenbein describes the Indians who today live in Oklahoma. In the nineteenth century, thousands of American Indians from the Eastern United States were forced to move to Oklahoma—the so-called Indian Territory. This forced migration was a bureaucratic solution to the Indian "problem" and it effectively destroyed the traditional native culture. Today, inhalant abuse is widespread among Indian children in Oklahoma.

The story of Shamattawa is valuable because it provides a modern-day example of the historical process of dislocation and self-destruction that afflicted Indian bands in most of Canada and the United States in the nineteenth century. Gasoline was not available back then, so Indians used alcohol to fuel the same process of self-destruction. In Shamattawa, the invasion of white culture did not begin on a large scale until the 1940s, so the effects have become visible only in the past two or three decades.

As a physician, Dr. Tenenbein knows he can do little to help the children of Shamattawa. But if he had unlimited resources to tackle the gasoline plague, he would not mobilize an army of medical workers. Instead he would try to create jobs and economic opportunities at Shamattawa. "It's not really a medical problem," he says. "It would be folly to send a hundred doctors up there. There's nothing we can do." The root of the problem, he believes, is "the social and economic upset, discord and disharmony." Dependency on welfare has given the people of Shamattawa "a total lack of self-worth," he says. "What could be more depressing than to wait for the government cheque?"

Shamattawa's crime rate has fluctuated considerably over the past two decades. At its peak, it was one of the worst in Canada. In 1985, for example, the RCMP reported 79 assaults, one attempted murder, 66 break-ins, 21 thefts, and 32 weapons offences in this community of only seven hundred people. By 1988, the RCMP had calculated that the crime rate at Shamattawa was six times greater than the Canadian average.

Outbreaks of violence in 1981 and 1986 forced teachers and nurses to flee from Shamattawa. "It's hell up there," said a nurse who left the reserve. She was assaulted and threatened several times during the six months she worked there. "The violence is everywhere," she said. "I spent one night huddled under my kitchen table with all the windows blown out."

In the fall of 1986, the door of the nursing station was blown down by a shotgun blast. Six weeks later, the windows of the nursing station were shattered by someone wielding an axe handle. The next day, two nurses and ten teachers abandoned the reserve, flying out in chartered aircraft. Less than a day later, vandals broke into a schoolroom and smashed the desks and chairs.

The worst was yet to come. On the day after Christmas, the bodies of Beatrice Dixie Hill and Alexander Redhead were found in their homes in Shamattawa. Both had been shot and killed. Two juveniles, aged fifteen and seventeen, were charged with second-degree murder. One of the juveniles was the son of one of the dead adults.

The band called an emergency meeting to discuss the situation. Chief Judah Miles and his band councillors asked the people whether they would support drastic measures to combat the crime and the sniffing and alcoholism that caused it. They asked those who supported the strong measures to stand up. Everybody rose to their feet.

The band passed a bylaw to prohibit alcohol on the reserve, and all band members were asked to give their guns to band officials for safekeeping. More than sixty guns were surrendered voluntarily. A 10:00 P.M. curfew was established, and any band employee found with alcohol was fined or dismissed. If welfare recipients were discovered with alcohol, their welfare cheques were cut off and they were given vouchers that could be used only to purchase food or clothing. Everyone who arrived at Shamattawa by airplane was searched for alcohol.

The campaign was a courageous effort against incredible odds. For a while, it was successful. Drinking dropped by 95 percent in the first two months after the shootings, and only four people were caught with alcohol in the entire month of January. School attendance went up; the crime rate declined dramatically. At one point, the RCMP completed a four-day patrol without opening a single file. An optimistic headline in the *Winnipeg Free Press* read: "Troubled Shamattawa turns it around."

The gasoline sniffing, however, remained as widespread as ever. By the spring and summer of 1987, the violence had returned. The band, realizing that the curfew was a futile gesture, no longer bothered to enforce it. Alcohol was smuggled into Shamattawa, and there was a series of stabbings and shootings. Later in the year, a forty-three-year-old man died of a skull fracture after he was knocked to the ground. A teenager was charged with second-degree murder in connection with the incident.

Larry Keddie, the Anglican missionary at the reserve, was angry. He had arrived at Shamattawa in June—just as the violence was escalating. He is an intense, bearded man who had been studying at a university in southern Ontario when he was asked to become the pastor of the Anglican church at Shamattawa. He accepted the job enthusiastically and immediately began learning to speak Cree so he could deliver his sermons in the native language. But he was horrified by the crime on the reserve. When he heard about an infant girl who came close to death as a result of a fire set deliberately by her intoxicated mother, he decided to do something.

In his next Sunday sermon, he condemned the drinking and the gasoline sniffing. He wrote an open letter to the band and posted it at the Hudson's Bay store, the nursing station, the band office, and the RCMP office. "The time has come for the church to speak out against the evils of Satan here in Shamattawa," the letter read. "The church cannot and will not remain silent any longer.... The people here have to take a stand against the drinking and sniffing that takes place here. Do not tolerate it around your home." He signed the letter: "Your friend and pastor, Larry."

For a week, the Indians stopped talking to Larry Keddie. He wondered whether they were angry at him or ashamed of their own behaviour.

Others doubted that the Anglican missionary's outburst would accomplish anything. Two other missionaries, Oyvind and Inger Marie Haukas, had been living at Shamattawa since March 1987, under the sponsorship of a church in Norway and an international non-denominational Christian organization. The Norwegian couple and their young daughter lived in an abandoned fire-damaged house in Shamattawa and gave Bible classes in their home for a handful of band members. When they heard about the pastor's sermon, they were uneasy. They did not believe that the people of Shamattawa needed to be reminded of their problems. "They are absolutely aware of the problems," Oyvind says. One band councillor told Oyvind that the Indians feel hurt when they are lectured by a white man.

Oyvind and Inger Marie have not lectured the people of Shamattawa—not even when a group of Indian children asked their four-year-old daughter to join the children in a sniffing binge. "When people are sober, you can go into any home," Oyvind says. "They are really nice and friendly. They receive you. It's just when they drink and sniff that they suddenly turn. Everything changes in one second.... I believe that the root of the problem is the inner feelings. It is a broken culture. They have to get everything from the white man. The lack of housing is a huge problem. They get so sick of it that they can't take it any more."

On a summer weekend in Shamattawa, the young white men who work at the Hudson's Bay store jump into their motorboats and go water skiing on Gods River. As they roar up and down the water, crowds of Indians stand on the banks of the river, staring in amazement.

The white people come and go, but it is the Indian people who remain at Shamattawa—people like George Redhead and Daniel Redhead, who have spent their entire working lives on the reserve. Today they are still quietly struggling to solve the overwhelming problems of their community. They are not discouraged. The story of Shamattawa is their story. It is a story of courage and endurance.

The young people walk down the gravel road. They are wearing faded black hockey jackets that read: "Shamattawa Snowbirds." On the door of an abandoned building, there are scrawled graffiti: "Victor Duck, I still love you, no matter what."

The northern lights are a ghostly presence in the night sky above Shamattawa. Sheets and plumes of luminescence shimmer magically through the winter sky. Colours begin to emerge from the plumes, and then, like a huge celestial curtain, they seem to billow in the cold wind.

CHAPTER TWO

From Lytton to Sabaskong Bay: Fighting for the Schools

The Ojibway people of Sabaskong Bay can remember the exact moment when they took control of their future. It was a cold day in November 1974, and the school bus had arrived at its usual time to pick up the Ojibway children and transport them fifty kilometres to a provincial school in the northwestern Ontario town of Sioux Narrows. But on this November morning, there was a strange silence at the bus stop. There were no children waiting. A boycott had begun.

For almost a century, outsiders had controlled the education of the children of Sabaskong Bay. Missionaries set up residential schools where the Ojibway children were confined day and night, with no family contact, while they were indoctrinated with the religion and culture of the white man. Even today, the elders at Sabaskong Bay have vivid memories of those schools. Some can remember being chased by priests and dragged onto school buses, then taken tearfully to a school in Kenora, where they were forced to memorize hymns and Bible lessons. They were separated from their parents and prohibited from speaking Ojibway. "I never did get to know my parents," one elder said.

Indian residential schools, founded and operated by Protestant and Catholic missionaries, were the dominant institution in Indian communities across Canada from the late nineteenth century until the 1960s.

The federal government allowed the churches to assume complete control of Indian education on reserves from Nova Scotia to British Columbia. The government, like the churches, believed the Indian culture was "barbaric" and "savage". The federal authorities were determined to transform the Indian children into faithful Christians who would abandon their traditional native spiritual beliefs.

For Indian children who did not live near a residential school, the government built a network of federal day schools. Many of these schools were poorly constructed and underfunded, and their teachers were often paid less than half the salary of teachers at provincial schools, where the white children were educated. The curriculum at the federal schools was supposed to be similar to the curriculum at provincial schools, but in fact the quality of education was inferior because of the low salaries and poor funding. The federal schools were imposed on Indian communities with little attempt to consult the native leaders.

Until the First World War, federal officials kept up the pretence that Indian parents had requested a Christian education for their children. In reality, however, the missionaries and the federal government's Indian agents put strong pressure on the parents to persuade them to send their children to the schools. The Indian agents used the sweeping legal powers they held under the federal Indian Act to deny food rations to Indian families who did not comply. In many cases, children went to the schools only because they were orphans, or because one of their parents had died and the remaining parent could not afford to raise the children.

In 1920, the pretence of voluntary attendance was dropped and amendments to the Indian Act made school attendance mandatory for Indians. The same amendments gave Ottawa the power to force Indians to give up their legal status as Indians. Those who wanted to attend university were encouraged to give up their status. Duncan Campbell Scott, deputy superintendent general of Indian Affairs, summarized the intent of the amendments: "Our object is to continue until there is not a single Indian in Canada that has not been absorbed into the body politic, and there is no Indian question, and no Indian department, and that is the whole object of this Bill."

A growing number of federally controlled day schools were established in the 1920s and 1930s, but there was also a dramatic increase in residential school enrolment. The total number of Indians in residential schools across Canada jumped by 110 percent from 1912 to 1932, and further amendments to the Indian Act in 1930 expanded the department's powers to enforce school attendance. Truant officers and legal penalties compelled children to go to school. Indian parents could be jailed or fined if their children did not attend. In fact, the federal department was given greater powers to enforce attendance among Indian children than the provinces could exercise over non-Indian children.

By the 1940s, about 8,000 Indian children—half the Indian student population—were enrolled in seventy-six residential schools across the country. Although the residential schools remained the most powerful institutions in native life, most Indian children could not thrive in them. They expressed their resistance by leaving the schools as fast as they could. In 1930, three-quarters of Canadian Indian students were in Grades 1 to 3, and only three in every hundred students went past Grade 6. (By comparison, almost one-third of white students in provincial schools went past Grade 6.) There was little change as the years went by. In 1950, only 10 percent of Indian students went past Grade 6, compared to 30 percent of white students in provincial schools.

If an Indian student somehow survived the residential school and wanted a higher education, it was rarely possible. As late as the 1940s, school officials and federal bureaucrats often required Indian students to leave school at the age of sixteen. At a residential school in northwestern Ontario, a federal inspector admonished the administrator for offering Grade 9 to the students. "If we let the Indian people go to Grade 9, then they'll want to go to Grade 10, and then they'll want to go to university. That's what we don't want," the inspector said.

Beginning in the early twentieth century, a growing number of Indian leaders began to oppose the residential school system. They complained repeatedly to the Indian Affairs Department but were ignored. In 1911, a Cree chief wrote to the governor general to ask for day schools to replace the residential schools. Indian children in the residential schools were being "torn from their mother's arms or homes," the chief wrote.

In 1931, the League of Indians of Western Canada passed a resolution asking the Indian Affairs Department to establish local schools on each reserve to replace the residential schools. One of the league's leaders, Edward Ahenakew, was a Cree who had graduated from the

University of Saskatchewan. He vividly described the dangers of the residential schools. Indian students "acted under orders" every day in the residential schools, Ahenakew said. "They never needed to use their own minds and wills…. When suddenly given their freedom they do not know how to use it. Their initiative is lost…." After leaving the schools, they "sit on the fence between the whites and the Indians, belonging to neither, fitting into neither world," he said. "You cannot make a white man out of an Indian. It is much better to make our children into good Indians, for we are Indians in our prison and in our thinking."

But the protests went unheeded. Residential schools continued to operate in Canada until the 1950s and 1960s, when the federal government adopted a new policy of integrating Indian students into the regular provincial school system. Under the new rules, most Indian children were ordered to attend provincial schools. By the end of the 1960s, almost all residential schools were closed or shifted to non-church control. Although the provincial schools were better funded than the federal schools, the threat of assimilation was much stronger there, where Indian students were overwhelmed by white teachers and white students and native culture was ignored or denigrated.

In the 1960s and early 1970s, the children of Sabaskong Bay were sent to Father Moss School at Sioux Narrows, an integrated provincial school for white and Indian students. Children from four Ojibway reserves were required to attend the school, yet their parents were denied any voice in the key decisions at the institution, which was controlled by a Roman Catholic school board. Indians could not vote or gain election to the board.

The Ojibway children were unhappy at Father Moss School. Absenteeism was high, and about 80 percent of the students dropped out before the end of high school. Many were as old as sixteen or seventeen by the time they reached Grade 8. Disputes between students and teachers broke out frequently, and Ojibway students were often expelled from the school for several days at a time. When an Ojibway education counsellor tried to resolve the disputes, the school officials ignored him.

The chiefs of the four bands asked for permission to set up their own schools. The Indian Affairs Department refused. So in 1974, the boycott began.

"Education is like love," says John Peter Kelly, the Grand Chief of the Ojibways of Treaty No. 3 in northwestern Ontario and a leader of the boycott. "We cannot delegate others to exercise it on our behalf."

In defiance of the Indian Affairs Department, the Ojibways of Sabaskong Bay hired their own teachers and set up classrooms in an old building on the reserve, thus becoming one of the first Indian bands in Canada to take control of the education of their children. Within a few weeks, the Indian Affairs Department agreed to fund the new school. Books, desks, and other supplies were transferred to Sabaskong Bay from the school at Sioux Narrows.

"Our citizens will no longer tolerate second-class citizenship, impoverished living and inferior education," the Sabaskong Bay band council told the Indian Affairs Department in a declaration of its new philosophy. "Education is the escalator that moves people from poverty and misery to human dignity and comfort.... We must not give up the dream."

By 1975, the three hundred people of Sabaskong Bay were running their own elementary school. For the first time, their children were studying Indian culture and history and the Ojibway language. An Ojibway teacher was working in the classrooms. Elders and parents were participating in the school. In 1977, a high school was added. Today, the dropout rate at Sabaskong Bay has declined dramatically. As many as seven students are graduating from Grade 12 each year, compared to an annual total of only one or two graduates before the takeover. "We are going to use education to regain control of our lives," John Peter Kelly vows.

Canadians often assume that Indian self-government would entail the creation of a sovereign state or a new level of government. But in reality, self-government has a much more practical meaning for most Indian bands. It begins with the freedom to regain control of individual elements of their community: their schools, courts, health system, and child welfare system. These are the institutions that affect people most directly. By asserting their right to make their own decisions in such vital areas, Indian bands are liberating themselves from a state of dependence and government control.

In the early 1970s the schools became the first major battleground in the fight for Indian self-government in Canada. Several years before the earliest steps were taken toward self-government in the justice and child welfare systems, aboriginal people were already struggling for control of their schools.

To understand why the schools were the first battleground, one must understand the crucial importance of the education system in Canada's assault on Indian culture from the 1860s to the 1960s. The schools were the chief weapon of the missionaries and the federal bureaucrats in their systematic campaign to destroy Indian culture. Today, thousands of Indians still bear the scars of that war of attrition.

In the spring of 1987, Jan Derrick More telephoned the RCMP. For eighteen months, she had been working as a family therapist in the small logging town of Lytton in the Fraser Canyon of British Columbia. Many of her clients were Thompson Indians, known today as the Nl'akapxm Nation, who live on a reserve adjacent to the town. As she listened to her Indian clients, some frightening evidence slowly emerged.

Derrick More started assembling a series of family trees for her clients, going back several generations. As she recalled what the Indians had told her, she noticed that all the disturbing stories and all the family trees were pointing in one direction. That was when she called the police.

For years, alcoholism and suicides had been tormenting the people of the Lytton reserve. The band's social worker, Mandy Brown, had tried everything. Again and again, she sent people away to alcohol treatment programs. They dried out, came back to Lytton, and began drinking again. Something unspoken was lingering in their subconscious memories.

At the meeting with the RCMP officers, Derrick More pulled out the family trees and spread them on a table. Then she explained the identical stories of childhood sexual abuse that were emerging from her clients. By the end of the meeting, the RCMP had agreed to launch an investigation.

Over the next few weeks, the RCMP interviewed 140 people in the area. The stories of sexual abuse were repeated again and again, and they all pointed to one source: St. George's School, an Indian residential school near Lytton. The investigators were stunned. "We had never realized how widespread it was," Derrick More says. "But when we found the pus beneath the surface, it all made sense."

In December 1987, the RCMP completed their investigation. Derek Clarke, a former dormitory supervisor at St. George's School, was arrested and charged with nineteen sexual offences. Three months later, he pleaded guilty to eleven counts of buggery and six counts of indecent assault. The crimes involved seventeen boys, some of whom had been as young as nine years old when they were victimized. Most had been Indian students at St. George's School.

Ever since it was established in the nineteenth century, the school had been controlled and administered by the Anglican Church. The sexual abuse of Indian children at St. George's had begun in 1964 and continued for eleven years. The children were beaten or punished if they refused to comply with Clarke's sexual demands. In 1974, several Indian boys at the school got up enough courage to tell the administrator that Clarke was molesting them. Clarke was dismissed from his job at the school, but the police were not informed.

At the sentencing hearing in 1988, Clarke's victims were allowed to speak to the court. In halting voices, interrupted by periods of silence and tears, they described the tragedies that had ravaged their lives after their childhood abuse at St. George's. They described lives of crime, drugs, alcoholism, and suicidal urges. "I had my 30-30 gun looking right at me," one of the victims told the court. "I was broken in all areas of my life. All my dreams were just about shattered." He said he'd had nightmares for twenty-one years after he was molested by Clarke. The nightmares did not end until he was able to talk about the abuse. "Twenty-one years of pain, shame, guilt, and hurt has finally stopped," he told the court.

Clarke was sentenced to twelve years in prison. Seven of his victims were among the local Indians who crowded into a small provincial courtroom to watch. After the sentencing, they tearfully embraced. "It's like a thousand-pound weight being lifted from your shoulders," one of them said. "The hell he put us all through. This tore our whole community apart and completely disoriented our culture." Another said: "It's finally over. Twenty years of carrying this. The cycle is complete. I feel set free."

In his sentencing judgment, Judge William Blair said Clarke was responsible for at least 140 sexual incidents and perhaps as many as 700 incidents or more. He said Lytton is a community "in great pain" because of the history of sexual abuse. "The community feels victimized by St. George's and by the Department of Indian Affairs. Suicide is a very common cause of death. The accused ought to have been aware of how culturally fragile this community is and was."

The judge said it was impossible to be certain how much of the suicide and alcoholism at Lytton was caused by the sexual abuse. But he identified the abuse as "a major contributing factor" which had "made the lives of the victims close to unbearable" in some cases. One of the victims "started drinking to get kicked out of school, and he's been drinking ever since," the judge noted.

Ruby Dunstan, the chief of the Lytton band, recalls at least ten suicides by former St. George's students. "We'll never know how many had to do with this and we'll never be able to reach all of them." In fact, one of Clarke's victims committed suicide in January 1988, just a week before the sentencing.

Jan Derrick More said the conviction of Derek Clarke had "cracked the secret" of the Lytton people. "In our work there always seemed to be a hidden problem. We'd get so far and then we would hit a brick wall. Now all the pain, suffering, and regression make sense."

As the long-hidden problem of child sexual abuse becomes better understood today, experts have found that Indian children are among the most vulnerable of the victims. Historically, missionaries and residential school teachers were in positions of great authority and power over Indian children. Perhaps inevitably, some abused that power.

One of Derek Clarke's victims had previously been a victim of William Douglas, a Salvation Army captain in the remote Indian community of Canyon City in northern British Columbia. Douglas was eventually convicted of twelve counts of gross indecency involving seven Nishga Indian boys. The boys were traumatized for decades. Several of the victims attempted suicide, suffered depression, or became alcoholics. "This wasn't just a crime of sex," a counsellor said. "It was also a crime of power."

In 1989, Roman Catholic priest Harold McIntee pleaded guilty to sexually assaulting thirteen Indian boys at a Catholic residential school near the town of Williams Lake in the British Columbia interior. The priest had assaulted the Indian children more than seventy-five times in the 1950s and 1960s.

Maggie Hodgson, an expert on sexual abuse who works at a native alcoholism foundation in Edmonton, has conducted seminars for Indians who spent their childhoods in residential schools. She discovered that as many as 80 percent of the Indians had been sexually abused at church-run schools. Like an infectious disease, the abuse is transmitted from generation to generation. The victims become the abusers. Research in some Canadian Indian communities has found that 75 to 94 percent of the residents have been sexually abused in their childhood.

Sexual crimes, however, are only one example of the misuse of power by white men who acted as preachers and educators in Indian communities. Protestant and Catholic missionaries, operating under authority given to them by the federal government, used the residential schools to serve their own purposes: to "civilize" the Indians and transform them into Christians. This was a task that required the exercise of power—an absolute command over the daily lives of Indian children.

St. George's School, which was located about four kilometres north of Lytton, was typical of Indian residential schools in Canada. A Protestant missionary, the Reverend J. B. Good, founded the school for Lytton Indian boys in 1867. He was inspired by William Duncan, the most aggressive and influential Protestant missionary in the early days of white settlement in British Columbia, who had established one of the earliest schools for Indians in 1857 at Fort Simpson. Duncan was determined to destroy the traditional Indian culture. Describing the Indian communities as "dens of darkness and iniquity", he claimed that their centuries-old culture was full of "atrocities" and "heathenism". He wrote: "The dark mantle of degrading superstition enveloped them all, and their savage spirits, swayed by pride, jealousy and revenge, were ever hurrying them to deeds of blood. Thus their history was little else than a chapter of crime and misery."

In 1862, Duncan created a new village, known as Metlakatla, in northern British Columbia. Here he brought together his Indian followers, built a massive new church, and required his followers to send their children to his school. He ordered the villagers to stop painting their faces, to give up their potlatch ceremonies, to rest on the Sabbath, to attend religious instruction, to be "cleanly and industrious", to be "liberal and honest in trade", and to pay a village tax.

Reverend Good, who was one of the thousands of white people pouring into the Fraser Canyon region after the gold rush of 1858, was impressed by Duncan's methods. Following Duncan's lead, he told the Lytton Indians that they must end "all their manifold hypocrisy, uncleanliness, and idleness, and many other sins and evil practices." Reverend Good decided that his new school for boys would instil "habits of instant obedience." He built the school a few miles from Lytton, in order to escape the "evil influences" of the Indian community.

At the same time, Catholic missionaries were establishing a series of Indian residential schools in British Columbia, especially in the lower Fraser Valley. In 1879, the residential school system was praised by a federal government report, known as the Davin report, which described the schools as "the principal feature of the policy known as 'aggressive civilization'." The report urged the government to use missionaries to "civilize" the Indians and "take away their simple Indian mythology" by carefully regulating their behaviour in boarding schools. Day schools would not be effective enough because they would allow Indian students to maintain some contact with their families, the report said. It added: "...if anything is to be done with the Indian, we must catch him very young."

A glimpse of daily life at St. George's School is provided by the annual reports of Indian agents and school principals in the Lytton area. The reports made no secret of the fact that the white preachers and educators held the Indian culture in complete contempt. Their goal was to transform the Indian boys into miniature Englishmen. The Indian children at St. George's School were taught reading, writing, arithmetic, geometry, dictation, singing, grammar, geography, and English history. For recreation, they were required to play English sports such as football, rounders, field hockey, and cricket. During the cold winter months, they were taught to play chess, dominoes, and draughts. The boys did most of the housework, washing, cooking, and clothes mending, and they worked every day on the surrounding 240-hectare farm to provide food and income for the school.

Every annual report by the principal of St. George's School included a section entitled: "Moral and Religious Training". In his 1904 report, for instance, principal George Ditcham wrote: "We have daily readings and instruction in the Bible, besides our daily prayers, and two services on Sundays with school from two to three o'clock in the afternoons. There has been no serious trouble with the morality of the school and the conduct has been excellent when one considers the natural deformities of these Indians." The school officials were convinced that the Indian boys would quickly become immoral if they were left alone. "Careful watch is kept over the boys to train them in honesty, truthfulness and uprightness, and instruction is given to this end," Ditcham said.

The philosophy according to which the residential schools operated was diametrically opposed to the traditional Indian philosophy of education. Before the arrival of the missionaries, Indian children learned by watching their parents and elders. Their family and their community were intimately involved in their education. The myths and stories told by their elders were an important part of the process of learning.

There is little doubt that the federal government regarded the Indian residential schools as a key weapon in a long-term plan to destroy all vestiges of the Indian culture. Some children were kept in the schools for several years at a time, with no holidays and no contact with their parents or their home communities. An official report in 1913 by an agent of the Indian Affairs Department made it clear that the schools were part of a systematic long-term plan. "It is considered by many that the ultimate destiny of the Indian will be to lose his identity as an Indian, so that he will take his place fairly and evenly beside his white brother," the agent wrote. "It is only by systematically building from one generation to another that this will be accomplished. The ex-pupils merely form the second link in a chain between barbarism and civilization. Some of them are married and have children attending the schools, but they will only be the third link."

From the viewpoint of the missionaries, the schools were a great success. As early as 1888, one anthropologist was having trouble locating any Indian communities whose original culture was still undisturbed. The anthropologist reported that the Lytton Indians "have been Christians for a long time." He added: "I hear very little about olden times."

The federal government believed that the Indian residential schools were tremendously successful. "Young native women trained at these institutions go out to service, and are much sought after, as nurse maids and general servants, and give great satisfaction to their employers," an official of the Indian Affairs Department boasted in the 1906 annual report of the department's British Columbia office. The British Columbia Indians were practising Christianity "with praiseworthy devotion," the federal official said. "Owing to the good and effective work of the missionaries, at the present time there are but few pagans among the Indians, over nine-tenths of the whole native population being now registered as members of one or other of the different religious denominations...."

The same sense of absolute self-confidence was displayed by the officials of St. George's School at Lytton. Year after year, they bragged that the Indian boys were being moulded into devoted Christians who spoke English and studied English history. "The children always follow attentively the daily readings of the scriptures," George Ditcham told his superiors in 1905. "They learn their Sunday lessons wonderfully well," he wrote in a 1908 report.

Yet beneath the glowing optimism of the official assessments, there were indications that the Indians were not entirely happy with the residential schools and their constant assault on the Indian language and culture. In 1911, after years of cheerful reports, George Ditcham admitted that the Indians had rebelled against the propaganda and punishment at the residential schools. "For various reasons and from various causes the attendance has been very bad," Ditcham said in a brief report in 1911. "There are only five small boys at school— some finished and others absconded, some from the school, some from Lytton hospital—one followed the other like cattle, and as the expense was too great for constables to bring them back and hold them at school, they are still away."

As a result of the policy reforms of the 1960s, St. George's School became a residence for out-of-town native students who were sent to provincial schools in Lytton. The former Anglican school was closed permanently in 1978. It was destroyed in a mysterious fire in 1983.

The ruins of St. George's School and the surrounding farm are still visible today, north of Lytton on the winding road to Lillooet. The beautiful stone chapel is still there, although its doors and windows are boarded up. Next to it is an empty plot of land where the school itself once stood, before the fire. There is a rusting skeleton of a set of children's swings and a decaying cluster of abandoned white-painted barns and farm buildings. Just below the ruins, close to the Fraser River, stands a new complex of senior citizens' buildings for Indian elders. But many of the elders are reluctant to live there. They say they can still feel "bad spirits" from the residential school.

Those spirits are a constant presence. The memory of St. George's School is like a ghost, haunting the people of Lytton. The older people feel the effects of the school most acutely: it is a shared experience, something they all suffered through. For a long time, they endured the painful memories in silence. Now, finally, they have mustered up the strength to confront the school's terrible legacy.

Ruby Dunstan, the chief of the Lytton band, was sent to St. George's from 1948 to 1953. She was six years old when her parents were told that they would be jailed and their children apprehended if they refused to send the children to St. George's. "I used to cry when my sisters went to school," Dunstan remembers. "Then it was my turn to go, and I cried to get out of the school. It was horrible. It was the worst five years of my life. They treated us like animals and they expected us to come out a happy person. As far as I know, nobody has ever come out of there happy."

Her parents knew what the school was like. But they knew the children would be hunted down and forcibly taken to the school if they were not sent voluntarily. Dunstan recalls that her parents "wanted to be law-abiding citizens."

At home, before she entered school, Ruby and her parents ate dried meat and dried salmon and berries. "We learned, as a family, how to gather food and prepare it. But at the residential school, they told us we couldn't eat it. They said it was heathen. I didn't know what heathen meant. But the way they took our food and threw it out, I thought it must be bad. And yet that was what we had always eaten."

The school officials were careful to regulate any visits from parents who wanted to see their children. Instead of being allowed into the dormitory, the parents were confined to one single room. If the parents brought traditional Indian food for their children, it was confiscated. "They tried so hard to tell us that our culture was no good," Dunstan says. "We couldn't eat our own foods, they wouldn't let us pray in an Indian way, they whipped the hell out of us. You were told you shouldn't be an Indian, but you knew damn well that you'd always be an Indian, you couldn't change."

One day, Ruby Dunstan tried to run away from St. George's, but she was pursued and picked up in a car and driven back to the school. "The principal strapped the hell out of me, on both hands. I swore I wouldn't cry. My hands were all purple that night. The next day, I couldn't even hold a pencil."

A young fellow student, seeing that Ruby couldn't hold a pencil long enough to do her schoolwork, offered to help her. But a teacher saw the two children talking together and whacked Ruby on the head with a big ring of keys. The scar is still visible today.

Every Indian child at St. George's School was assigned a number, which was stamped on his clothing and his locker. In 1950, a young Indian girl named Charon Spinks became Number 473. The number is still burned on her consciousness today. "Any time I see that number, those days just flash through my mind," says Spinks, who now works as an alcohol counsellor at Lytton. "We were always in line, like the military. We had to learn a kind of discipline that was against our grain. We got punishment for things we didn't understand. I didn't know why I was being hurt. I've still got scars on my fingers from being whacked with key rings and yardsticks. They suspected we were worshipping some object. But we weren't—it was just nature."

Charon Spinks remained a student at St. George's School from 1950 to 1959. Her memories of the school are painful. "I remember crying without tears. My heart felt like it was breaking. That's how lonely I was. I would find girls crying, girls who couldn't speak English, and I would console them—even though I would need consoling myself. I was always worried about my younger brother and sister. I felt sick, just worrying about them."

From her experience as a counsellor, Charon Spinks is convinced that the residential school is a major factor in the alcoholism and family breakdown at Lytton. Some people drink "to get rid of the pain," she says. "It affects your spouse, your children, your children's friends. It just goes on and on. They've lost their identity. They feel confused about themselves. They feel they're not accepted by their own people. They feel they don't belong in either world."

Charon Spinks began to understand the long-term damage caused by St. George's School when she heard two teenaged Indian girls talking about themselves. "They said they wished the Indian part of them could be cut out. I still haven't gotten over that, and that was fifteen years ago."

Charon Spinks and Ruby Dunstan survived the residential schools through sheer determination and perseverance. But others became alcoholic or suicidal. "Some of them have just given up," Dunstan says. "They're on a lost road."

A culture cannot survive without its language. The language is an expression of the culture—it is the backbone, the identity of the people. When the language is lost, the culture is crippled. And so it was the language that was the first target of the residential schools. The school officials were determined to destroy the Indian languages, to ensure that the Indian children would be assimilated into the white culture. In many cases, they were successful. Today, it is estimated that fifty of Canada's fifty-three native languages are in danger of extinction. Thirteen languages are considered extremely endangered because they are spoken by fewer than a hundred people. Once they disappear, they will be gone forever. There are no foreign countries where the languages will be preserved.

The Thompson Indian language of the Lytton Indians came to the brink of extinction by the 1960s. "Something has happened to us," says Charon Spinks. "We can't communicate with each other. It's like a cut. It's had a traumatic effect."

The Lytton Indians were punished if they spoke their language at the residential school. They were taught to be ashamed of it and so were reluctant to teach it to their children. Now those children are adults, unable to understand the words of their elders. "They laugh at us," Charon Spinks says. "They say, 'You sound like you're talking Chinese.' "

Gladys Granier, another survivor of St. George's School, remembers being taunted because she could not speak English when she arrived at the school at the age of seven. "The teacher called me a dumb Indian. She said, 'Look at the dumb Indian, she can't speak English.' She rounded up the other children and made fun of me in front of them. I remember saying, 'I'll learn this stupid language.' "

She stayed at the residential school from 1954 to 1961, painfully learning English. Then she forgot her native language. For years, she never spoke the Thompson Indian dialect of her own people. "It's only now that some of the words are coming back to me. I have a hard time when I speak my own language. I feel like I'm sneaking something. I find myself hesitating before I speak. I guess I learned my lesson so well that it's hard to change."

Almost every generation at Lytton has been affected by the residential school. Most of those who are now forty-five or older lost their native language at St. George's and could not teach it to their children. When they eventually regained some of their language, it was too late to pass it on to the next generation. Most of their children, now twenty-five to forty years old, never heard the language spoken in their homes as they grew up. But now the school-age grandchildren of the St. George's students are learning the language at the provincial school in Lytton. And they, in turn, are teaching a few words to their parents.

Between the generations, there is still a communication gap. The residential school has forcibly divided them. Often an elder who still speaks the Indian language will wander into the Lytton band office—and none of the younger band officials will be able to talk to him. That is part of the legacy of St. George's.

The people of Lytton were among the first Indians in Canada to recognize "residential-school syndrome"—a term coined by psychologists who are beginning to notice a distinctive set of symptoms in their Indian clients. They compare it to the grief cycle that a person undergoes after the loss of a close relative. But instead of losing a parent or a spouse, the Indians have lost a culture. Something they were born with, a part of their soul, was wiped out by the missionaries and the teachers.

Jan Derrick More, the therapist hired by the Lytton band who helped uncover the history of sexual abuse at St. George's School, has been assisting in the healing process at Lytton. In seminars and counselling sessions, she has worked with about five hundred of the Lytton Indians.

Ironically, one of Derrick More's ancestors was a missionary and another worked in an Indian residential school. She believes that white Canadians must learn to acknowledge the role their ancestors played in establishing and perpetuating the residential schools. "It's a white issue. It's all about white society's inability to understand. White supremacy consolidated itself in the residential school. It was the key that locked the door to the Indian culture."

When she began holding workshops at B.C. Indian reserves to discuss the psychological effects of the residential schools, the most common reaction was anger and denial. "They were saying: It's dead and behind us, don't bring it up. You people were responsible for it."

But the sexual abuse trial at Lytton shocked many Indians into confronting the reality of the residential schools. After the trial, Derrick More was flooded with telephone calls from native people across British Columbia who wanted to tell her their personal stories. Many said they were now finally understanding the reasons for the behaviour of their parents, who had attended residential schools.

The counselling and therapy sessions in Lytton have traced the poison of the residential school as it is passed from generation to generation. Sometimes the worst effects of residential-school syndrome are felt by the children and grandchildren of the survivors of the school. Here, from Jan Derrick More's case files, is an illustration:

Two young boys, seven and nine years old, were referred to Derrick More because their father had committed suicide. The father, a victim of sexual abuse at St. George's School, had killed himself with a shotgun. The youngest boy was withdrawn, angry, and suicidal. Both were constantly involved in fights. After talking to the boys, Derrick More sensed that they had a "missing mother". They lived with their grandparents and had received no nurturing and little physical contact from their mother. Derrick More decided to ask the mother to join the therapy sessions.

The mother, a woman in her early twenties, agreed to participate. In therapy with one of her sons, she eventually told him—for the first time—that she loved him. The boy cried. The mother's sister then joined in the therapy, and when the two women talked about their own mother, they began to realize that they had never received love or warmth from her. Derrick More invited this woman, the grandmother of the boys, to participate in the therapy.

The grandmother, a woman in her late fifties, proved to be the key to the riddle. She was a classic victim of residential-school syndrome. As a child, she had spoken the language of her people. She was hugged and loved by her parents and grandparents. But then she was sent to St. George's School, where she was strapped when she spoke the Indian dialect. For years, she lived in complete confusion and panic. Eventually she became determined that she would never speak her own language again.

Today the woman regrets those lost years at the residential school. She remembers the moment when her own grandmother realized that they could no longer talk together in their own language. "She remembers the sadness in her grandmother's eyes. She decided she was a bad person. She became lost between two cultures. She was seeking love."

By the age of sixteen, she was locked up inside herself. She began drinking heavily, and several of her five children were taken away from her.

All of the people in this jigsaw puzzle—the boys, their mother, their aunt, and their grandmother—were "longing to be loved," Derrick More said. But the residential school had stripped the grandmother of her skills as a parent. Her trauma was transmitted from generation to generation. "If you're constantly running up against people who tell you that you're bad, you begin to see yourself that way. The school was telling six-year-olds that everything they learned from their parents was wrong."

There is a quiet rage among the survivors today. "The stereotypical silent Indian is an angry Indian—someone who knew he could be beaten up if he opened his mouth," Derrick More says. "People had to block their feelings in order to survive."

Today, however, the native culture in Lytton is recovering its strength. The wounds are not neglected any more. "There are a lot of miracles happening," Derrick More says. "It's acceptable to heal now."

The stories told by the survivors of St. George's School have been echoed countless times by Indians across the country who endured residential schools in their own regions. In most cases, the schools functioned as prisons and indoctrination centres, rather than educational institutions.

Daniel Kennedy, a Saskatchewan Indian chief at the turn of the century, recalled being "lassoed, roped and taken to the [residential] school" in the Qu'Appelle Valley of Saskatchewan in 1886 when he was twelve years old. As soon as he arrived at the Catholic school, his long braided hair was cut off by the school administrators.

There was little improvement in the first half of the twentieth century. Jane Willis, a Cree from the James Bay region of northern Quebec, remembers her troubled childhood in an Anglican residential school in the 1940s and 1950s. "For twelve years I was taught to love my neighbour—especially if he was white—but to hate myself," she wrote. "I was made to feel untrustworthy, inferior, incapable, and immoral. The barbarian in me, I was told, had to be destroyed if I was to be saved. I was taught to feel nothing but shame for my 'pagan savage' ancestors.... When I had been stripped of all pride, self-respect, and self-confidence, I was told to make something of myself...."

About two thousand Nova Scotia Micmac Indians were sent to a residential school at Shubenacadie from 1929 to 1967. Micmacs who attended the school describe it as "a house of horrors". One survivor, Isabelle Knockwood Toney Shay, has interviewed dozens of her classmates so she can write about the school—the writing itself is a form of therapy. "I was psychologically traumatized from the experience of witnessing what happened to my little friends," she says. "When I interview people, we cry a lot together.... I think reading and writing about my abused childhood at the residential school is the only way I will know who I am and how to deal with abuse in all its forms."

At the Baptist Mission residential school in Whitehorse, Indian children tried to sneak away from the school to speak their Tutchone language because teachers strapped any children who were caught speaking in their own tongue. "If they heard you speaking Indian they said it was the devil talking through you," said an Indian woman who was sent to the Baptist school in the 1940s. In the summer, the children were required to attend a Bible school, forcing their parents to abandon their traditional summer hunt for caribou and moose. "It was cultural genocide," the woman said.

At the Port Alberni residential school on Vancouver Island, Indian children who spoke their Tseshaht language in the 1920s were punished in almost unbelievable ways. Randy Fred, whose family attended the school for generations, recalls that the teachers pushed sewing needles through his father's tongue when he spoke Tseshaht. The Indian children were required to wear grey prison-style shirts, denim over-alls, and army-style boots. A wire fence enclosed the school grounds, and the students were not permitted within three metres of the fence.

In the Sudbury region of northern Ontario, federal Indian agents knocked on the doors of local Indian homes and ordered the parents to surrender their children. Once apprehended, the Indian children were sent to the Catholic residential school in the village of Spanish, where their heads were shaved and they were given identical uniforms of corduroy breeches and beige shirts. Basil Johnston, a survivor of the residential school in Spanish in the 1940s, said the name of the village "inspired dread from the first time that we Indian boys heard it…. It was a word synonymous with residential school, penitentiary, reformatory, exile, dungeon, whippings, kicks, slaps, all rolled into one."

Blue Quills, a Catholic residential school, began operating in 1931 near the Saddle Lake reserve in northeastern Alberta. Its Indian students were required to follow a strict daily schedule, rising at 6:00 A.M. and going to bed at 7:30 P.M. They had to maintain complete silence during meals. If they tried to run away from school, their heads were shaven and they were kept barefoot. Students from the school's early years remember the teachers using a pictorial catechism, showing white people ascending a road to heaven and Indians descending on a road to hell. The children were told that they should prevent their parents from going to Sun Dances because the Sun Dance was forbidden by God.

The regimentation continued into the 1950s. Each student was assigned a number and the teachers often addressed them by their numbers, as if they were in the army. The numbers were stamped on their clothing and eating utensils. The private property of the students, including their mail, was subject to scrutiny by school officials. "Going to Blue Quills was like going into a room and not being let out," one student said later.

At almost every residential school, the Indian children tried to resist. At one Anglican school near Sault Ste. Marie in northern Ontario, truancy and homesickness were widespread among the Indian children. "Some of them, when homesick, seemed to lose all control over themselves and made an unearthly noise; others would watch for their opportunity and run away," said Reverend Edward Wilson, the school's founder.

The residential schools and the missionaries who ran them are viewed with cold fury by today's generation of Indian leaders. Two native activists, Eric Robinson and Henry Bird Quinney, have described their rage at the cruel lessons taught by the church-run schools: "The burning of sweetgrass and tobacco was 'heathen' ritual, but praying with their burning incense was supposedly the only sacred way. Songs with the Drum were 'barbaric', but Latin chants were okay. Dancing to honour the return of the birds in springtime was wrong, but kneeling in the dark confines of chapels with rosary beads was right."

At a ceremony in 1986, the United Church of Canada officially apologized to Indian people for organized religion's history of suppressing Indian culture. Two years later, a Jesuit missionary in Ontario apologized for the way that the Catholic church had attacked native culture for so many decades. However, he admitted that some Jesuits still believe they have nothing to apologize for. He asked the Indians to forgive the missionaries.

After the Second World War, new social trends began to influence the federal government's Indian policies. As society became more secular, the notion of turning Indians into Christians was less important. At the same time, Canadians were beginning to adopt more liberal attitudes, and some of the most blatant forms of discrimination against Indians were becoming unpopular. In 1948, a parliamentary committee recommended that Indians be permitted to vote in federal elections. The same committee recommended that Indian children be educated with non-Indians in integrated provincial schools.

Despite the committee's report, Indians were not allowed to vote in federal elections until 1960. In the meantime, however, Ottawa took its first steps toward dismantling the residential schools. As a result of amendments to the Indian Act in 1951, the federal government was authorized to make agreements with the provinces to allow Indian children to attend regular public schools—the same provincial schools that non-Indian children attended. Gradually, during the 1950s and 1960s, Indian children who lived within driving distance of a provincial school were pushed into the provincial system. Most were bussed to the nearest school, usually in a town or city. The residential schools were slowly phased out.

The new policy resulted partly from vague feelings of egalitarianism, but it also stemmed from a desire to assimilate Indian children into white society. The provincial school system was now perceived to be the most effective way of absorbing Indian culture into the dominant white culture. Indian leaders had not asked for a policy of assimilation, but the policy was introduced, nevertheless.

Under the new education policy, Ottawa agreed to transfer money to the provinces to pay for the education of Indians in public schools. Joint agreements were struck between the federal government and individual school boards, whereby Ottawa gave each school board an annual fee for each Indian student who attended a school under the board's jurisdiction. In most cases, this fee was paid in September. Once the money was received, there was no incentive for the provincial schools to keep the Indian children in school. If an Indian student dropped out in October or November, the school boards still received the full fee.

The new education policy was only slightly more enlightened than the old philosophy. At the provincial schools, the Indians were submerged in large classrooms of white students and taught by white teachers who had little interest in the native culture. Administrators and teachers at the provincial schools made the same basic assumption as the people who ran the residential schools: that the educational system should teach Indians to adopt the white European viewpoint of the world.

Like the residential schools, the provincial schools were located at a distance from the Indian reserves, so Indian parents and the Indian community had little involvement with them. Indians were not allowed to sit on school boards—or even vote in school board elections.

For the Indian children, the experience of attending the provincial schools was almost as traumatic as going to a residential school. "We were not prepared for it at all," said one student who was transferred from a residential school to a provincial school in Alberta in the 1960s. "We were so used to being with our native peers that we were not used to being around white people. Just the nuns and priests were the only white contacts we ever had…. And all of a sudden you're thrown in with a bunch of white kids that laugh at you because everybody is wearing coveralls. We were very vulnerable to insults from the white kids."

In many cases, the white teachers in provincial schools simply assumed that their Indian students were slow learners. The Indian students were assessed with standardized tests that had been designed for white middle-class English-speaking urban students. At one provincial school, where the 1,400 students included 189 from a nearby Cree Indian reserve, the teachers applied those standardized tests and concluded that 164 of the 189 Indian students were "ineducable". The results were carefully entered into the permanent records of the Indian students.

The textbooks in the provincial schools only added to the alienation of Indian students. In *Teaching Prejudice*, an analysis of Ontario social studies textbooks carried out in 1971, researchers found that Indians were portrayed less favourably than any other ethnic group. They were described as primitive, unskilled, aggressive, and hostile. In history books, descriptions of Indians killing white people were called "massacres", but when a group of Indians was killed by Europeans or Euro-Canadians, the books described the incidents as "fights" or "battles".

It soon became obvious that the provincial schools were not a solution to the question of Indian education. The dropout rates and failure rates for native children continued to be high. About 94 percent of Indian students in the public school system were failing to graduate from high school.

In 1969, a group of Indians from the Saddle Lake reserve in northeastern Alberta took the first steps toward self-government in education. They began by demanding the hiring of Indian teachers at the nearby Blue Quills residential school. A few native teachers were hired as a result of the request. But in October 1969, a native woman overheard a federal bureaucrat discussing a plan to shut down the school permanently as part of the shift to provincial control of Indian education. She telephoned the Saddle Lake School Committee, a group of parents, and other band members from the Saddle Lake reserve. The committee members wanted a chance to try running the school. When they asked for a meeting with a senior Indian Affairs official, the request was denied, so in July 1970, they launched a sit-in at Blue Quills school.

Within a few days, about 250 people had joined the original group of 60. For several weeks they sang and danced in the school gymnasium while Indian elders prayed and held pipe ceremonies. A group of young native men went hunting every day to provide food for the protestors.

Eventually the federal government bowed to the pressure, and in September 1970, Blue Quills became the first Canadian school to be controlled by an Indian community. Courses in the Cree language became part of the curriculum. Attendance began to increase, and the school expanded to cover high school as well as elementary school grades. Within fifteen years, the school had produced 135 high school graduates.

The next step was taken by the National Indian Brotherhood, the main native group in Canada and the forerunner of today's Assembly of First Nations. In 1972 the National Indian Brotherhood produced *Indian Control of Indian Education,* a landmark paper on the issue of native education that proposed a dramatic shift in federal education policy. "Until now," they wrote, "decisions on the education of Indian children have been made by anyone and everyone, except Indian parents.... If we are to avoid the conflict of values which in the past has led to withdrawal and failure, Indian parents must have control of education with the responsibility of setting goals." Using Blue Quills as their model, the National Indian Brotherhood proposed a system of band-controlled schools in which Indian parents would at last have a voice. Within a year, Ottawa agreed to the principle of Indian control of Indian education.

Today, about 28 percent of Canada's 82,000 Indian elementary and high school students are attending schools controlled by Indian bands. There are about 240 band-controlled schools in the country—mostly in British Columbia and the Prairies. A few regional Indian groups—including the Nishgas of British Columbia and the Cree of northern Quebec—have established their own school boards. Most band-controlled schools, however, operate on a smaller scale. Funding is provided by the Indian Affairs Department, but committees of parents make the key decisions for each school.

Indian Affairs continues to exercise some influence over the band-controlled schools, since the department decides how much money a band should receive for the annual budget of its school. But once the money arrives, the Indian community has the power to allocate its education budget in any way it chooses—as long as the community sends regular financial reports to the department and submits to an annual audit.

In most cases, the band-controlled schools have decided to follow the basic provincial curriculum, with modifications to allow native languages and culture to be taught. These modifications require extra funds, of course, yet band-controlled schools receive less money per student than provincial schools. The average federal spending on an Indian in a provincial school in 1985–86 was $4,263, while the average spending on an Indian in a band-controlled school was $3,916. Often band-controlled schools cannot afford to develop their own textbooks and teaching materials. Nor can they afford to match the salaries that teachers receive at provincial schools. As a result, they sometimes find it difficult to attract good teachers.

The Indian Affairs Department has rarely provided adequate training or preparation for Indian bands that decide to take control of the schools on their reserves. A federal report in 1982 said the policy of transferring control to Indian bands was undermined by the fact that bands were not given enough time to prepare for the new responsibility. According to the report, the federal policy was "riddled with inconsistencies" because it lacked any guidelines for band takeovers. Frequent conflicts between the bands and the Indian Affairs Department have made the problem worse. For all these reasons, dozens of bands have gone through a painful transition period as they have struggled to learn the administrative skills necessary for running a school.

After taking control of education policies on their reserve, the Ojibway band at Sabaskong Bay was uncertain how to hire teachers or purchase school supplies. Their students ended up sharing books and desks for the first year, and several teachers were hired and then fired. Teachers spent weeks trying to establish a line of credit from book publishers. "It was chaotic," said Darlene Bob, education counsellor at Sabaskong Bay. "It was really overwhelming. We were totally unprepared. All of a sudden we had all the control. No one from the department came down to help us. We made a lot of mistakes. Some of our people didn't even know what kind of teachers to look for. They didn't know that some teachers had a degree and others only had a certificate."

The four Cree bands at Hobbema, Alberta, have learned from the difficulties that other bands have experienced. They have decided to keep their students in federal and provincial schools because they are unhappy with the lack of preparation and training offered by Ottawa before takeovers. "It hasn't been a positive experience for other bands," said Brian Wildcat, director of education for the four bands. "We want a transition period. But the department just wants us to take over on September 1. There would be years of growing pains."

Once the short-term pain is over, however, the band-controlled schools tend to be much more successful than their federal or provincial counterparts. Bands that control their own education have reversed decades of high dropout and failure rates and high rates of absenteeism. Year after year, Indian-controlled schools across the country are producing proportionately more graduates than the federal or provincial schools where Indians are enrolled. The result is a dramatic improvement in the overall level of Indian education in Canada. In 1972, before the band takeovers, only half of the Indian students in Grade 8 were returning to school the following year. By 1985, two-thirds of the Indian Grade 8 graduates were remaining in school. From 1972 to 1985, the number of Indian students enrolled in grades 10 to 12 almost doubled.

In 1981–82, only half of the Indian students at the Alexander reserve northwest of Edmonton were attending classes at the reserve's federal school. There were no Indian teachers at the school, the dropout rate was 100 percent, and the federal school had not produced a single Grade 12 graduate in the previous decade. In their level of education, most of the Indian children were lagging three to five years behind non-Indian students in provincial schools. But in 1987, five years after the band took control of the school, the dropout rate was reduced to just 2 percent. Attendance exceeded 90 percent and nine students had graduated from Grade 12. Most students were progressing at the same rate as the provincial average. Many native teachers and teacher assistants were employed at the school. At the beginning of every day, a traditional sweetgrass ceremony was performed. Cree was widely spoken among the students, the teacher assistants, and some of the teachers.

At the Kahnawake reserve near Montreal, Mohawk parents withdrew their children from a Montreal high school in 1978. With virtually no funding, the band created a makeshift school with volunteer teachers at a temporary location on the reserve. Within a few years, the Mohawks had established the Kahnawake Survival School for about two hundred Indian students in grades 7 to 11. The band members controlled the school through an elected committee, which effectively served as a school board for the reserve. By 1985, more than half of the school's forty staff members were Mohawk, and a six-person team was drafting a new curriculum for the school, with particular emphasis on the Mohawk culture and language. While public schools across Canada feature large portraits of the Queen and Prince Philip on the walls, the Survival School has pictures of the sacred eagle.

Indian self-government in education has allowed bands to begin teaching their native languages to their students. At some band-controlled schools, especially those where English is the first language spoken at home by Indian children, the native language is taught once a day as a separate subject. At the Saddle Lake reserve, for example, children study Cree language and culture for eighty minutes every day. At other schools, including the Nishga schools in northwestern British Columbia, bilingual programs allow students to choose their native language as the primary language of instruction for a number of classes. And a few schools, such as the Kahnawake Survival School, have immersion programs in which the native language is the primary language of instruction for all classes.

Bilingualism is one of the key goals of Indian educators. They want their young people to be fluent in English or French, so that they are not shut out of jobs and other opportunities in Canadian society, but they also want them to become fluent in their native tongue. Language is still essential to preserve their native heritage, to promote pride in native culture, and to transfer that culture from one generation to the next. Researchers have also found that Indian children learn better if they are taught in their mother tongue.

Indian-controlled schools have been widely acclaimed. "The teaching of native studies, native languages and native culture is instilling in students a pride in their heritage and respect for their culture," the Canadian Education Association concluded in a 1983 report. "Native teachers are providing positive adult role models for children.... From all indications, it would appear that native children in band schools are achieving greater academic success and are remaining in school longer than those in provincial school systems or those attending federally operated reserve schools."

New training programs, allowing Indian students to remain in the north as they earn their degrees in education, have produced several hundred native teachers in the past fifteen years. These programs are usually affiliated with universities, but the actual training courses are often given in classrooms on Indian reserves to ensure close contact between the student teachers and the community. The training programs are beginning to achieve their goals. A decade ago, only 3 percent of the teachers in northern Saskatchewan were of native ancestry. Today, one-quarter are native. Studies have shown that native students are more responsive in the classroom and participate in classroom discussions more frequently when their teacher is native.

In western Canada, where the Indian population is largest, several Indian-controlled colleges have been established. They have produced hundreds of graduates. The best-known of these is the Saskatchewan Indian Federated College, which is affiliated with the University of Regina. Beginning in 1976 with only a handful of students, it soon became one of the fastest-growing colleges in North America. By 1989, nearly eight hundred part-time and full-time students were enrolled. In the space of a decade, the Indian-controlled institution gave degrees and diplomas to more than four hundred graduates. A further four hundred graduates are expected by 1991.

The college is guided by ten elected chiefs and two Indian senators who sit on its board of governors. The faculty is led by Indian professors who have doctorates and master's degrees. Native elders conduct pipe ceremonies every morning and meet the students individually to help them learn about their heritage. Visiting professors and exchange students come to the Saskatchewan college from around the world.

In 1988, a milestone was reached at the University of Regina. For the first time in the university's history, a student from the Saskatchewan Indian Federated College was awarded the President's Medal—the top academic prize at the university. The student, Doreen Johnson from the Alkali Lake reserve in British Columbia, graduated with an average of 87.4 percent in her social work courses. She was also awarded the University Prize in Social Work. During her years at the college, she served as editor of the student newspaper, tutored fellow students, and organized a support group for battered native women. Perhaps most remarkably, she achieved all of that as a single parent with four young children and a nephew living with her. When the award was presented at the 1988 fall convocation, Doreen Johnson carried an eagle feather as she walked onto the stage. "I wanted everyone to know that I'm an Indian," she said later.

Despite the overwhelming evidence of the benefits of Indian self-government in the schools, almost half of all Indian students are still sent to provincial schools today, and a further 23 percent are still attending federally controlled schools. There are serious problems in the current system, with its confusing mixture of jurisdictions. A federal review in 1982 said the system is plagued by "extreme fragmentation".

At the federal schools, there is often a high turnover rate and poor morale among the teachers because of their low salaries and the dilapidated school buildings they must work in. Federal principals are not required to have the same qualifications as principals in the provincial system, and the teachers usually have no training in native culture or language. Indian parents have virtually no control over the education that their children receive in the federal schools.

Federal schools on Indian reserves are frequently so decrepit that they are routinely shut down because of leaking roofs or fire hazards. Students sit at home for days or weeks as they wait for the schools to be patched up. A federal school at the St. Theresa Point reserve in northern Manitoba was shut down for more than a month in 1988 because fuel-oil fumes were leaking into the classrooms. The Fort Albany band in northern Ontario waited twenty years for a new school, enduring regular shutdowns every year. As late as 1988, the children of Fort Albany could reach the school only by crossing a narrow causeway that was swamped by water and ice every spring. A federal official described the school as "a monster" because of its fire safety violations.

Federal officials have acknowledged that forty schools on Ontario Indian reserves need to be renovated or replaced. A study in 1988 by the Assembly of First Nations estimated that at least $411 million is required to repair schools on Indian reserves and build new ones.

Meanwhile, 49 percent of Canadian Indian children are sent to provincial schools, which continue to receive guaranteed payments from the Indian Affairs Department even if the Indian students drop out of school. Federal money, intended to pay for Indian education, ends up going to the benefit of the white students who remain in the schools after the Indians drop out.

In Alberta, the children from four Cree reserves near Hobbema are scattered among thirty-five schools in the central region of the province. Few of the provincial schools make any effort to include native culture in their curriculum. There is a disastrously high dropout rate among the Hobbema children—beginning as early as Grade 4. By the senior years of high school, the dropout rate is 90 percent. "Something is terribly wrong," says Lillian Potts, a councillor and former chief of the Montana band at Hobbema. "We're not all dumb."

In the Cree culture, children learn to avoid eye contact with others. But at the provincial schools, the teachers tell them, "Look at me." In the Cree culture, children learn quietly by watching the example of others. There is no compulsion, no constant instruction. Silence has significance and meaning—it implies thoughtfulness and reflection. But at the provincial schools, the education system is based on mandatory rules, strict instruction, and prompt responses from the students. Teachers expect obedience from their students. "The children are taught one thing at home, and when they go to school they're taught that it's wrong," Lillian Potts says. "It's a culture shock. The ones who succeed are those who are more adaptable to the dominant society."

Because of the widespread criticism of the provincial school system and its treatment of Indian children, the Alberta government appointed a committee to study the issue. After holding several months of public hearings, the committee confirmed that the criticism of the provincial schools was valid. "The failure to respond to the special needs of native students has been a shameful act of intolerance and misunderstanding," the committee said in its 1984 report.

The committee, headed by Calgary lawyer Ron Ghitter, concluded that native students "are being treated as second-class citizens by our educational system." It said there is "much to be done to redress the neglect, ill-conceived policies and paternalistic approach that has for too long symbolized the state of native education."

Research by the Ghitter committee found that the dropout rate for native students was as high as 85 percent in some provincial schools. Provincial teachers often lack the training necessary to make their classes relevant to native children, and testing procedures in provincial schools are often biased against Indian children, the report said. "It is a feat of courage, perseverance and dedication for a native student, particularly from an isolated community, to complete high school in Alberta."

Despite some improvements in the Indian education system in recent years, much remains to be done. An estimated 80 percent of Indian students across Canada are still dropping out of school before completing Grade 12. The dropout rate for non-Indian students, by comparison, is only 30 percent. The education system for Indians is fragmented, underfunded, and still largely controlled by white institutions.

Indian leaders have a vision for the future—a vision based on the unfulfilled goals of the National Indian Brotherhood's 1972 policy paper on Indian education. They believe that Indian bands must settle for nothing less than complete jurisdiction over the education of their children. They must have the authority and the resources to control their schools, to set the standards for their education system, to use their own language in the schools, and to develop their own curriculum and textbooks whenever the provincial curriculum is inadequate.

Certainly, progress has been made. But roadblocks and obstacles always seem to emerge to delay the advances. The number of Indian post-secondary students, for example, increased sharply from about 1,000 students in 1971 to more than 14,000 in 1987. Then the federal government decided to clamp down on its financial assistance. In 1989, a ceiling was placed on Ottawa's assistance to Indian post-secondary students, making it inevitable that hundreds of qualified candidates would be unable to get assistance.

In the spring of 1989, a group of Indian students staged a five-week hunger strike to protest the restrictions on federal aid. They were supported by rallies and sit-ins by Indians across the country. They argued that the new policy was illogical and self-defeating, since education is still the surest way of helping Indian people avoid the prisons and the welfare rolls. "If Canada continues to cap our education dollars, we will perpetually be in a situation where upwards of 90 percent of our people are unemployed, and we will continue to be a drain on this country," said Georges Erasmus, national chief of the Assembly of First Nations.

The government responded by pointing to a technical loophole in its treaty obligations. The nineteenth-century treaties had promised that the federal government would provide an education for Indians who chose it, but the treaties did not mention universities and colleges— because virtually none existed anywhere in Canada at the time. For decades, Liberal and Conservative governments have accepted that they should help finance a post-secondary education for any Indian student who wants it. But the present Conservative government has rejected that obligation, on the grounds that the treaties did not explicitly refer to post-secondary education.

At Sabaskong Bay, a dozen students were unable to attend college or university because of restrictions on federal aid. "They were all enthusiastic, but I had to tell them they couldn't go," Darlene Bob said. "It was difficult to tell them. Now they're all sitting at home, doing nothing."

David Kelly, a young Ojibway from Sabaskong Bay, is one of the fortunate ones. He has managed to stay in university, despite the federal cutbacks. A product of the new era of Indian self-government in the schools, Kelly was educated at the band-controlled high school at Sabaskong Bay. His teachers talked to the students about Indian issues. Elders came into the classroom to demonstrate the harvesting and preparation of wild rice. A trapper was invited to one of his classes to show the students how to skin animals. "It was very important to the reserve," Kelly says. "If that school wasn't there, a lot of kids wouldn't be in school. They wouldn't have diplomas or anything. I don't know if I would have made it through."

Today, David Kelly is studying at Lakehead University in Thunder Bay, working toward a Bachelor of Arts and a Bachelor of Education. His aim is to become a teacher—to continue the work of forging a new future for his people.

CHAPTER THREE
Inside the Reserves

The city of Sydney is dominated by the tall stacks of its steel mill. Plumes of orange dust belch out of the stacks, staining the sky and casting a pall over the frame houses and churches nearby. It is a historic city—the steel mill was built in 1889 and some of the houses date back to the late 1700s. But the glory days of industrialization are long past, the steelworks are now debt-ridden and heavily subsidized, and the rusting plant is surrounded by tar ponds and slag heaps. The local economy is depressed; unemployment is high.

More than a century ago, a band of Micmac Indians lived on a small reserve on the outskirts of Sydney—a picturesque spot on the banks of the Sydney River overlooking the harbour. Today there is no trace of the reserve. In its place stand a cluster of motels, asphalt parking lots, and modern medical offices. Cars and trucks speed past on Kings Road, a busy commercial route that follows the Sydney River.

Above the river, looking down on Kings Road, is a comfortable middle-class neighbourhood whose streets have names like Castle Drive and Holyrood Avenue. Up the hill, away from the river and past the big homes on Castle Drive, an unassuming road called Membertou Street cuts through a bleak tract of garbage-strewn brush and eventually leads to the Membertou reserve—the home of the native people who disappeared from their dwellings on the Sydney River in the 1920s.

The five hundred Micmacs of Membertou are within the town limits, but they are isolated behind the ring of swampy brush. Only one street leads into the reserve, and there are no sidewalks. Outsiders do not enter the reserve unless they have a specific purpose. "Don't go up there at night," a taxi driver tells a visitor. He claims it is unsafe. In reality, the reserve is as safe as any other neighbourhood of Sydney, but the townsfolk still perceive it as dangerous.

It was here, on the Membertou reserve, that Donald Marshall grew up. As the eldest son of the Grand Chief of the Micmac Nation, he was in line to become the next Grand Chief—the spiritual leader of the Micmac people. But in 1971 he was uprooted from Membertou and shipped to prison, where he was locked away for eleven years for a murder he did not commit.

The story of Donald Marshall is, in a way, the story of his people. Like the native people in the rest of Nova Scotia and across Canada, the Micmacs of Membertou were uprooted again and again by the legal and political institutions of white society.

Almost five centuries ago, the Micmacs became the first native North Americans to encounter Europeans. When the first European explorers arrived, there were 10,000 to 35,000 Micmacs living on the east coast of Canada. They migrated between the ocean and inland lakes, looking for fish, lobster, crabs, wildfowl, moose, bear, and beaver—all of which were in abundant supply. The Micmacs were healthier than many Europeans at the time. Studies of Micmac skeletal remains from the pre-European period have shown that they had an average life expectancy of thirty-four to forty years—a lifespan that the average European did not achieve until the nineteenth century.

The Micmacs had their own political structures, boundaries, laws, and a sophisticated culture and language. Their language, which is often compared to Latin, has been described as one of the most beautiful in the world. One word in Micmac can express a thought that may require several English words to express, and a single verb can have more than two hundred different endings. Although English has one of the richest vocabularies of any language in the world, Micmac surpasses it by far. It is believed to have five times as many words as English has.

The early European settlers did not recognize or respect the subtleties of Micmac culture. They set about converting the Micmacs to Christianity and involving them in the wars between the French and the British. The intruders also introduced diseases, alcohol, and new kinds of food—all of which soon reduced the Micmac population.

Early in the eighteenth century, as British settlements began to spread across Nova Scotia, the Micmacs launched a guerrilla war to resist the encroachment on their territory. The British responded with a sustained campaign of genocide. In 1749, Nova Scotia's English governor, Colonel Edward Cornwallis, ordered his troops to "annoy, distress, take or destroy the Savages commonly called Mic-macks, wherever they are found." He established two companies of volunteers to hunt and kill Micmacs, offered a reward of ten pounds sterling for every Micmac scalped or taken prisoner, and ordered his troops to burn the forests to make it difficult for the Micmacs to subsist. The campaign of genocide continued relentlessly for more than a decade. Hundreds of Micmacs were massacred. Some bands of Micmacs were shot as they slept.

In the early 1760s, peace agreements were reached, but over the next few decades, the Micmacs faced constant pressure as British settlers flooded into Nova Scotia. Starvation and smallpox decimated their population. Hepatitis and tuberculosis, caused by poor living conditions and inadequate diet, killed many more. By the 1840s, the Micmacs were on the brink of extinction. Only 1,300 remained alive. "Almost the whole Micmac population are now vagrants, who wander from place to place and door to door seeking alms," a government official wrote. "They are clothed in rags. Necessity often compels them to consume putrid and unwholesome food." In 1853 the Nova Scotia Indian commissioner concluded that the Micmacs were "fast passing away."

Although the Micmacs had signed treaties of coexistence and friendship with the British, at no point did they agree to surrender their land. The British government simply assumed that the entire colony belonged to the Crown. And so the Micmacs received no compensation when their land was taken over by European settlers.

In the early nineteenth century, after the Micmacs pleaded for land of their own, the government allocated about a thousand acres for the

Indians in each county of Nova Scotia. By the end of the century, about forty small reserves had been set aside for the Micmacs.

Most of the reserves were inadequate for agriculture or any other form of economic activity. A survey of the Bear River reserve, for example, found that "the greater part is stoney, and of little value." Any Indian land that was discovered to be fertile was soon taken over by white settlers who built houses and farms on the reserves. In 1859, the Nova Scotia Legislature authorized these trespasses by allowing the settlers to gain title to the Micmac land. Stripped of any substantial resources, the Micmacs were effectively kept in a state of poverty. A few survived on small-scale farms, but most were forced to seek employment outside their reserves.

During the industrial boom of the late nineteenth and early twentieth centuries, some Micmacs were able to earn a steady income as labourers on the fringes of industry. But by the 1930s, the Maritime economy was falling into permanent decline as shipbuilding and lumber operations were scaled down and layoffs began. Micmac workers were among the first to be dismissed. "The local employer, in his endeavour to keep down local employment costs, never hesitated to give preference to the white man," a federal official reported in 1941.

Hundreds of Micmacs became so desperate that they moved to Boston, where jobs were plentiful, racism was less of a barrier, and ethnic minorities were easily accepted into the cultural melting pot. By the 1960s, several thousand Canadian Micmacs were living in New England.

The reserve system, introduced by the British in some of their early treaties with the Indians of Upper Canada, was extended and entrenched by the Canadian government in the nineteenth and twentieth centuries. Like all other Canadian Indians who lived on reserves, the Micmacs of Nova Scotia were governed by the Indian Act of 1876. It was this legislation that gave the federal government most of its powers over the lives of aboriginal people. To a large extent, those federal powers still exist today, enshrined in an amended Indian Act.

The reserves were created to remove Indians from the path of white settlement and to assimilate them by transforming them into farmers. In some cases, the reserves were still blocking urban growth and industrial development, so they were expropriated and relocated. In the end, most of the reserves were too small and infertile to permit any significant amount of farming. Indian leaders sometimes compare their reserves to "postage stamps"—an accurate description if they are compared to American Indian reservations. Less than 0.2 percent of Canada's total area is reserved for Indians, while in the United States the proportion set aside for Indians is twenty times larger.

In 1983, the small size of Canadian Indian reserves was criticized by a House of Commons committee on Indian self-government. The committee noted that the total size of the reserves is just one-fifth as large as the amount of land set aside for national parks. The reserves are equally small in comparison to the land set aside for airports and military bases. And the amount of land available for the average Indian is falling steadily as the Indian population increases. "The committee does not dispute the need for parks, defence bases and airports; but surely the land rights of the aboriginal inhabitants of this continent deserve as much or more attention," the committee said.

The Indian Act defines a "reserve" as "a tract of land, the legal title to which is vested in Her Majesty, that has been set apart by Her Majesty for the use and benefit of a band." In other words, reserves are legally controlled by the federal government, although Indians are permitted to "use" the land. Although land has always been central to the native economy and the native way of life, Indians remain vulnerable to expropriation and dislocation because they do not have legal title to their land. Under Section 35 of the Indian Act, the federal government has the authority to transfer land on an Indian reserve to a provincial or municipal government or to a corporation, without obtaining the consent of the Indians who live there.

For more than a century, the sweeping powers of the Indian Act have allowed Ottawa to keep the Indian population under its thumb. The Act applies to "status" Indians—those who are registered in Ottawa as official members of a recognized band, usually living on a reserve. Non-status Indians may be full-blooded Indians, but, for a variety of reasons, they were never registered in Ottawa. Until recently Indian women lost their status if they married a white man. The term Métis was originally applied to people of French and Indian descent but now applies more generally to any mixed-blood native people who identify themselves as Métis.

Until 1960, Indians were not permitted to vote in federal elections unless they were prepared to give up their Indian status in a formal process known as enfranchisement. New Brunswick and Prince Edward Island did not give Indians the franchise until 1963, and Alberta and Quebec refused to let Indians vote until 1965 and 1969, respectively.

The Indian Act effectively bars Indian bands from mortgaging their land—through Section 29, which guarantees that reserve lands cannot be seized as collateral for a loan. Since mortgages are one of the most common ways for entrepreneurs to raise funds for new economic ventures, this provision makes it difficult for bands to launch their own business enterprises. Without this tool, Indian bands must hope for government loans or other sources of revenue. Bands are allowed to lease out parcels of reserve land, but not without first surrendering their rights to the land to the federal government. The hunting and fishing rights of aboriginal people are also weakened by the Indian Act. Section 73 allows the federal government to pass regulations to limit hunting and fishing on the reserves, and Section 88 allows provincial governments to put reserves under the jurisdiction of provincial game conservation laws.

The Indian Act also imposes severe restrictions on the political power of Indians. The band council, headed by a chief, is supposed to be the elected authority at each reserve, yet the powers of the band councils are curtailed by Section 82, which gives the Indian Affairs minister the authority to disallow any bylaw passed by a council. Even when the minister permits a bylaw to be passed, it is likely to relate to an insignificant issue. Section 81 allows the band councils to pass bylaws over minor matters such as "the destruction and control of noxious weeds" and "the regulation of bee-keeping and poultry-raising".

The federal government has not hesitated to exercise its veto powers—even on relatively trivial matters. When the Membertou band in Sydney passed a bylaw to enforce speed limits on the reserve in 1979, the Indian Affairs Department disallowed it because, according to the department, the bylaw exceeded "the scope of the powers enumerated in Section 81 of the Indian Act".

The combined effect of the paternalistic restrictions in the Indian Act has crippled the economies of most reserves. In 1981, a federal memorandum admitted that the government's policies had created "dependent and alienated Indian societies which demonstrate many of the characteristics of underdeveloped nations in Africa, Asia, and Latin America."

Until the 1960s, the provisions of the Indian Act were enforced by federal employees, known as Indian agents, who had enormous powers over the reserves. In the Prairies, for example, Indians had to seek a special permit from the agents before they could sell their crops or cattle. Even the purchase of farm implements required a permit from the agent. This system became a disciplinary tool. If an Indian annoyed the agent in some way, he could lose his permit to sell crops. "It is most wretchedly humbling to many a worthy fellow to have to go, with assumed indifference, to ask or beg for a permit to sell one load of hay that he has cut himself, on his own reserve, with his own horses and implements," the early Cree leader Edward Ahenakew once wrote.

The Indian agents had other powers too. They had the authority to prosecute Indians on the reserves and to preside over band council meetings. They could prohibit an Indian from leaving his reserve without a pass, and they suppressed native spiritual ceremonies such as the potlatch and Sun Dance. Some of the Indian agents operated almost like dictators. "Here I was a young kid in his early twenties and I was absolutely astounded at the power I had over the life of these people," one former Indian agent recalled.

By the late 1960s, the Indian agents were gone. However, some of the power of the Indian agent has reverted to the federal bureaucrats who control the flow of money from the Indian Affairs Department to the reserves, thereby controlling the quality of life of the people who live there. On most reserves, vast sums of federal money are spent on welfare and other forms of social assistance—the largest single item in the budget of the Indian Affairs Department. "As a result there has been a short-fall in funds for job creation, economic development and community infrastructure," a federal discussion paper acknowledged in 1981. The department's budget puts its emphasis on welfare dependence, rather than economic self-sufficiency.

With such sweeping powers at its disposal, it has been easy for the Department of Indian Affairs to make decisions that fail to take into account the interests of native people. In cities such as Sarnia and Victoria, the department has expropriated Indian land and pushed native communities out of the city. But some of the most blatant abuses of federal power took place in Nova Scotia, where Micmacs were arbitrarily moved to inferior locations twice in the space of a quarter-century.

Helen Martin was born on the Kings Road reserve in Sydney in 1922. Her father was Ben Christmas, chief of the Sydney Micmacs for forty-two years. Today she sits in her small house on the Membertou reserve, where the Micmacs were sent in the 1920s, and looks at a scrapbook of memories. She points to photographs of the Micmac houses on the old Kings Road reserve. "Look at the houses," she says. "They're not bad."

Many of the two-storey houses on the old reserve were bigger than the bungalows that were allotted to the Micmacs after they were forced to move in 1925. The bungalows were so small that some of the children had to sleep in the kitchens. "My father built our old house," Helen Martin recalls. "He said our old house was bigger. We had three bedrooms upstairs and one bedroom downstairs. He said we got a raw deal. He was always a fighter."

Helen Martin has grey hair and a brown face. Her front teeth are missing, and she is puffing on a cigarette and wearing a housecoat. As her grandchildren scamper through the house, she sits at her kitchen table, writing stories of Micmac history and folklore on the sheets of looseleaf paper that pile up around her. Among her people, she is recognized as the unofficial historian of Membertou.

She remembers how the Micmacs refused to move for a decade after they were ordered to leave. "It's a very sad story, how the Indians were moved. They tore everything down. We weren't good enough for the white man. They took us away from that reserve because of racism."

The Kings Road reserve was established in 1882, after the Micmacs had lived on the site for decades. It was a tiny patch of land—barely two acres. In 1888, the Intercolonial Railway arrived in Sydney, and two-thirds of an acre was expropriated from the reserve to make room for the railway. The Micmacs were given $550 in compensation and were left with just 1.4 acres for the entire band, which had several dozen members.

In the meantime, a prominent citizen named Joseph Gillies had purchased land on the northern boundary of the Micmac reserve. Gillies was the solicitor for the town of Sydney, the owner of the town newspaper, and a Conservative MP from 1892 to 1900 — a powerful figure in Nova Scotia politics. And he was determined to get rid of his Micmac neighbours.

Gillies said the Indians annoyed him "to a point really beyond endurance." In 1899 he wrote to the federal Department of the Interior, demanding to be "rid of the nuisance speedily." He recruited the support of Sydney's mayor, who recognized that the Kings Road property had become much more valuable after the influx of population that occurred when the Sydney steelworks opened. The Micmacs were seen as an impediment to commercial development and a damper on property values.

The federal Department of the Interior, which was responsible for Indian affairs at the time, spent several years trying to persuade the Micmacs to surrender their land, but the band refused to move. Gillies became frustrated. "It is too sad to think of a big department like the Department of the Interior, that it should be beaten by a band of Indians," Gillies told a federal official.

In 1914, a tall barbed-wire fence was erected to prevent the Micmacs from entering the property of their neighbours on Kings Road. The neighbours circulated petitions to demand the relocation of the entire band. The following year, the Exchequer Court of Canada held a hearing to decide whether to remove the Micmacs from Kings Road. Twenty-one witnesses spoke at the hearing. Almost all were white. Their testimony was peppered with racist remarks, fuelled by their desire for financial gain. Gillies argued that the Micmacs "are a most undesirable class to have near one.... Where you get an undesirable class anywhere, they certainly depreciate the value of the property." Businessmen testified that the Micmacs were "an objectionable feature in the matter of selling real estate out in that direction."

Gillies and his neighbours complained that the Micmac reserve was filthy and unsanitary, yet the Sydney medical officer testified that the sanitation at the Kings Road reserve was no worse than it was in other sections of the town. The neighbours said the Micmacs were drunk and rowdy, yet a Sydney magistrate revealed that only seven Micmacs had appeared before him in the previous ten years. "The record of the Indians as a whole is good," the magistrate testified.

Gillies and the other neighbours complained that the Kings Road reserve was too crowded, with 122 Micmacs living on the tiny site.

But when Micmac leader Joe Julian suggested that the government could purchase land from a neighbour named Frank Neil to expand the reserve and relieve the overcrowding, the idea was flatly rejected. The testimony went like this:

> *Julian*: Can't we enlarge our place, where we are now?
> *Gillies*: No, I don't think so.
> *Julien*: From Frank Neil's?
> *Gillies*: We want to get you away from the Kings Road.
> *Julian*: Is that the question?
> *Gillies*: It cannot be enlarged. I don't want to sell any of my place.
> *Julian*: That is the way, we do not want to sell ours.

Two other Micmac leaders, Ben Christmas and Joe Christmas, confirmed that the Micmacs wanted to stay on the Kings Road reserve. If they were relocated, they would soon face complaints from their new neighbours, who would try to make them move again, Ben Christmas told the court. His words were prophetic. Less than thirty years later, the government would attempt to move the Micmacs from the new Membertou reserve to an even poorer location.

In his ruling in March 1916, Mr. Justice L. A. Audette of the Exchequer Court admitted that the Indians were "reasonably well-behaved" and "healthy" at their Kings Road reserve. But he argued that the reserve was too small and congested. This was a cruel irony. The size of the reserve had been determined by government edict in 1882, and now it was being used as an excuse to remove the Indians.

"No one cares to live in the immediate vicinity of the Indians," the judge wrote in his ruling. "The removal would make the property in that neighbourhood more valuable for assessment purposes—and it is no doubt an anomaly to have this Indian reserve in almost the centre of the city, or on one of its principal thoroughfares.... The overwhelming weight of the evidence is to the effect that the reserve retards and is a clog on the development of that part of the city."

The judge agreed with Gillies that the Micmacs were morally inferior. "The racial inequalities of the Indians, as compared with the white men, check to a great extent any move towards social development.... I do therefore, without hesitation, come to the conclusion, on this branch of the case, that the removal of the Indians from the reserve is obviously in the interest of the public." He declared that the Micmacs "will not suffer anything serious" from their relocation.

The Micmacs could not fight back. Like all other Indians in Canada, they were not permitted to vote in federal or provincial elections, and they had virtually no legal rights. They were powerless to oppose the judge's decision.

Following the ruling by Mr. Justice Audette, there was a delay of a number of years while an alternative site was sought for the Micmacs. Eventually the government acquired a 66.5-acre tract of land on the southern fringes of Sydney—a worthless plot of swamp, rocks, and woodland. This was the Membertou reserve—the new home of the Micmacs. Over a period of several years, beginning in 1925, the Indians reluctantly moved away from the banks of the Sydney River. They began to clear the trees and settle into their new life.

The Micmacs had always been a maritime people who depended on fishing and canoeing, but at the new site, for the first time in their lives, they had no access to the water. It was a psychological and economic blow to the Micmacs. Joe Julian had tried to explain to the Exchequer Court that the Micmacs needed a river or a lake, but he had been ignored.

Water is "a vital element in the Micmac culture," says Bernie Francis of the Membertou band. "Micmacs in Membertou have difficulty exercising their customs now because they are no longer near water. The feeling of being close to the water was taken away from the people. It's like being chained."

The Indian Affairs Department built bungalows at the new reserve in the 1920s and 1930s, but they were not connected to the Sydney water lines until the mid-1950s. Because of the rocks and swamp, the reserve was poorly drained and the bungalows were often flooded. The dampness caused illnesses among the children. Ben Christmas, the long-time chief, pleaded for assistance from local politicans and federal bureaucrats in the 1930s, but his petitions were dismissed. The Indian Affairs Department branded him "an agitator and troublemaker".

The Membertou reserve is too small and barren to allow any significant economic development, and commercial enterprises are almost impossible because the site is isolated from the prime business districts of Sydney. It combines the worst of both worlds—too remote to allow commercial development, but not remote enough to allow hunting or fishing. "We can't fish any more because the harbour is polluted," says Donald Marshall, Sr., the Grand Chief of the Micmacs, who still lives on the Membertou reserve. "And I'd starve to death if I depended on hunting on this reserve—unless I shot the dogs." With some bitterness, the Micmacs now realize that they could have created successful enterprises if they had been permitted to remain on the busy commercial thoroughfare of Kings Road. "The economic opportunities would have been great," says Dan, an official with the Union of Nova Scotia Indians who lives in Membertou. "We look down there and see hotels right where we were located. We lost that advantage."

In the early 1940s, while the Sydney Micmacs were still reluctantly adjusting to life on their barren new reserve, the federal government decided to proceed with a plan to "centralize" all the Micmacs of Nova Scotia. The idea had been developed in 1918 by H. J. Bury, a senior federal official in Nova Scotia who argued that it would "simplify" the federal administration of Indian reserves. He drew a sketch of how all the Micmacs would be neatly clustered into three areas. For more than twenty years, Bury lobbied for centralization, promising that the scheme would cut government expenses in half. Moreover, it would placate the white residents of Nova Scotia, who were accusing the Micmacs of trespassing on private property. The white residents complained that the Micmac women were "temptations" to their sons.

A federal inquiry in 1941 concluded that centralization would save money, since the Micmacs would need fewer schools and medical services. Spurred by the rising cost of the Second World War, the government acted on the inquiry's advice. It planned to sell the vacant reserves after the Micmacs were uprooted from their homes.

Instead of being shipped to three reserves, as Bury had originally proposed, all the Micmacs would be crammed onto two existing reserves: Eskasoni, about fifty kilometres southwest of Sydney on Bras d'Or Lake, and Shubenacadie, about sixty-five kilometres northeast of Halifax. Both were remote locations, away from the major towns and cities. Neither site had sufficient land or resources to support a large number of Micmacs. Despite the obvious shortage of land on those two sites, the centralization policy was authorized in 1942 by a federal order-in-council. Hundreds of Micmacs were uprooted from their homes. Their homes, farm buildings, and schools were burned to the ground.

Federal bureaucrats were proud of the centralization policy. One official described it as "an experiment in rural sociology". A newspaper in Sydney said the policy was "being watched with interest throughout Canada and may lead to a pattern for the establishment of similar projects."

The bureaucrats assumed that most of the Micmacs would become farmers after they were shipped to Eskasoni and Shubenacadie. But the government ignored the advice of the Nova Scotia Economic Council, which had warned against the notion that unemployed people with little or no farming experience could be sent to live on farmland. "Any further attempt, involving public money, to settle inexperienced, unemployed workers on farms in the hope of making them self-supporting is not justified," the economic council said in a report in the late 1930s.

Indian agents and priests pressured the Micmacs to move to the designated reserves. They frightened the Indians by warning that the old reserves would no longer have schools or medical services. Food supplies and government services were actually terminated at some reserves to make it difficult for the Micmacs to remain in their homes.

About half of the Micmacs were eventually relocated, despite their strong resistance. Hundreds of Micmacs signed petitions to oppose the policy. "We cannot understand why it is being done," one petition said. Ben Christmas, the long-time chief of the Membertou band, pointed out that Eskasoni had a high unemployment rate and a shortage of fuel wood and timber. He said the reserve could not possibly support a life of hunting, fishing, or farming. The chief predicted, quite accurately, that centralization would lead to an increase in drunkenness and lawlessness.

The government continued to push ahead with centralization, despite the protests. J. A. MacLean, the federal Indian agent at Eskasoni, said the opposition was stirred up by "left-wingers" and contended that centralization was "the nearest solution" to making the Micmac "a decent chap". If properly "developed", the Micmacs would be "one of the greatest tourist attractions the province has to offer," he said.

In 1945, however, MacLean resigned from his position as Indian agent, admitting that Eskasoni did not have enough land or resources to support the Micmacs. Centralization of the Micmacs "will only add to the additional cost of maintaining them, without any benefits," MacLean said in his letter of resignation. His warning was ignored.

Many of the Micmacs had fought overseas for Canada in the Second World War, but when they returned home to Nova Scotia they were shocked to discover that they were not entitled to the normal federal land grants for veterans unless they moved to Eskasoni or Shuben-acadie. Federal funds for building repairs were severely curtailed on reserves that the Micmacs were supposed to vacate.

In the late 1940s, federal officials began to admit that agriculture and other forms of employment were nearly impossible to establish on the centralized reserves. "Just what am I going to do when I get 1,200 Indians on a reserve who are away from most industries and away from employment?" asked the new Indian agent at Eskasoni. Another official said the Micmacs must be educated for jobs outside the reserve. "If we fail there, centralization will be one of the worst steps we have ever taken," the official said. In 1949, the government finally abandoned the idea of moving every Micmac to one of the two designated reserves. But by then, almost half of Nova Scotia's Micmacs had been crowded into Eskasoni and Shubenacadie, and several of the old reserves had lost two-thirds of their inhabitants. One reserve, Malagawatch, was completely vacated.

There were shortages of food at the designated reserves, and some of the Micmacs came close to starvation. In 1953, the people of Eskasoni pleaded for rations "to relieve our unfortunate situation." Some tried farming, but soon gave up because the land was infertile. At least three-quarters of the Micmacs became dependent on welfare. One man remembered his old home at the Afton reserve: "Afton used to be a really lively place.... The Indian people involved themselves in farming and growing crops, and they helped each other in planting and harvesting. But after centralization, people started changing their attitudes toward helping each other. They started drinking heavier... and they depended more and more on Indian Affairs to provide for their living."

The government tried a few schemes to create income for the people at the designated reserves. Oyster cultivation and blueberry harvesting were briefly considered. Twenty beavers were moved to Eskasoni in a futile effort to create a trapping industry. Sawmills opened and closed. Finally the government encouraged the Micmacs to seek employment outside the reserves.

In 1957, the federal government admitted that centralization had "not proved too successful" and gave the Micmacs the "privilege" of returning to their old reserves—at their own expense. Today, largely as a result of centralization, Eskasoni has more than two thousand residents and Shubenacadie has about nine hundred. (A parliamentary committee that investigated the Nova Scotia reserves in the late 1940s concluded that Eskasoni could provide a reasonable standard of living for only twenty families, while Shubenacadie could accommodate only one-tenth of the intended number.) Rates of suicides and alcoholism at both reserves are high. A study in 1980 found that the number of deaths caused by cirrhosis of the liver at Shubenacadie was fourteen times the national average. "The social conditions are just a breeding gound for alcohol and drugs," said Dan Christmas of the Union of Nova Scotia Indians.

Lisa Patterson, who has documented the history of the centralization plan, wrote that the federal scheme "reflected the arrogance, insensitivity, paternalism and lack of expertise in Indian Affairs at the highest levels." She added: "The relocation scheme may have appeased a few of the municipalities that were complaining about Indian squatters, but the cost was enormous. A price is still being paid by both the government and the Indians for the hasty adoption of a policy that excluded Indian opinions as thoroughly as it tried to exclude their persons."

Every summer, the Micmacs of Malagawatch return to their deserted reserve. They gather at the site of an old cemetery, where fifty of their ancestors are buried in unmarked graves. Standing under the spruce and poplar trees, they gaze out over the blue water of Bras d'Or Lake and listen to a priest as he gives mass and communion. An overgrown foundation and the tangled remains of a few pastures are all that remain of a once-thriving Micmac community. Sometimes the elders say to each other: Pe'kwaptm. Roughly translated, the Micmac word means: "I feel good, seeing this familiar place."

Until the 1940s, the Micmacs had managed to sustain several small farms and a school at Malagawatch. But under the centralization scheme, the school was dismantled and carted away, the houses were destroyed, and the farms were deserted. As the shoreline eroded, the bones of the dead Micmacs fell into the salt water of Bras d'Or Lake and washed into the sea.

Four decades later, on a sunny winter afternoon, Albert Julian stamps his feet on the snow-covered ground of the cemetery. His aunt is buried somewhere here. He isn't sure exactly where. The only markers are three white wooden crosses, a white iron cross and a crude sandstone marker with a Micmac name scratched on it.

Albert and his wife, Mary Rose, remember the trauma of centralization. "People were disoriented and dislocated," Albert says. "We were coerced into moving to Eskasoni. We were just totally ignorant of our human rights back then. We were promised pasture. But there was no pasture. We were given swamp, covered with alders. The cows ate alder leaves in the swamps. You could taste the alder sap in the milk." Almost overnight, the population of Eskasoni doubled. "People were so hungry," Mary Rose recalls. "They were taking things from other people's gardens."

Many years later, the elders are still scarred by the pain of centralization. One old woman at Eskasoni had vivid flashbacks to the day when all her worldly possessions were piled in boxes on a nearby road. "She kept on worrying and worrying about her boxes," Mary Rose says. "Her children didn't know what she was talking about. They mentioned it to me, and I said, 'That's centralization she's talking about.'"

Albert Julian is now the administrator of the Eskasoni band. He helps supervise about $5 million in annual welfare payments to the people of the reserve. "There's an almost total dependence on welfare," he says. "It's become a way of life. The welfare dependency is a direct result of the centralization. It's been ingrained in generation after generation."

Albert has a weather-beaten face and piercing eyes. He wears a plaid shirt, jeans, and a baseball cap. He has a wry smile and a Cape Breton accent when he speaks. He and his wife sit in their bungalow at Eskasoni, overlooking Bras d'Or Lake, as a bald eagle soars past the house.

The people of Eskasoni live in hundreds of bungalows strung along the highway, hemmed in between the lake and the Cape Breton highlands. Because of the steep slope of the hills, only about 20 percent of their 3,500 hectares can be used for housing. That leaves virtually nothing for farmland. "Land got so damned scarce," Albert says. "We're bounded by the hills and the lake. There's just not enough acreage."

There were about a dozen farms at Eskasoni before centralization, but they gradually dwindled away as the reserve was subdivided again and again to make room for more houses for the overcrowded population. "We've become eternally dependent on the fool's gold— the rations and the welfare cheques," says Alex Denny, a long-time Micmac activist who lives at Eskasoni.

Aside from welfare, the Micmacs have few options for survival. Some try to hunt and fish to supplement their modest incomes, but it is virtually impossible to find animals on Nova Scotia's overcrowded reserves. And when they hunt in the wilderness outside the reserves, they are severely restricted by the province's game laws—despite the hunting rights guaranteed to the Micmacs by treaty and by court judgment.

In 1985, the Supreme Court of Canada upheld the validity of a 1752 treaty that gave Micmacs the right to hunt at all times of the year. The court warned that Indian treaties should not be given a narrow, technical interpretation, but a broad interpretation, to reflect the understanding of the Indians who signed the treaties. The Supreme Court quashed the conviction of James Matthew Simon, a Micmac from Shubenacadie who was charged with carrying a shotgun on a public road in a season when hunting was prohibited by provincial law.

Yet the Nova Scotia government and the federal government immediately adopted a narrow, technical interpretation of the Supreme Court decision. They questioned whether the Supreme Court decision had any application outside the reserves. And provincial authorities continued to arrest Micmacs who hunted out of season.

Tensions between the Micmacs and the provincial government grew worse in 1987 and 1988 as the government showed no signs of accepting the Supreme Court ruling. "Anyone who hunts out of season will be prosecuted to the full extent of the the law," the government said bluntly in a communiqué, ordering the Micmacs to obey the provincial rules.

In September 1988, the Micmacs organized an out-of-season moose hunt in the Cape Breton highlands to assert their treaty rights. They were met by RCMP officers who stopped them and laid charges against fourteen of the hunters. And in December 1988, two game wardens were assaulted after they stopped a group of hunters. Four Micmacs were charged with assault. The violence was inevitable, Micmac leaders say. "It was an extreme result of the frustrations," says Terry Paul, chief of the Membertou band.

A single moose can provide 130 to 180 kilograms of meat—enough to feed a Micmac family for months. "There are people on welfare who rely on hunting for food," says Roy Gould, a Micmac newspaper publisher in Membertou. "We're proud that we have educated them on their rights. They're asserting their rights—especially the young people. They don't have the patience that the older people do. There's going to be more confrontations."

The anger and frustration are also products of the unemployment and overcrowding on the Nova Scotia reserves. At the Membertou reserve in Sydney, the Micmacs find it almost impossible to gain employment in local shops and factories—even in low-skilled, entry-level positions. "There's still a racial barrier," says Dan Christmas, who encountered the barriers himself when he worked as the employment coordinator for the Union of Nova Scotia Indians. "If you go to the department stores or the fast-food places, you never see a Micmac working there. You never see a Micmac waitress at the hotels."

In 1987 and 1988, a provincial inquiry into the wrongful jailing of Donald Marshall heard evidence of widespread racism at all levels of white society in Sydney. Several white witnesses said their parents and friends had told them not to spend any time with Indians. One white woman testified that her friends could not understand the fact that she had a Micmac boyfriend. According to her, they asked, "How could you ever go out with an Indian boy?"

At an elementary school in Sydney, white children used derogatory terms such as "redskin" and "squaw" to refer to their Micmac classmates, the inquiry was told. One witness recalled a schoolteacher who grabbed Micmac children by the ear, shook them, and said: "You Indians."

The Micmacs are convinced that these prejudices have influenced the attitudes of businesspeople in Sydney. In 1988, only two Micmacs from Membertou were employed in retail stores in the city, and only one band member was employed at the steel mill. "A lot of the young people have stopped trying for jobs," Roy Gould says. "They know they'll just get a cursory interview. It's pretty obvious that priority is given to the non-Indians. It's a redneck town. We know we don't stand a chance. Our school marks are too low, we're too shy, or we're too visible as Indians."

Today, about 90 percent of the Micmac adults at Membertou are unemployed or underemployed. Most band members are living on welfare. "The employment that does develop is in the form of make-work projects on a short-term or seasonal basis," a recent report on economic development at Membertou pointed out. "The yearly activity does little to resolve the real problem of total economic dependence. In Membertou, 99 cents of every dollar in our community is one or another form of government subsidy to maintain a basic existence. A continuous cycle of poverty persists."

The living conditions at Membertou are not as bad as those on the average Indian reserve in northern or western Canada, and the rate of alcoholism and drug abuse is relatively low. Yet conditions are still much worse than in the rest of Sydney. The reserve is seriously overcrowded, with about 30 of its 104 houses occupied by two or more families. There is a large backlog of houses needing repairs, and many band members are living outside the reserve because of the shortage of housing.

Almost everywhere in Canada, the increasing Indian population is constricted by the small size of the country's reserves. At the same time, because of poverty and welfare dependence, Indians must wait for government-constructed housing. The result is severe overcrowding on most reserves. A 1985 study by Ekos Research Associates, commissioned by the Indian Affairs Department, found that 7,700 houses on Indian reserves (about 18 percent of all reserve houses) are occupied by two or more families. A house is normally considered to be overcrowded when it has more than one person per room. By that standard, 36 percent of all households on Indian reserves are overcrowded, according to the Ekos study. By comparison, only 2 percent of the Canadian population lives in overcrowded conditions.

Even if a house on an Indian reserve is not overcrowded, it is likely to need major repairs. The Ekos study found that 47 percent of houses on reserves are substandard, very poor or beyond repair. All of these houses need "immediate, serious rehabilitation," the study said. Only 11.5 percent of houses on reserves are in good or top condition.

One-third of all houses on Canadian Indian reserves have no running water. Drinking water is usually collected from a river or an outdoor tap, and outdoor latrines are commonly used. More than half of all houses on Indian reserves have no central heating. Instead, they are crudely equipped with cooking stoves or wood stoves, often homemade ones, constructed from empty barrels. The stoves are a major cause of respiratory diseases and fires on Indian reserves.

Even without the crude heating system, the small wood-frame houses on Indian reserves are firetraps. When a fire begins, they are often destroyed within a few minutes. Deaths are inevitable because on many reserves there is no basic firefighting equipment. In Manitoba, for instance, only sixteen of the province's sixty Indian bands have enough equipment and trained staff to fight fires properly.

When a house caught fire at the Fairford reserve in central Manitoba in November 1988, the Indian band could not respond. It had only one firefighter and a fire truck that could not work in the winter because its pumps were frozen. The band telephoned a local fire department, but the department refused to help because the band owed $4,600 for previous firefighting services. A three-year-old boy died in the blaze. The rate of fire deaths on Indian reserves is six times greater than the national average—largely because the Indian housing is such a fire hazard. "We are living in paper shacks," said Ed Anderson, chief of the Fairford band. "If there is a fire in a building, it is only a matter of minutes before it is engulfed in flames."

Massive spending by the federal government—more than $600 million in the past decade—has reduced the number of Indian houses that urgently need replacement. However, the Indian Affairs Department acknowledges that 2,000 houses are still desperately needed on Indian reserves. A further 10,000 families on Indian reserves are on waiting lists for housing. And there has been no improvement in the overall percentage of Indian reserve households living in substandard conditions. The housing on many reserves is barely above the level of shelter in a Third World village.

In some cases, government spending has simply created more substandard houses. Much of the new housing construction has been cheap and quick. According to the Ekos analysis, 15 percent of all housing constructed by the federal government on Indian reserves from 1983 to 1985 is physically substandard because of poor design or poor construction. A typical example is the Fisher River reserve in Manitoba, where thirty-seven houses were constructed by the federal government in 1983 and 1984. Because of poorly built septic fields and leaking septic tanks, sewage flooded into the basements of twenty-four of the houses, and they became uninhabitable. Several families were forced to abandon the houses as children became sick from the fumes.

Meanwhile, the federal government has argued that it has no legal obligation to provide housing on reserves. It claims that neither the Indian Act nor the nineteenth-century treaties make any mention of an Indian right to housing. As a result, a growing proportion of federal Indian housing funds is delivered by the Canada Mortgage and Housing Corporation (CMHC)—the same agency that provides housing subsidies for non-natives—rather than by the Indian Affairs Department.

Indian leaders have resisted this trend, arguing that they have a special relationship with the federal government because of their historical position as the first nations of Canada. They believe the housing on Indian reserves should be delivered by a single, distinct agency that could eventually be Indian-managed. They propose two other major changes: a significant increase in annual federal spending on Indian housing and an improvement in federal consultation with Indian people before housing projects are approved. Money is certainly part of the solution, but greater Indian control of housing programs could help avoid the kind of fiascos that occur when cheap housing is imposed on Indian reserves as a band-aid measure.

The poor housing on reserves has led to serious health problems. According to a national survey commissioned in 1985 by the Indian Affairs Department, 60 percent of nurses on reserves had seen outbreaks of disease and illness caused by the overcrowding and the lack of running water and proper sanitation. The reserves had become a breeding ground for infectious and parasitic diseases.

Canada's native people are still dying from Third World diseases such as tuberculosis, gastroenteritis, and pneumonia—illnesses that rarely cause death among non-native Canadians. Tuberculosis, for instance, is widespread in Africa and other parts of the Third World, but it is almost never encountered among non-native Canadians. Yet tuberculosis is still a deadly reality on Indian reserves, occurring ten times as often among natives as among non-natives.

In 1988, when Nelson Mandela was stricken with tuberculosis in a South African prison, the Western world was shocked. Observers said Mandela's illness was "a terrible indictment" of prison conditions in South Africa. It is an equally damning indictment of conditions on Canadian Indian reserves.

The rate of TB has declined among Indians since the Second World War, but the decline has been slow. Some experts believe that the reduction in the number of TB cases merely reflects the natural decline of tuberculosis in this phase of the epidemic—and the decline has stalled in the past decade. The statistics suggest that the comparison to the Third World is still valid. In the African country of Tanzania, the TB rate is 50 to 100 per 100,000 people. On Indian reserves in the Canadian Prairies, the rate from 1970 to 1981 was 161 per 100,000.

Infant mortality is another indicator of the poverty on Indian reserves. The infant mortality rate among Canadian Indians has improved in recent decades, yet it is still twice as bad as the rate among non-natives. From 1980 to 1985, the rate among Canadian Indians was 19.6 per 1,000 births. During the same period, the rate for non-natives was 7.9 per 1,000 births.

If an Indian child survives infancy, there is still a strong chance of premature death. A study in Manitoba found that the death rate for Indian children up to the age of fourteen was four times greater than the rate among non-native children.

Most of the infant deaths on Indian reserves are caused by violence, or illnesses such as pneumonia. Many of these deaths are linked to substandard housing conditions. In 1980, for example, poor sanitation and lack of running water were the major causes of an epidemic of gastroenteritis among Cree Indian infants in the James Bay region of northern Quebec. At least eighty children were hospitalized and eight children died.

The same story can be told for the vast majority of diseases and illnesses. Intestinal infections, respiratory diseases, skin and infectious diseases, and disorders of the nervous system are all much more common among Indians than among non-Indians.

A few examples can illustrate the point. Rheumatic fever, which frequently results from poverty and overcrowding, occurs four times as often among Manitoba Indians as among the province's non-natives. Rickets, a bone disease in infants caused by a lack of Vitamin D, is still a problem at some Indian reserves, even though it is virtually unknown among non-natives today. Meningitis and hepatitis are much more widespread among Indians than among non-natives. Almost half of Manitoba Indian children suffer from ear infections in the first few years of their lives, largely as a result of overcrowding and poor housing, and they often end up with impaired hearing because of infections. Vitamin and iron deficiencies are routine among native children.

Nor do the problems disappear as an Indian grows older. A survey of nearly five hundred Saskatchewan Indians found severe health problems among middle-aged and elderly Indians. By the age of fifty, the native people were suffering problems normally experienced only by senior citizens. Almost half of those who were fifty or older found it difficult to walk more than two blocks at a stretch.

Some might suggest that the dramatic difference between natives and non-natives is simply a result of geographic isolation: Indians in remote reserves have difficulty getting access to physicians and hospitals. Although this could be a factor contributing to their health problems, there is strong evidence to demonstrate that it is not the only one. For example, the rate of hospitalization in white communities in northern Saskatchewan is close to the provincial average, but the hospitalization rate in nearby native communities is much higher. Indians in the Peter Ballantyne band in northern Saskatchewan are hospitalized for respiratory infections at a rate four times higher than the rate in the nearby non-native community of La Ronge. Even in southern Ontario, where medical services are easily available, the rate of hospitalization for Indian infants is four times as great as the rate for non-natives.

Some native illnesses are caused by the sudden transition from a traditional life of hunting and trapping to a modern sedentary life of welfare dependency. As traditional foods are replaced by store-bought foods, some native people are consuming large quantities of sugar, fat, and carbohydrates for the first time in their lives. As a result, there has been a dramatic increase in diabetes among Indians. On some reserves, almost half the residents are diabetic. In 1985, a committee of Manitoba health experts reported that diabetes had become an epidemic among Indians.

Reserve conditions have not been kind to Canadian Indians. When European explorers and fur traders arrived in Canada in the seventeenth and eighteenth centuries, they found that the native people were healthy and strong. In 1767, one fur trader wrote that "the Indians in general exceed the middling stature of Europeans; are straight and well-made people, large-boned but not corpulent.... Their constitution is strong and healthy; their disorders few...." Others made the same kinds of observations. "The Indians are in general free from disorders; and an instance of their being subject to dropsy, gout or stone, never came within my knowledge," the eighteenth-century explorer Alexander Henry wrote. Some researchers believe that the Indians were probably healthier than the traders and explorers at the time. Yet by 1905, after epidemics of smallpox and influenza, a physician in northern Ontario reported that the Indians were "far below the average size and weight of the white man.... Their muscles and bones undeveloped; stature stooping, with a long, narrow, thin chest."

Government officials often boast that the disease rate among Canadian Indians has declined in the past fifty years. However, the decline has been agonizingly slow, and the gap between natives and non-natives is still dramatic. If there has been any drop at all in the disease rate among natives, it is outweighed by the worsening death rate from accidents, violence, alcohol, drugs, fires, and suicide. Overall, some experts believe the health of Indians is growing worse, not better.

The death rate from accidents and violence among Indians has increased sharply in the past thirty years. In 1964, about 22 percent of all Indian deaths resulted from accidents and violence. Today, that figure is 35 percent—one of the worst records in the world. Aboriginal people are also four times more likely to be murdered than non-natives. The death rate among Canadian Indians from accidents and violence far exceeds the rate in the Third World or almost anywhere in the industrial world. By comparison, only 5 percent of deaths among non-natives are due to accidents and violence.

Disease and violence have sharply curtailed the life expectancy of Indian people. In 1961, the life expectancy of non-natives was ten years greater than the life expectancy of natives. In 1981, the gap was still ten years. The average Canadian Indian today can expect to live to be sixty-six years old, while the average life expectancy for non-native Canadians is seventy-six.

The federal government is not completely blind to health problems on the reserves. The medical services branch of the Health and Welfare Department has established nursing stations at virtually all of the isolated northern reserves, and it airlifts patients out if they need a doctor's attention. However, the health services are provided largely by white nurses and doctors who usually do not know the local native language or the traditions of native healing. Their communication with their patients is hampered by the cultural gap.

In recent years, federal and provincial training programs have produced a growing number of native doctors and nurses who understand native culture and languages. But there are still frustrations on the Indian reserves because Ottawa continues to control the administration of native health services. "What is needed by a community is best known by the people who live there," says Richard Saunders, director of operations at the Alberta Indian Health Care Commission. "It cannot be assumed and then imposed by outsiders, no matter how experienced or well-intentioned."

The federal government has agreed to the principle of allowing Indian bands to control their own health services. So far, however, there has been little progress in the transfer of control to the bands. Indian leaders say a transfer of control will be meaningless unless it includes an increase in financial resources so that the bands can tackle their health problems. The federal government "simply wants to transfer the responsibility for what is really a dreadful situation to Indian band councils without the resources to improve it," says Gregg Smith, president of the Indian Association of Alberta. "Transfer on this basis is not acceptable."

Native leaders are also calling for a greater recognition of the role of traditional healers—elders and midwives who traditionally performed many of the tasks now assumed by white doctors. And they believe there should be a greater number of native mental health workers in each community. In fact, mental health may be the most neglected aspect of health services on the reserves.

While better health programs can help alleviate the problems on the reserves, they cannot eliminate them. Sickness and violence on Indian reserves are just symptoms of the larger problems of poverty and underdevelopment. The Indian Act, with its restrictions on native autonomy, and the reserve system, with its patchwork of tiny reserves on infertile land, have locked Indians into a cycle of unemployment, overcrowding, poor health, and dependence on welfare.

In the mid-1960s, after years of official neglect, the federal government began a belated effort to improve the economies of Canadian reserves. But it was not until the 1970s that substantial amounts of money were spent on economic development. In 1970–71, the Indian Affairs Department was spending only $10 million on native economic development—barely 4 percent of its total budget for Indians and Inuit. By 1977–78, the spending had risen to $55 million.

However, much of this money was wasted on short-term make-work projects and poorly planned business schemes. Often the government failed to consult Indian bands before ploughing money into a project on a reserve. At one point in the 1970s, the government poured $1.5 million into four business projects at the Fort Hope reserve in northern Ontario. All four failed. An independent analysis blamed the Indian Affairs Department for its heavy-handed control of the projects and its hiring of outsiders to supervise the enterprises. The band did not even legally own the businesses—the department owned them. A former chief of the Fort Hope band, describing one outsider who was appointed as an economic development officer, said: "He took away our pride. You see, it was always his ideas that were being developed and not ours."

Some of these problems were corrected in 1984 when the Native Economic Development Program (NEDP) was launched. This federal program, which had a budget of $345 million over five years, put greater emphasis on helping aboriginal groups plan their own projects. The program provided funds for feasibility studies, native-owned development corporations, native-controlled trust companies, and community-based business enterprises.

NEDP was the biggest single government initiative in the history of native economic development. However, it must be remembered that the total budget of NEDP was divided among all aboriginal people, including status and non-status Indians and Métis and Inuit. The Assembly of First Nations has estimated that status Indians alone will need $1 billion over the next four years to keep their economies progressing.

Some bands have succeeded in using federal grants and loans as a springboard for economic development. The 1,800 Cree of The Pas reserve in northwestern Manitoba, for example, now control $21 million in assets, including a large shopping mall and 15 businesses, employing about 250 people. The unemployment rate on the reserve is about 40 percent—much lower than the jobless rates of 80 to 90 percent routinely recorded at most northern reserves.

The success of The Pas band can be attributed partly to the favourable location of its reserve—adjacent to a large town whose six thousand residents provide a captive market. Many other reserves are too small and too isolated to develop local markets. And if they try to sell their products to markets in southern Canada, the cost of freight is often prohibitive because of their remote location.

Another obstacle to economic development at many distant reserves is the lack of a hydro supply. In northeastern Manitoba, for instance, the reserves are not connected to the main provincial hydro transmission line. Their electricity is supplied by diesel generators, which restrict each household to a 15-amp power service—barely enough power for a refrigerator and a couple of light bulbs. Of course, most businesses cannot operate with such a limited power supply, and the cost of installing an adequate supply can run to thousands of dollars.

The Cree band on the Shamattawa reserve in northeastern Manitoba cannot even obtain enough electricity to open a laundromat, let alone a larger industry. The band has been paying $400 a month for a limited power supply to operate a small band-owned grocery store that has three freezers and a milk cooler. Shamattawa's diesel generator frequently breaks down, disabling everything on the reserve.

In 1987, when the Shamattawa band discovered that it would cost $16.5 million to bring a hydro line to its remote northern location, it placed an ad in a Winnipeg newspaper urging readers to write to their MPs and MLAs to support the project. "We're going to have to take drastic action to get their attention," said John Michaluk, economic adviser to the Shamattawa band. Today, the band is still waiting for its hydro line.

Michaluk believes the federal economic development programs are fundamentally flawed because they ignore the shortage of electricity and the astronomical cost of transportation to the isolated reserves. "Shamattawa lacks a lot of the basic infrastructure to develop the businesses that might be possible," Michaluk said. "A lot of the recent programs help businesses, but it's very difficult to get funding for infrastructure. We have to solve the energy crisis in the community."

At the Gods Lake Narrows reserve in northeastern Manitoba, a Cree entrepreneur named Louis Watt became the first Indian businessman to survive a battle with the local branch of the Hudson's Bay Company. Challenging the traditional monopoly of the legendary trading company, he opened a modest little convenience store on the reserve in 1984. He stayed open on weekends and late at night when the Hudson's Bay was closed. Within four years, his annual sales had jumped from $150,000 to $400,000, and the Hudson's Bay manager was worried enough to start checking the prices at Louis Watt's store.

Watt had to overcome some major obstacles on the way to economic success. After spending $3,700 in hook-up fees to install a 30-amp power supply for his small store, he was faced with a hydro bill of $300 a month. His grocery supplies had to be flown into the reserve, at a cost of 57 cents a pound, and then they had to be trucked from the airport to the lake and shuttled to the store by motorboat. "It's hard work, and there are a lot of frustrations along the way," Watt says.

The Gods Lake Narrows band has applied for grants from every conceivable government program, but the funding is just "a drop in the bucket," says Lawrence Okemow, the economic development coordinator at the reserve. "I find it very discouraging. So far, we haven't made much headway."

According to a national survey in 1983, less than one-third of the businesses on Indian reserves had survived for five years or longer. By comparison, about 60 percent of non-Indian businesses had survived for five years or more.

"There's no tougher issue in the country," says Michael Decter, a Winnipeg consultant and former civil servant who has studied the issue of native economic development. "We've made progress in the past fifteen years, but the reality is still pretty grim. It's going to take generations. It's slow and painful."

For many Indians, a life of unemployment and overcrowding on the reserves is too much to bear. Thousands of native people are abandoning the reserves and migrating to the cities, where the job opportunities are better. Even the slum housing of a decaying inner-city neighbourhood is more attractive than the wooden shacks on the reserves. The jobless rate among urban Indians is estimated to be 25 to 45 percent, yet that is better than the unemployment rate of 50 to 90 percent on the reserves. The average income on Indian reserves is one-third of the average income of non-native Canadians, and more than 80 percent of Indians have an annual income of $10,000 or less. And the situation is growing worse. In the mid-1960s, about 36 percent of Indians were receiving welfare cheques, but by the 1980s, between 50 and 70 percent were on welfare.

For the past two decades, a wave of migration from the Indian reserves has radically altered the face of most cities in western Canada. In the mid-1960s, only 16 percent of all Canadian Indians were living outside the reserves. Today, about one-third have left the reserves. In some provinces such as Saskatchewan, more than half of the Indian population is now living in towns and cities. There are an estimated 20,000 to 60,000 natives living in Winnipeg, for example, and a further 17,000 to 35,000 in Regina. At some inner-city schools in the Prairies, more than half of the children are Indian or Métis.

Those who choose to leave the poverty and poor housing of the reserves are soon confronted by the racism and discrimination of landlords and employers in the cities. Turned aside by those who hold such attitudes, many of the migrant Indians become transients, moving from city to city in search of housing and employment. Some non-native city dwellers have admitted openly that they believe in discrimination. A survey of more than 1,000 Saskatoon residents in 1986 found that only 27 percent would definitely be willing to rent a housing unit to an Indian or Métis tenant. Similar attitudes exist in other Prairie cities. "There's a definite problem of racism in Regina," the city's social development director says. "Every year, the city gets lots of telephone calls from people who want to know if the city has rules to restrict native housing. They say there are two or three native units on their block already."

An investigation by the Manitoba Association for Rights and Liberties (MARL) found a number of cases of blatant discrimination against Indian tenants in Winnipeg. The association organized teams of native and non-native volunteers to see whether landlords were discriminating against natives. In one instance, a landlord told a native couple that they could not look at an apartment because it had already been taken. Shortly afterward, a white couple visited the building and were told that the apartment was still available. The landlord said he had rejected the native couple because he did not want "their kind" in his building.

Discrimination against Indian and Métis tenants is so widespread that a native housing counsellor in Winnipeg was forced to keep two separate lists of landlords. One list contained the names of landlords who accepted native tenants and the second contained the names of those who refused to rent their housing units to natives.

Karen Zacharias, a former employee of two Winnipeg rental agencies, remembers how the agencies instructed her to prevent any natives from renting units in several dozen of their best buildings. "This is a nice block, we want clean people, no people on welfare, no natives," the owner of one agency said to her. Native applicants were informed that they did not have enough references from previous landlords, or they were sent to slum buildings, or the agency would simply not process their applications. "We'd say that the apartment was taken," Zacharias recalls. "Or we'd say we were still checking the references, and that would give us time to find another tenant." The manager of one agency told Zacharias that she would rather see an apartment sit vacant if the only alternative was a native tenant. "She'd say, 'They're like cockroaches—if one of them gets in, you get a lot more of them hiding there.'"

Theoretically, native people looking for rental housing can complain to the provincial Human Rights Commission when they suffer discrimination, but it can take several months for the commission to investigate a complaint, so they soon give up. "They become a very easy group to target because they're not aware of their basic rights," says Garry Charles, manager of the Winnipeg Regional Housing Authority. "They've probably lost faith that the system can work. If you don't believe that the system will protect your rights, you don't bother banging your head against the wall."

The Canada Mortgage and Housing Corporation has funded a non-profit housing program for natives in the cities, but the program is hampered by an angry white backlash in many neighbourhoods. Because of this reaction, the CMHC tries to restrict its native housing units to a maximum of two houses per block. "Whenever you have native housing in a certain area, property values go down," says Clifford LaRocque, an administrator at a native housing corporation in Regina. "That's the rationale for the limit."

Sometimes the neighbourhoods send delegations of a dozen or more people to complain about native housing. "They want to know what the hell we're doing, putting Indians in their community," says Glen Gordon, manager of another native housing corporation in Regina. He has been forced to arrange meetings between Indian tenants and their neighbours to ease the tensions. "We don't want our people to be harassed," he says. "Sometimes there are slogans written on the walls, rocks thrown through the windows, verbal abuse, children beaten up."

When the struggle to find housing is over, the search for employment begins. Job prospects in cities are not as hopeless as on the reserves, but they are diminished by the barriers of discrimination and poor education. As a result, unemployment among urban natives is much higher than among urban non-natives. In Edmonton, according to a 1985 survey, one-third of the city's native residents were unemployed, and the average annual income for a native family was $9,926, compared to an average income of $31,177 for non-natives. In Winnipeg, almost half of urban natives have annual incomes below $10,000, according to census data.

In the Prairies, the poorest of the urban poor—those who rely on food banks, soup kitchens, and emergency shelters—are overwhelmingly Indian or Métis. About 90 percent of those who depend on the Winnipeg food bank are native people. Two-thirds of the clientele of the Saskatoon food bank are native. An analysis of emergency shelter dwellers in Winnipeg in 1986 found that 57 percent were native.

Seeing the steady migration of native people to the cities, federal politicians and bureaucrats have sometimes assumed that the reserves should simply be dismantled and native people should all move to regions where jobs are available. That school of thought—essentially a philosophy of assimilation—was embodied in a White Paper produced by Pierre Trudeau's Liberal government in 1969, which recommended the elimination of most special programs for native people. But aboriginal leaders have always resisted the notion of complete assimilation. To lose the reserves, despite all the problems they entail, would be to lose their spiritual home, the heart of their community.

Even on reserves with the bleakest living conditions and the highest rate of unemployment, a sense of communal spirit prevails. A survey of Ojibway Indians at the Fort Hope band in northern Ontario found that 86 percent felt it was easier to live in their own community than in a city. At least 80 percent of the band members said the reserve had a better social life and a greater sense of security than the city. "I feel at home," one band member said. "That's not the way I feel in the south because when I'm there I'm just an Indian and people react in a different way."

If the reserves were dismantled and Indians were scattered into the cities, the values and social relationships of the Indian community would be lost. "There's a lot of beautiful things at home," says Lyle Longclaws, former president of the Manitoba Indian Brotherhood, who grew up on the Waywayseecappo reserve. "You're closer to each other. Our only resource is ourselves, so we build on that. We have a solid family life and a solid community life. It's the whole clan system. In the city, you're lucky to get the first name of your neighbour. You miss your own people."

An Indian on a reserve is really a member of an extended family. On many reserves, almost everyone is related to everyone else by blood or marriage, and there is a tradition of interdependence and mutual help. Band members have the security of belonging to a tightly knit community, sharing a common history and a sense of kinship. On a summer day, the doors of the houses are open. People drop in to visit each other for a few hours—or for a few weeks, if they are returning from the city and need a place to stay.

"My father and his friends would come to Winnipeg and get jailed for vagrancy because they had no identification and no money in their pockets," Lyle Longclaws remembers. "But on the reserve you don't need identification or money. It's a much different value system."

Dismantling the reserves might seem to be the easiest solution to the problems of native people, but native leaders say the solution lies in doing the exact opposite—in strengthening the reserves through economic development, land claims, and self-government, so that the economic momentum on the reserves is as powerful as their sense of community.

When economic development is successful, it stems the flow of Indians from the reserves to the cities. In 1976, more than half the members of the Westbank Indian band in British Columbia were living outside the reserve. Today, after a series of profitable business ventures, about 90 percent of the band members are living on the reserve.

The transformation began when Ron Derrickson was elected chief of the Westbank band in 1976. Derrickson had already become independently wealthy by developing a cattle ranch and a trailer park on reserve land in the Okanagan Valley near Kelowna. When he became chief, most band members were living in poverty, without running water or proper sanitation. But over the next decade, Derrickson helped the band create seventeen companies and develop real estate and trailer parks in the Okanagan region. Most of the Westbank band members now have comfortable homes in a subdivision on the reserve.

Education and social programs are essential elements in the development of a thriving economy on the reserves, Derrickson believes. "You have to start with a healthy home. It's hard to think of economic development when children are dying and old ladies are sick from the lack of running water."

He also advocates the dismantling of the Indian Affairs Department and the repeal of the Indian Act. "Let the Indians develop their own policies. You can't have civil servants running the lives of Indian people."

Derrickson is constantly frustrated by the restrictions imposed on his reserve by federal officials. When he wanted to lease a parcel of reserve land to a company he owns, he had to complete an eighty-eight-page federal lease document. The document was sent back to him with fifty-eight amendments by federal bureaucrats. "The Indian Affairs Department is a hindrance to any economic development. The hoops we have to jump through are almost not worth it."

Derrickson is convinced that there could be an economic revival at any reserve in the country if the federal restrictions were eased.

"It's not impossible. I've never seen a reserve yet that doesn't have something that can be developed. But the system is what kills us."

CHAPTER FOUR
Hobbema: Oil and Suicide

With its grain elevators and its shopping mall, Hobbema could be any small town in the Prairies. Its administrative buildings are strung along a busy highway, eighty kilometres south of Edmonton. Hundreds of truckers and motorists speed past it every day, perhaps noticing an auto dealership and a service station before they are surrounded by farmland again. There is nothing in Hobbema's anonymous exterior to suggest that this town had one of the highest suicide rates in North America from 1980 to 1987.

The story of Pamela Soosay, a teenaged Cree from Hobbema, was just one small part of the nightmare. In the autumn of 1986, she hanged herself with an electrical cord. Her sixteen-year-old boyfriend, Leo Cattleman, found her body hanging from a tree. A year later, he put a gun in his mouth and pulled the trigger. In the same year, a pregnant seventeen-year-old girl shot herself. At the peak of the suicide epidemic in Hobbema, sixteen people killed themselves in a single year.

The town of Hobbema is located at the centre of four Cree Indian reserves. For over a century, these reserves have been the home of four Cree bands—the Samson, Ermineskin, Louis Bull, and Montana bands, which today have a total population of about 6,500. A traveller who turns off the highway and follows the gravel roads into the countryside soon realizes that these reserves are far from ordinary. There are none of the overcrowded, rundown shacks that pass for housing on most Prairie reserves. Most of Hobbema's band members live in split-level or ranch-style homes, worth at least $100,000 each. Roofed with cedar shakes, landscaped and bordered by decorative wooden fences, these homes exude an air of prosperity. Satellite dishes have sprouted up beside some dwellings, and late-model cars and trucks are parked outside the shopping mall. Among the local business enterprises are the Hobbema Fireplace and Stove Centre and the Little Cree-ations toy store. The mall contains an insurance office, a trust company, a law office, a hair salon, and a grocery store.

Forty years ago, an oilfield was discovered at Pigeon Lake, the traditional fishing ground of the four bands. The oil wells began production in 1950, but the royalties that the oil companies paid to the bands were not substantial until the mid-1970s. Then the money began to flood into Hobbema. By 1983, at the peak of the oil boom, the four bands were receiving $185 million in annual royalties.

Over the past fifteen years, more than $2.1 billion in oil and gas revenue has poured into the bank accounts of Alberta Indian bands. The bulk of this money, however, has gone to just a handful of bands: the Sawridge band at Lesser Slave Lake, the Enoch band near Edmonton, the Stoney and Sarcee bands near Calgary, and the four Cree bands at Hobbema.

In the history of Canada, very few communities have ever been transformed from poverty to wealth so suddenly. As the oil money poured into Hobbema, the social upheaval was traumatic. Alcoholism increased, cocaine arrived on the four reserves, families broke apart, and the suicides mounted steadily.

From 1985 to 1987, there was a violent death almost every week at Hobbema, and the suicide rate for its young men was eighty-three times the national average. There were as many as three hundred suicide attempts by Hobbema Indians every year. The oil money "stripped them of self-respect and dignity," a Samson band social worker said. Automobile accidents, usually related to alcohol, were skyrocketing. A dozen residents of Hobbema died in highway accidents in 1987 alone.

A culture can be destroyed as effectively by money as by disease or war. The influx of money at Hobbema was an invasion by a foreign value system into a culture that had been based on hunting, fishing, and a subsistence economy for most of its history. "When we had no money, we had a lot of family unity," recalls Theresa Bull, a councillor in the Louis Bull band and the vice-chairman of the Hobbema health board. "Then we had all this money and people could buy anything they wanted. It replaced the old values. If you weren't sure of the old values of the community, money brought in a value of its own. It doesn't bring happiness. It put more value on materialistic possessions. The family and the value of spirituality got lost."

Under the system of oil royalties for Indian reserves, as much as 70 percent of the net revenue from the oil wells was placed in a trust fund in Ottawa, where it was administered by the Indian Affairs Department, which allocated the money for the "use and benefit" of the bands. The oil royalties gave the average Hobbema family $3,000 or more in monthly payments. At the age of eighteen, each of the younger band members became eligible for a trust-fund cheque of $30,000 or more. This system is still operating today.

"There was so much money that people thought it was growing on trees," said Eddie Littlechild, chief of the Ermineskin band. "The money played a big part in the abuse of alcohol and drugs. The people weren't interested in going to work. The younger people don't know what it is to work for their money. We didn't realize the problems that the money would create."

To families living in desperate poverty, the monthly royalty cheques at first seemed like a welcome relief. Unlike the Alberta government, which also profited from oil royalties, the Hobbema bands had no financial experts who might have advised them to channel their royalty payments into a fund for economic development. The decision to issue royalty cheques to individual families seemed reasonable at the time: after years of living in poverty, why continue suffering while waiting for long-term economic development projects to pay off?

The Indian Affairs Department could have provided the necessary expert guidance, but it made little effort to help the bands adjust to their strange new circumstances. "There was no assistance to prepare us to spend wisely," said Simon Threefingers, chief of the Louis Bull band. "In the last ten years, the federal government has just pulled out. They say, you have money, that's it, period. They're glad we have money because they can have nothing to do with us."

Leroy Little Bear, a professor of native studies at the University of Lethbridge, says the Hobbema Indians were "at the bottom of the social scale" when the oil money began to arrive. "They were not ready, mentally, for that large flow of money. They had no courses on economic planning or budgeting. It was an endless flow of money without the requisite training. It's like dropping candy among kids. The kids are going to go wild."

Robert Laboucane, a senior official of the Indian Affairs Department in Alberta, criticized Ottawa for failing to provide management training for the oil-rich Indians. "There was just no preparation," he told a reporter in 1986. Laboucane was immediately dismissed from his position as superintendent of economic and employment development in southern Alberta.

The story of Hobbema is proof that money by itself cannot repair the damage that has been done to native culture for more than a century. When the flow of money is too great and too sudden, it becomes yet another threat to traditional cultural values. The shift from poverty to wealth was as wrenching as the shift onto the reserves in the nineteenth century.

The fate of any community is a product of a complex web of factors. At Hobbema, the influx of money was certainly one factor. The lack of proper management and control of the money was another. And the history of the community—a history of dire poverty and harsh treatment at residential schools—had an equally important influence. The invasion of the oil money was the culmination of a century of turmoil, just one more way in which the harmony of an Indian community was destroyed by powerful outside forces.

In the mid-1800s, the four bands of Hobbema were among the Plains Cree who hunted buffalo and wandered through the area now covered by Alberta and western Saskatchewan. But by the 1870s, the buffalo were fast disappearing as the white settlers arrived. Eventually, the Indians were reduced to eating horses, dogs, gophers, and mice. Treaties were signed in the late 1870s, and the four bands settled onto reserves at Pigeon Lake and the surrounding Bear Hills region.

At first, the bands tried to support themselves by fishing in Pigeon Lake, where the whitefish were abundant. But the fishery began to fail in 1883. Shortly afterward, an epidemic of measles wiped out one-third of the band members. Famine was widespread. In 1885, the Indians of Bear Hills finally fought back by joining Louis Riel's rebellion, which was sweeping across the Prairies that year. They raided a farm, killed a number of cattle, gutted a Hudson's Bay trading post at Battle River, and forced almost all of the white settlers to abandon the region. When the Riel Rebellion collapsed, the Indians of Bear Hills gave up the fight, and white settlers soon returned to the area.

Most of the white people had complete contempt for the Indians of the four bands at Pigeon Lake and Bear Hills. General Thomas Strange, who led the Alberta Field Force against Riel in 1885, refused to shake hands with two of the chiefs—including the original Chief Ermineskin—even though they had remained peaceful during the Riel uprising. One of the general's top volunteers, Major Sam Steele, described the Bear Hills bands as "the most depraved in the north west". He complained that the Indians did not want to make "an honest livelihood", and he called them "coffee-coolers of the worst type".

The Indians continued to suffer from famine and disease. But the next step in the destruction of their culture would eventually prove to be the most devastating of all. In 1887, a religious school was established on the Ermineskin reserve. For the next eighty years, the federal government allowed the school to have complete responsibility for the education of the four bands. Under the careful supervision of zealous Catholic missionaries, the teachers forced the Indian children to speak English, to follow the Christian faith, and to learn the "habits of labour" of white European culture. Later, in a book of local history, a white author praised these teachers for attempting "the near-impossible" and persevering in "this discouraging and thankless task."

In 1891, a railway from Edmonton to Calgary was completed, and a simple flag station was established near the Catholic mission at Bear Hills. The station was named Hobbema, in honour of Meindert Hobbema, a Dutch landscape painter. This became the name of the mission and the town—a symbol of the foreign culture that was being imposed on the Cree people.

By the early years of the twentieth century, the Hobbema Indians had become figures of amusement for the white settlers. The Cree women were invited to participate in cart races in the annual agricultural fairs, and Chief Ermineskin was reduced to giving demonstrations of Indian war dancing at the agricultural fairs. In the summer, white settlers went sun bathing on Indian land at Pigeon Lake, which came to be regarded as one of the finest swimming spots in Alberta. Some of the white families camped on Indian land at Pigeon Lake for the entire summer. "After the initial attack of hot blistering sunburn, the days of summer were spent fishing, berry-picking and splashing in the lake," the local historian wrote.

In 1923 the Indian Affairs Department purchased a strip of Indian land on the beaches of Pigeon Lake. The land was then subdivided, and within a year forty cottages had sprung up on the beach.

The Sun Dance, an important spiritual ceremony that had been performed by the Prairie Cree for centuries, was outlawed by an amendment to the Indian Act in 1895. The Catholic missionaries at Hobbema helped to stamp out the tradition, warning the Indian Affairs Department whenever they heard of plans for a dance. In 1923, when the Hobbema Indians were permitted to hold a Sun Dance (under the strict supervision of the RCMP), the Catholic missionaries immediately fired off a letter of protest to the Indian Affairs Department, complaining that the revival of the Sun Dance would allow "the old paganism" to survive. They demanded the suppression of the ritual.

Meanwhile, the residential school was continuing its efforts to destroy the Indian language and spiritual beliefs. Like native people in many other parts of Canada, the adult members of the four Hobbema bands have painful memories of their church-run education. It was a boarding school, so the Indian children were effectively separated from their parents. "There was a cut in the family," said one Samson band member. "There was a loss of culture and language. In the classrooms, we weren't allowed to speak our language. A lot of our customs practically died out."

The residential school brought the Hobbema Indians dangerously close to losing their traditions and their language forever. "I took my grandchildren to the Kehewin reserve for Indian Days last year, and they couldn't understand any of it," said Eddie Littlechild. "It's really sad to see Indian people losing their language."

Simon Threefingers spent seven years at the residential school, from 1944 to 1950. "The nuns told us that our spiritual beliefs were a sin. So we lost that. I didn't believe any of those spiritual things until I had a family of my own."

*

Hobbema's residential school was finally shut down in the 1960s, and the slow process of healing began. But within a few years, the oil money arrived—and Hobbema was plunged into turmoil again. By the 1980s, the suicide rate was soaring.

How could an influx of money precipitate an increase in suicides? It might be logical to assume that the wealth would lead to stability and fewer social problems. However, the link between Hobbema's high suicide rate and its new-found wealth can be understood if the oil money is recognized for what it was: a crisis for the Cree community. A crisis can be caused by economic disaster or by sudden prosperity. The circumstances are different, but the result is the same. Almost a century ago, the French sociologist Emil Durkheim described collective crises as "disturbances of the collective order"—and he found a strong connection between suicide and collective crises. Regardless of whether the crisis is caused by a sharp upturn or a sharp downturn in social circumstances, the disruption can be traumatic— and it can sometimes lead to an epidemic of suicides.

In his 1897 study of suicides, Durkheim looked at the rate of suicide in Italy in the late nineteenth century. During this period, large-scale industrial growth began in Italy and economic prosperity suddenly increased. Incomes skyrocketed by 35 percent from 1873 to 1889. Suicides, which had been stable, jumped by 36 percent from 1871 to 1877 and by a further 28 percent from 1877 to 1889. Durkheim found exactly the same trend in Germany in the same period, following the unification of the country and a sudden spurt in industrial growth. Suicides rose by 90 percent in that country from 1875 to 1886. "Whenever serious readjustments take place in the social order, whether due to sudden growth or to an unexpected catastrophe, men are more inclined to self-destruction," Durkheim wrote in his classic essay.

A study of Alberta's oil-rich Indian bands in 1984, commissioned by the Department of Indian Affairs, confirmed that the syndrome described by Durkheim was taking its toll of human lives a century later in another culture. In the study, Edmonton consultant and former Indian leader Joe Dion concluded that the sudden wealth was causing "social disruption" among several of the Alberta Indian bands. The unexpected influx of money was leading to alcoholism, drug addiction, and suicide, Dion wrote. "The penalties in loss of life and limb...are heavy and tragic." The oil money "has in some instances broken up families, and the effects have extended out to weaken the social fabric of entire communities." He added: "The suicide rate seems to be higher in the [oil-rich] bands, in spite of the money (and in some cases because of the money) which should be bringing them a better standard of physical and mental health."

In an interview, Joe Dion criticized the Department of Indian Affairs for failing to prepare the Indian bands to cope with their changed financial circumstances. "I don't think the government cared how it was done. Nobody thought about counselling when this money came in. I think the department was remiss and irresponsible. There could have been a plan, a policy, to prepare for the use of this money." His 1984 report recommended the appointment of an independent trustee to take over Ottawa's role as the administrator of Indian oil money. It also recommended that the trustee set up a technical advisory committee to give managerial training to the Indians, so that the bands could eventually assume full authority for the oil money.

In the absence of any attempt to cushion the Indian communities from the impact of the sudden wealth, the effects were damaging. "There's no doubt that there's a relationship between the amount of money available and the rate of [school] dropouts and suicides," Dion said.

When the money came pouring into Hobbema, alcohol and drug abuse grew steadily worse. In the 1980s, most of the suicides and other health problems at Hobbema were linked directly or indirectly to alcohol, solvent abuse, cocaine, or other drugs. Tests on the body of Pamela Soosay, for example, found that she had a blood-alcohol level three times higher than the legal driving limit when she killed herself.

Public health officials reported twenty-one deaths from alcohol or drug abuse in one eighteen-month period at Hobbema. In fact, 40 percent of all deaths at Hobbema in the late 1970s and early 1980s were caused by accidents, poisoning, and violence, mostly related to alcohol or drugs. About 70 percent of adult admissions to hospital were a result of alcohol abuse, and an estimated 25 to 30 percent of the parents at Hobbema were failing to provide proper care to their children, largely because of alcohol abuse. "Many of the diseases for which Indian children are admitted are diseases of neglect that involve infections that should be treated early," a study of health conditions at Hobbema in 1982 reported.

An influx of money is not the only kind of crisis that has led to social disruption and suicide among Canada's aboriginal people. Since the arrival of Europeans in North America, native communities have been hit by social crises much more frequently than non-native communities. Pressure from the encroaching white culture has produced the kinds of collective disruptions that Durkheim warned about. Oil exploration, logging, mining, and hydro projects have destroyed the natural rhythms of hunting and fishing at many Indian and Métis communities. Other communities have been uprooted and relocated. Residential schools and the seizure of native children by child welfare authorities have robbed children of normal family lives, leading to troubled family relationships in subsequent generations. The result, inevitably, is a crisis in the social order of the native community. Not surprisingly, the suicide rate among Canada's aboriginal people is far worse than the suicide rate among non-natives.

In the 1980s, the Cree bands at Cross Lake and Norway House in northern Manitoba were hit by suicide epidemics after their traditional economy of hunting and fishing was severely damaged by hydro flooding. Because of the hydro projects, water levels in some northern Manitoba lakes and rivers have fluctuated wildly, dropping by as much as 2.5 metres every summer. Weeds, rocks, and mud flats made it almost impossible for the Cree to continue fishing. Hunting and trapping became difficult because thousands of animals were drowned.

Multi-million-dollar compensation packages were provided to the Cree, but the compensation could not ease the pain and frustration of trappers and fishermen who were left idle. Their pride and their sense of self-reliance were stripped away. From 1985 to 1987, there were 126 suicide attempts at Cross Lake, and 20 band members killed themselves in one eight-month period. The suicide rate was roughly ten times the provincial average. The community was forced to establish a crisis committee to fight the suicide epidemic. "For a whole year I remember this community was in mourning because of one death after another," a band councillor said.

At the same time, there were as many as fifteen suicide attempts each month by the Cree at Norway House. "There's just a feeling that they're being exploited, they're being used, their whole way of life can be overturned so casually," said Alan Ross, chief of the Norway House band. For the first time in centuries, band members realize there is no point in teaching their children the traditions of fishing and hunting. " I cannot pass on what was passed on to me, I can't pass it on to my kids and they won't be able to pass it on to their kids," one band member said.

The suicide epidemics at Cross Lake and Norway House were just two examples of the frightening trend toward self-annihilation in native communities that so often follows the disruption of the old way of life. A study of Manitoba suicides from 1971 to 1982 found that the suicide rate among Indian teenagers was eleven times higher than the rate among white teenagers. According to the study, native males were "by far the highest-risk group" in Manitoba. The loss of their traditional native culture was one of the major reasons for the high rate of suicide among native people, the study concluded.

For Canada as a whole, the suicide rate for Indians under the age of twenty-five is about six times higher than the rate for non-natives in the same age group. One-third of all deaths among Indian teenagers are suicides. Each year, Indians lose almost five thousand potential years of life because of suicide. As shocking as these figure are, they may be underestimates. Violent deaths account for 36 percent of all Indian deaths, and a large portion of these are believed to be unreported suicides. Often an apparent suicide is officially recorded as an accident because the victim was intoxicated and the coroner is reluctant to record that the victim took his own life. Many drownings and car crashes may also be hidden suicides. Researchers believe the true rate of Indian suicides may be twelve times the national average.

Some experts have concluded that the suicide rate among Canadian Indians is the highest of any racial group in the world. Menno Boldt, a University of Lethbridge sociologist who specializes in the study of suicide, says he has not found another racial group with a suicide rate nearly as high as the rate among Canadian Indians. "Even the worst ghettos in U.S. cities don't have as high a rate," he says.

Dr. Michael Moffatt of the University of Manitoba believes that Indian youths are often vulnerable to suicide because they feel trapped between two cultures—traditional native culture and modern white culture. "They don't feel they belong in either one. They know they can't go back to hunting and trapping because those days are over. Suicide is much more prevalent in communities that have a high degree of disorganization, alcoholism and loss of cultural values."

Durkheim's observations support this connection. In 1897, Durkheim warned that suicides will increase if a community's collective values are weakened. "Suicide varies inversely with the degree of integration of the social groups of which the individual forms a part," he wrote. "The more weakened the groups to which he belongs, the less he depends on them, the more he consequently depends only on himself and recognizes no other rules of conduct than what are founded on his private interests…. There is, in short, in a cohesive and animated society a constant interchange of ideas and feelings from all to each and each to all, something like a mutual moral support, which instead of throwing the individual on his own resources, leads him to share in the collective energy…. Social man necessarily presupposes a society which he expresses and serves. If this dissolves, if we no longer feel it in existence and action about and above us, whatever is social in us is deprived of all objective foundation. All that remains is an artificial combination of illusory images, a phantasmagoria vanishing at the least reflection…. Thus we are bereft of reasons for existence."

At most Alberta reserves where oil and gas are being extracted, revenue from royalties has been more modest than the incredible sums received by the Cree of Hobbema. Even so, the royalties for many of these communities have added up to tens of millions of dollars over the space of a decade. At the peak of the boom, the Saddle Lake band in northeastern Alberta was receiving close to $9 million in natural gas revenue each year. Half of that money was retained by the band for construction projects and economic development, and the rest was distributed among the band members, providing about $100 per month for each member. Bonus payments, as large as $500 per member, were distributed twice a year. In total, some families at Saddle Lake received as much as $1,000 in a month at the peak in 1984.

Even this windfall—which nevertheless represented only one-twentieth of the money received by the Hobbema bands at the peak of the oil boom—was not enough to overcome the effects of a century of poverty at Saddle Lake. Most of the houses on the reserve are still overcrowded today. In many cases, three or four families are living in a single house. Every year there are about two hundred applicants for the twenty houses constructed annually at the reserve. And the poor housing brings cases of tuberculosis and other diseases associated with overcrowding and poverty. A local nurse is working full-time to alleviate the tuberculosis problem at seven Indian bands in the region. There are enough TB cases at Saddle Lake alone to justify a full-time nurse if one was available, the band says.

"Just about any illness you can name, we've got it here," says Jim Cardinal, administrator of the Saddle Lake health centre. He describes cases of infectious diseases, meningitis, and children born with fetal alcohol syndrome. Malnutrition is common at Saddle Lake, especially among elderly people who are disabled. Houses are frequently fumigated to combat outbreaks of bedbugs. "Poverty is probably the major contributor to ill health here," Cardinal says.

Although the monthly payments at Saddle Lake were smaller than the payments at Hobbema, they still represented a disruption to the community. "It brought in a lot more alcohol and substance abuse," Jim Cardinal says. "As a result, there are a lot of family breakups." Melvin Steinhauer, the tribal administrator at Saddle Lake, also has bitter words for the gas revenue. "A lot of people have been hurt by it. It's a real killer. It kills the initiative and the responsibility. It kills a lot of things. People don't want to work, people don't want to go to school. They just live day to day. Most of them are worse off than before the money came. They don't know how to deal with it. People got into trouble because they had a spare $100 a month in their pocket to spend. There were deaths. Young people were killed in car accidents and suicides. That's the impact of the royalty distribution. It didn't improve anything, really."

In recent years, the gas revenue has declined drastically and there are no more monthly payments to band members. Millions of dollars have poured into Saddle Lake in the past decade, yet the money was not enough to overcome the massive obstacles that the community still faces. The problems of disease, poor housing, and unemployment at Indian reserves are the product of centuries of social and economic pressure. They cannot be solved overnight by sudden wealth.

The Enoch band, located about twenty kilometres west of Edmonton, reaped as much as $15 million in annual royalties during the oil boom.

Each of the one thousand band members was given a $500 monthly payment, so a typical family could easily receive $2,000 or $3,000 a month. The remainder of the money went to the Enoch band as a whole, making it one of the most prosperous Indian bands in the province.

With its portion of the oil revenue, the band made extensive investments in land and business ventures—to the point where it now owns a racetrack, a stable with room for 120 thoroughbred horses, a 2,000-hectare cattle ranch with about 1,000 beef cattle, a 2,400-hectare grain farm, an industrial building where trailers are manufactured, a construction company, two golf courses, a marina, a daycare centre, and an arena. The band also owns about one-third of a high-technology company in Edmonton and has invested in a hotel and a large hog farm. Housing on the reserve is good, and the band has constructed roads and recreational facilities.

Enoch's transformation from poverty to wealth was extremely rapid. For many decades before the oil boom, most of the band members were struggling, low-income farmers. "During my stay at the agency, there were daily calls for food assistance by able-bodied men," Enoch's federal Indian agent wrote in 1908. The oilfields were discovered in the late 1940s, but the revenue for the Enoch band was relatively small at first. Enoch remained a tightly knit community and alcohol abuse was rare. Almost every weekend, there were get-togethers for sports or social activities, and virtually everyone participated.

In the late 1970s, however, the Enoch band's oil revenue became a flood, surging into band members' bank accounts. As at Hobbema and Saddle Lake, the sudden prosperity did not create a utopia. Raymond Cardinal, a band councillor and former chief of the Enoch band, believes the influx of oil money was "a bad thing" for band members. "They weren't prepared for it," he said. "It was the younger people who got hurt." The current chief, Howard Peacock, says the oil money had a jarring effect on band members. "They had more spare time. They didn't know what to do with themselves, so they went to drugs and alcohol." In spite of some recent progress, about half of the Enoch adults still have alcohol problems, according to Leonard Cardinal, director of the alcohol and drug counselling program on the reserve.

"The community attitude in the 1950s was better," Cardinal says. "There was a community spirit then. There was less money and people had more respect for it. Now there's more money and people have less respect for it." Cardinal can see that the people of Enoch are more isolated from each other today. The community is less integrated, and there is less communication among band members.

"There was not enough budget training when the money came in," says Romeo Morin, a councillor and former chief. As at Hobbema and Saddle Lake, the Indian Affairs Department made virtually no effort to prepare Enoch for the influx of money. The department adopted a "hands-off policy," Morin says.

In 1985, the international price of oil plunged to $8 a barrel. "That's when the world came crashing down on us," Raymond Cardinal says. Oil royalties at Enoch eventually fell to $1.2 million per year, compared to a peak of $15 million annually during the boom years. The monthly payment to each band member fell from a high point of $500 to just $25.

The band was forced to slash its spending and cut back its public works projects. About one hundred band members were laid off. But the chief and his councillors also launched some useful programs to help cushion the band from the shock of the drop in oil revenue. Courses in "lifeskills" were set up to help Enoch's young adults learn how to compete for jobs, how to budget their money, and how to· resist the temptations of alcohol and drugs. The band began work on an ambitious plan for economic development, aiming to make Enoch self-sufficient when the oil money runs out. Hoping to capitalize on its proximity to Edmonton and the West Edmonton Mall, the band is building golf courses, an amusement park, and a trailer park for tourists.

Its efforts to be economically self-sufficient have not always been successful, however. Since 1972 the Enoch band had been working on a subdivision development plan which would have provided housing for 25,000 people on reserve land at the western edge of Edmonton. At one point it even reached an agreement with a major western Canadian development company that was eager to act as the band's partner in the project. The subdivision would have given the Enoch band enough income and employment to allow it to achieve its dream of economic self-sufficiency. But the project was delayed and ultimately blocked by a series of legal and bureaucratic problems.

One of the most troublesome of these was the fact that Indian land is governed by federal legislation. Because the land is immune from provincial laws, the owners of homes on Enoch land would not receive the security or services provided by provincial statute—a difficulty that makes prospective purchasers reluctant to buy homes in the subdivision. This kind of problem, of course, would almost never arise for non-native businessmen.

The subdivision plan was hampered by other obstacles too. The Enoch band had to deal with three levels of government in order to get approvals for the townsite, and the red tape was suffocating. Administrators and urban planners raised questions about "everything you could think of," Raymond Cardinal recalls. "It seemed like we had a clear road, but then an obstacle would be thrown in our way," he says.

Enoch was not the only Alberta band to encounter legal troubles when it tried to develop reserve land. When the Sarcee band created a subdivision on its reserve near Calgary, it hoped to sell 1,600 residential lots to the public. But the legal difficulties, including the issue of federal jurisdiction, hindered the project. Six years after the development began, only two hundred lots had been sold.

Self-sufficiency is an elusive goal for the four Hobbema bands too. Like the other oil-rich bands, they are required to keep most of their oil revenue in trust funds in Ottawa, controlled by the Indian Affairs Department. When the bands want to use their revenue for economic development projects, they have to persuade federal officials that the project is worthwhile. If the bureaucrats suspect that a band's proposed business venture might not be profitable, the money remains in the trust fund—even if the band disagrees with the official evaluation.

The Indian Affairs Department defends its strict policy by arguing that it legally has a trust responsibility for Indian money. The department is worried that it could be sued by band members for breach of trust if it allowed a band's trust fund to be spent on a money-losing venture. But there are weaknesses in this argument. If the money must be held in a trust fund, why not allow it to be held by an Indian-controlled trust company or investment firm? In fact, that alternative was recommended by the House of Commons special committee on Indian self-government in 1983. The committee was sharply critical of the current system, which essentially requires the Indian Affairs Department to function as the banker for Indian bands. "The department is ill-equipped to function as a bank," the committee said in its final report. "Holding the Minister responsible for managing Indian band monies, as if Indian people were incapable of doing so themselves, is the antithesis of self-government."

Some of the Hobbema bands have found it difficult to persuade Ottawa to release money from their trust funds, especially in cases where a business project is designed to provide important social benefits such as employment for band members, rather than simply to generate a profit. The social benefits are often disregarded by federal officials, who tend to focus on the bottom line.

The Indian leaders find it humiliating to be denied access to the money that flows from their land. "Let us make our own mistakes," Theresa Bull tells the bureaucrats. "We know what our people need. How can people who have never met us make decisions for us? You can't be paternalistic forever. The dependency that you've created for the bands has really hurt us."

Every weekday morning at the Enoch reserve, about fifteen students participate in a lifeskills class for alcohol abusers. It begins with a sweetgrass ceremony and a prayer. Then the students move into a regular classroom with a blackboard, and an instructor who teaches them how to prepare for job interviews and how to do monthly budgets. Once a week, they attend an Alcoholics Anonymous meeting. The sweetgrass ceremony and the native prayer, which were introduced into the lifeskills class in 1988, are examples of the revival of native culture at Enoch and other Alberta reserves. This cultural revival is one of the keys to survival for the Indian bands that were deluged with oil money in the 1970s.

At Hobbema, the local Cree newspaper advertises a 1950s-style rock-and-roll dance with an "American graffiti" theme—and yet in the same week, a traditional Sun Dance is held in a clearing in the bush near Hobbema. In 1951, after being banned for more than half a century, the Sun Dance was finally legalized, and in the 1960s and the 1970s the ceremonies were revived and strengthened.

An intricate, complex ritual, the Sun Dance cannot be held until an elder has received a vision. A large teepee-like structure is built with a tall pole in the centre and outside walls formed of small trees and green branches. When the four-day ceremony begins, drumming and singing are performed inside the tent and sweetgrass is burned to help cleanse the spirits of those who participate in the dance. Children place their hands on the centre pole to be healed by the Great Spirit. Young men, many of whom have been fasting for several days, hold feathers as they dance. Blankets and other gifts are given away to band members and visitors. Outside, in the clearing, there are poles and marks on the grass from Sun Dances of past years. "The dance is an expression of the joy and ecstasy of a religious life, of being thankful for life, the beautiful creation, the rain, the sun, and the changing seasons," says Chief John Snow, the long-time chief of the Stoney Indians in southern Alberta.

In the mid-1980s, the Indian leaders at Hobbema launched new programs to stop the suicide epidemic and to bring economic stability to the reserves. In late 1987 a leader of the Enoch band was dispatched to Hobbema to speak to the Samson and Ermineskin band members about economic planning. He warned the Hobbema Indians about the layoffs that became necessary at Enoch when the oil royalties began to decline. Armed with this strong warning, the Hobbema chiefs and councillors were able to resist the pressure from band members for greater monthly royalty payments. It became clear that the oil royalties had to be handled more carefully and invested for long-term self-sufficiency.

In recent years, the four bands have made wiser investments and planned their economic development strategy more thoughtfully. The Louis Bull band, for example, created ninety jobs by investing $5 million in a twenty-four-hour restaurant, service station, and grocery store for truckers on nearby Highway 2. The band also owns a small oil company, as well as several shopping malls and apartment buildings in Edmonton and Red Deer.

The Samson band, meanwhile, has established a trust company (Peace Hills Trust Co., which has branches in Edmonton, Winnipeg, and Hobbema), an insurance company (Peace Hills General Insurance Co., with agents across Alberta and $13 million in premiums written in 1987), and a shopping mall in the resort town of Lake Louise. It also has a minority interest in the Canadian Western Bank and a computer company in Edmonton.

The most important of the new initiatives, however, was a decision by the Hobbema bands to hire an addiction expert to create a comprehensive treatment program for the entire community. The program, one of the most innovative in Canada, began in early 1987 and now has an annual budget of $300,000 and a staff of seven counsellors. Instead of focusing only on alcohol and drug abusers, the counsellors talked to everyone on the reserve—including abstainers, moderate drinkers, recovering alcoholics, and the relatives of alcoholics. The objective was to change the thinking of the whole community and to build support for the battle against addiction.

A distress line, staffed twenty-four hours a day, was established to provide counselling to those who were suicidal or caught in crises. Alcohol and drug counsellors were frequently called out to an Indian home in the middle of the night to talk to a suicidal band member. Not once, after their intervention, did a band member go ahead with a suicide attempt.

Two counsellors were assigned to work full-time in the Hobbema schools, reaching each student at least once every two weeks to talk about alcohol and drugs. A psychologist travelled to Hobbema three times every week to talk to the band members. Workshops and seminars were organized to teach the Cree how to recognize the signs of a possible suicide attempt by a friend or relative, and a total of sixty band members signed up for a two-day suicide intervention course. In the summer of 1987, the people of Hobbema watched a troupe of native actors perform a dramatic version of a young Indian boy's decision to resist the temptation of suicide.

And in the real world of Hobbema, after a long struggle, death was vanquished. The suicide rate declined by 74 percent from 1987 to 1988, the alcoholism rate was reduced by at least 25 percent in the same time period, and the number of deaths from motor vehicle accidents fell from 12 in 1987 to just 2 in the following year.

Slowly, pride began to return to the people of Hobbema. A boxing club was established by the Samson band, and nearly one hundred Indian youths became enthusiastic boxers. Within a few months, several of them were winners at a regional boxing tournament. Meanwhile, the Hobbema Indians rallied around a favourite son, Willie Littlechild, who was seeking the Conservative nomination in the federal riding of Wetaskiwin. Nearly one thousand people from Hobbema purchased Conservative memberships and packed the nomination meeting to ensure his victory.

The destructive consequences of the influx of oil money were a temporary phenomenon for the people of Hobbema. By reviving their cultural traditions and by making a massive effort to tackle their social problems, the bands eventually recovered. Suicide is still a serious problem at Indian reserves across Canada, but Hobbema's community treatment program could become an inspiration for other native communities. "I think it's a good model," says Clive Linklater, a Saulteaux schoolteacher who became the director of the Hobbema counselling program. "It's really had dramatic results here. It could apply in any reserve. You have to have clear goals and a comprehensive approach."

By involving everyone in the community, the Hobbema treatment program has helped bring stability to families and social life on the four reserves. "A lot of programs are too narrow in focus," Linklater says. "We start with everybody."

In the space of two years, the suicide problem at Hobbema has been virtually eliminated. Similar programs could have a major impact on the suicide epidemic on other Canadian Indian reserves. "We could reduce it to zero," Linklater says. "We can wipe it out."

CHAPTER FIVE

Defence of the North: The Native Economy and Land Claims

Elias Martin is a husky, mustachioed Cree who speaks quietly and slowly as he shivers in the chill October air of northern Manitoba. Wearing a black T-shirt and jeans, he stands on a wooden doorstep, letting his eye wander over the small frame houses of Moose Lake, his home reserve. He is thinking about the violent youth gangs that are terrorizing the reserve's residents. "You have to live here to know the feeling," Elias Martin says. "People are scared. It affects the whole community."

A pot-holed gravel road stretches sixty kilometres through the barren brush of northwestern Manitoba before ending abruptly at the Moose Lake reserve and its adjoining Métis community. There is a hitch-hiker on the road, a young transient Cree from Saskatchewan who sometimes travels to Moose Lake to visit his girlfriend. He does not like to stay very long—the reserve is too dangerous, too frightening, he says. There is a bad feeling at Moose Lake. So he sees his girlfriend briefly and then leaves.

It is the gangs and the constant violence that trouble the hitch-hiker. Almost every weekend, the gangs are involved in beatings or brawls, and every night the people of Moose Lake have to barricade themselves into their houses, pushing chairs and logs against their doors and using rope or chains to keep them shut. They know that the youth gangs sometimes break into houses at night, searching for liquor. "If they find some poor guy inside, they beat him up," Elias Martin says.

"A lot of people won't report crimes because they're afraid of the intimidation," says Staff-Sergeant Ove Larsen of the RCMP detachment at The Pas, the nearest town. Gang members who commit crimes are often permitted to roam freely on the reserve because witnesses are afraid to testify against them. In some cases, the RCMP persuade a witness to testify at a trial, but at the last minute, on the day of the trial, the witness backs out and refuses to testify. The RCMP have tried to persuade the Moose Lake band to establish a justice committee or a neighbourhood watch group to provide protection for the people on the reserve. "But they're afraid to set that up because of a fear of retaliation," Larsen says.

There are two rival gangs at Moose Lake, each with about two dozen Cree and Métis members, ranging in age from fourteen to thirty-five. They arm themselves with rocks, sticks, chains, and knives. In a community with an unemployment rate of 85 percent and very few recreational facilities, the gangs are a lure for idle youths. "They have nothing else to do," Elias Martin explains.

The tragedy of Moose Lake is that the reserve was once a thriving, prosperous community. Located on the fertile soil of the Saskatchewan River delta, it was rich in wildlife—animals, fish, and birds. Its hunting and trapping grounds were regarded as among the best in the province, and the band at Moose Lake was one of the most peaceful and self-sufficient in Manitoba. According to one study, commissioned by four Cree bands in the region, "crime and vandalism were practically non-existent in 1960. The community prior to the flooding had no marked social problems but rather a high degree of coherence."

But in the early 1960s, thousands of hectares of wilderness—including about two-thirds of the land on the reserve—were submerged in water by the construction of the Grand Rapids hydro dam. Many reserve residents were forced to relocate to a new site, where the houses were jammed together on a small patch of land.

Before the hydro project, there were an estimated two thousand moose and large numbers of deer in the wilderness surrounding the Moose Lake reserve and the nearby Chemawawin reserve. About 380 moose were harvested every year. The ancestors of the Moose Lake and Chemawawin Indians had decided wisely when they chose the sites of their reserves in the nineteenth century. The Saskatchewan River delta was one of the last great breeding marshes for ducks and geese in North America, and its soil was rich enough to support grain and vegetable crops and a ranch of top-quality Hereford cattle. Even a successful muskrat ranch was established at Moose Lake. In the 1950s, the reserve and the surrounding region produced about $150,000 worth of muskrat pelts each year. Beavers and other fur-bearing animals were trapped in the wild, and the duck hunt brought in another $207,000 annually. There was a commercial fishery, and thousands of kilograms of whitefish were sold by band members every year.

But this traditional native economy was shattered by the hydro flooding of 1963 and 1964. Eighty million kilograms of cement were poured into the ground to create a massive dam twenty metres high, with dikes extending twelve kilometres on each side. Water levels on Cedar Lake were elevated by four metres, creating the fourth-largest lake in Manitoba. More than 2,200 square kilometres of delta land were intentionally flooded.

The cattle and muskrat ranches of Moose Lake were wiped out, the crops and gardens were destroyed, and the supply of moose fell sharply. After the flooding, Indian hunters often needed at least a week of hunting to find a single moose, and even then they sometimes returned empty-handed. "Moose populations are almost non-existent in the now deeply flooded area and [exist in] much fewer numbers in peripheral areas under shallow water," a provincial bureaucrat wrote in a 1969 report.

Incredibly, the Moose Lake band was given only $10,000 in cash compensation for the flooding. The band tried to sue the provincial government, but they were frustrated by procedural tactics that delayed the court cases.

Crime and alcoholism soon became a serious problem at Moose Lake. "Stress, anxiety and fear have been much in evidence since the flooding," a study of Moose Lake reported in 1978. Elias Martin, who works as an alcohol and drug counsellor at Moose Lake, now estimates that 90 percent of the community's adults are abusing alcohol or drugs. In 1986, alcohol helped spark a near-riot in which a number of band members were hospitalized and forty-one were arrested.

Jim Tobacco, chief of the Moose Lake band, says the crime rate on his reserve is one of the highest in Manitoba. "There's a very hostile attitude in the community. Our young people are always beating each other up. My people don't know who the hell they are. They live month to month, on welfare.... Our way of life and our resource base has been destroyed. We were promised benefits from the hydro project. Today we are poor and Manitoba Hydro is rich. The crime and violence, the gang warfare, are the price we pay for Hydro's vision of progress."

The impact of the flooding was even worse among the Cree people of Chemawawin, who lived nearby on the shores of Cedar Lake in the Saskatchewan River delta. Before the Grand Rapids hydro dam was built, they enjoyed the same abundant resources as the Moose Lake band and had a prosperous traditional economy of hunting, trapping, and fishing. Alcohol abuse was rare and crime was virtually unknown. "There are no apparent community problems," a provincial official reported in 1963. Another official said that the "thriving economy" was "the most striking aspect" of the reserve at Cedar Lake. The only people receiving welfare were single-parent families and disabled adults.

But all of that was radically altered by the Grand Rapids hydro project and the flooding. In the end, nearly the whole reserve disappeared under water, and the Cree were forced to relocate to a vastly inferior site about sixty kilometres southeast, on the opposite shore of Cedar Lake.

Manitoba Hydro had begun planning the Grand Rapids project in 1957, but the people of Chemawawin were not informed about it until the fall of 1960. The provincial government, acting on behalf of the Crown-owned hydro company, simply told the Cree residents of Cedar Lake that they would have to relocate within four years. The band was so isolated that it had virtually no experience in dealing with governments, and the Cree were not even told of their right to hire a lawyer. Moreover, the chief and most other band members spoke little English. Because the Cree had no legal counsel, it was relatively easy for the Manitoba government to persuade them to move. They were pressured into signing a final agreement in 1962.

The federal government made no effort to help the band. Using its powers under the Indian Act, the government simply expropriated the Chemawawin reserve and transferred the land to the province.

There is clear evidence that the federal and provincial governments were fully aware of the damage that the hydro dam would inflict on the people of Chemawawin and Moose Lake. In 1960, an official at Indian Affairs predicted that the flooding would cause the economic collapse of the Chemawawin and Moose Lake bands. "Although a great deal of thought and effort has gone toward the selection of a new site for the bands concerned, the record does not indicate how or where these people are going to earn their living when their reserves have been flooded," the official wrote in an internal memorandum. "It is very doubtful if the wildlife resources will provide anything like the livelihood which has been available in the past and which was the primary reason the reserves were originally selected by these bands."

Provincial officials were privately forecasting that the hydro dam would cause a drastic decline in the populations of moose, waterfowl, and fish. "The economic values impaired would, no doubt, be greater than any compensation," one provincial memorandum warned. Later, a senior provincial official admitted that he had seen a tragedy brewing as early as 1962, two years before the flooding. An environmental impact study, commissioned by the Manitoba government, confirmed that the flooding would cause serious damage—but its results were kept secret. In a confidential memo, a federal official warned Ottawa that "many of the resources from which the people derived a livelihood…will be lost or seriously depleted for a number of years and in some cases, possibly forever."

Publicly, the Chemawawin Cree were given a completely different story. They were told that they would live in a modern town, with electric stoves, and a new highway to connect it to the south. In a formal letter of intent in 1962, a senior provincial bureaucrat promised that the Cree would not be hurt by the hydro development. "On behalf of the Manitoba government, we agree to take every step possible to maintain the income of the people of Chemawawin at the new site," the letter said. Premier Duff Roblin gave the Indians the same assurance in a letter in 1964. He told the band members that they "will in fact be able to earn as good a living as before and, we hope, a better living."

It soon became obvious that the government's assurances were just empty rhetoric. The Chemawawin band's new location, known as Easterville, was far removed from its traditional rich hunting and trapping areas. The site had been chosen by the Manitoba government primarily because it was closer to the south and would be cheaper to service. The wilderness surrounding the new site was almost entirely muskeg and swamp, and the reserve itself was covered with rock and gravel. Trees were sparse and stunted, leaving the reserve hot and dusty in the summer. James Waldram, an anthropologist who has documented the Easterville story, describes the site as "one of the most uninhabitable and depressing places one could imagine." Its nickname was "The Rock Pile".

Because the soil at Easterville was full of fractured limestone, the band was unable to dig pit latrines. Buckets had to be used for sewage, causing an increase in airborne bacteria, which led to serious infections among infants on the reserve. The poor sanitation also contaminated the water supply.

The band suffered a steep decline in its hunting and trapping, and there was a 93 percent reduction in the number of fish caught. As a result of the hydro dam and the flooding, Cedar Lake was choked with floating logs and debris, and the water level often fluctuated, so that it became dangerous to fish on the lake. Sometimes it took three separate trips before the Cree hunters could find a single moose.

By the late 1960s, alcohol abuse was spreading rapidly through the Easterville reserve. Vandalism had become common, and children were often neglected. In 1966 a report commissioned by a federal-provincial committee concluded that the situation at Easterville was "desperate" and could soon become "a social disaster". Four years later, the commercial fishery on Cedar Lake was closed because mercury was leaching from the soil into the flooded areas—a common problem in hydro projects.

Manitoba Hydro, meanwhile, was boasting that the relocation of the Chemawawin band was a huge success because of the construction of new houses and schools at Easterville. In its public relations brochures, the corporation described Easterville in idyllic terms. "The brightly painted houses, nestled in a background of evergreens and birches, convey the impression of a lakeside summer resort."

The Cree sued the Manitoba government for breach of contract in 1970, but the government used a series of stalling tactics and legal maneuvers to prevent the case from going to court. As the community disintegrated, it became difficult for the band's lawyers to keep the case going, and the lawsuit eventually fell apart. By 1980, about 90 percent of the Cree were living on welfare, and a study found that mental depression was widespread among the people of Easterville.

Today, the Easterville Cree still occasionally travel across Cedar Lake to the old community of Chemawawin. They stare at the abandoned buildings. Sometimes, as they drift silently in their boats, they push an oar into the water and touch the submerged headstones of a flooded cemetery where their ancestors are buried.

In 1986, a consultant to the Easterville and Moose Lake bands said the people of Easterville had suffered "a profound trauma" as a result of the flooding and relocation. "There is certainly no evidence that the Chemawawin have recovered from the trauma of the move, the loss of their treaty lands and their resource base," the consulting firm of E. E. Hobbs and Associates concluded. "Whatever wider benefits the Grand Rapids hydro project may have brought to Manitoba, for the Chemawawin Cree it has meant the destruction of their traditional way of life. Today the band has no viable economic base, few prospects for the future, a wide range of accelerating social problems and a diminished level of confidence and self-esteem, the inevitable outcome of the decline in the band's fortunes since the flooding."

Early in 1989, the Manitoba aboriginal justice inquiry heard the story of the hunters and fishermen who had lost their way of life. "We hope that when you come to write your report, you will cover not just the crimes of today but also name the guilty people who have done so much damage to our communities," Easterville chief Alpheus Brass told the judges.

The judges listened to a group of Easterville school children describe the effects of the flooding. "It hurts to see my community this way," said Waylon Munroe, a twelve-year-old student. "When people get bored they start to drink and break into stores. Sometimes we fight each other. Teenagers commit suicide or try to escape by getting drunk, but I know that is not going to solve our problems."

The root cause of the Easterville tragedy was the government's refusal to let the band control its own future, Alpheus Brass told the inquiry. The lack of self-determination "was a poison poured into our community," he said.

Industrial development in native homelands is normally rationalized with the argument that the projects are required for "the common good" or "the public interest". It is the same argument that is used to justify the expropriation of a farm or a cottage to make room for a highway or a transmission line. Yet there are major differences between the expropriation of the property of an individual white landowner and the expropriation of traditional native hunting grounds.

First, a white landowner who loses his land can usually be adequately compensated with money. It is relatively simple for a farmer, for example, to use this money to purchase farmland somewhere else. A native community, in contrast, cannot maintain its way of life if its traditional homeland is gone. Historically, Indian bands have chosen to live in places where wildlife is abundant—but in the late twentieth century it is often impossible for a dislocated Indian band to find a vacant site with adequate supplies of wildlife. The result, in many cases, is a life of welfare dependency.

Second, a white landowner has legal title to his land, which makes it easier for him to insist on compensation. But since reserve land is legally controlled by the federal government, Ottawa has the power to transfer Indian land to a provincial government or sell it to a corporation with only token compensation to the natives. In the past, this federal power has paved the way for quick transfers of Indian land to make room for hydro dams or other projects.

Third, a white landowner usually has experience in dealing with lawyers and bureaucrats, and he is aggressive in defending himself. But the residents of most native communities in remote areas of Canada are inexperienced in negotiating with governments. Language can also be a barrier.

Finally, white landowners will usually benefit from the industrial projects for which expropriations are conducted. By consuming the electricity or minerals that are taken from the land, they are included in the "public interest" which profits from a development. But native people rarely gain any benefits from expropriations. They do not consume large amounts of electricity or other resources extracted from their land. The pattern is consistent: the power of expropriation is used against native people to the benefit of non-natives. Native people recognize that the "public interest" does not include them.

The Chipewyan Indians of northern Saskatchewan have been hunting and fishing on the wind-swept shores of Wollaston Lake for hundreds of years. Their traditional hunting grounds stretched north to Hatchet Lake and the Cochrane River and almost to the present-day border of the Northwest Territories. Because of their isolation, their traditional economy was undisturbed for centuries. And so the Chipewyan were unprepared for the sudden upheaval in their hunting territory in the early 1970s when the first uranium mine began its operations there on a massive scale.

Gulf Minerals Canada Ltd. had gained an exploration permit from the Saskatchewan government in 1968. Within a few months, the company discovered the Rabbit Lake ore body on the western side of Wollaston Lake, about thirty-five kilometres from the Chipewyan reserve, and began preparing the site for the start of production. No public hearings were held. Bulldozers roared, massive buildings sprang up, and roads and fences soon criss-crossed the hunting grounds of the Chipewyan. In 1975, Gulf began extracting uranium from the site.

The Chipewyan, inexperienced in the strange world of provincial politics, did not know how to fight the development. Instead they learned to endure the bulldozers and the fences, and they found new wilderness areas where they could hunt and trap. A few of them even found jobs at the mine.

Today, however, private companies and Crown corporations are planning a dramatic expansion of the uranium industry in northern Saskatchewan. Within a decade, there could be six mines on the western side of Wollaston Lake, bringing more turmoil into the lives of the native people who live at the Wollaston Lake reserve and the adjoining Métis community.

"Pretty near everybody doesn't like the mines," said Tony Dzeylion, a Chipewyan trapper whose trapline is just a few kilometres from the Rabbit Lake uranium mine. He watched his trapline fall into steep decline after the mine was constructed. "There's roads all over the place now. There's no trees because the bulldozers broke the trees.

There's drilling all over the place. I've seen the beavers floating dead—they don't like the iron and the oil. There used to be lynx. Now there's no lynx at all. And the fox and the mink are gone too. If there's too strong uranium in the water, the fish are going to die."

The uranium mines of northern Saskatchewan have produced more than $2 billion in revenue and royalties for their corporate owners and the provincial government. Meanwhile, the Chipewyan and Métis people of Wollaston Lake have been suffering outbreaks of tuberculosis and hepatitis—a result of their deplorable housing conditions, severe overcrowding, lack of running water, and the decline of their traditional way of life. "Regardless of how productive they are at their traditional pursuits, they are finding it increasingly difficult to pursue this lifestyle in an area dotted by exploration camps, road building crews and mining activities," a consultant's report said in 1981.

Often there is a token attempt to consult native people before a major development proceeds, but in the case of northern Saskatchewan's uranium mines, consultation did not take place until after the fact. The Cluff Lake Board of Inquiry held public hearings into uranium mining in 1977—two years after the Rabbit Lake mine began operating. The inquiry recommended the establishment of a nine-member Northern Development Board, including several native representatives, to regulate the uranium mines. In 1978, the provincial government established a "monitoring committee" to scrutinize the uranium industry. However, the Northern Development Board was never established, and the monitoring committee was abolished in 1982. Once more, in the face of new mining developments, the people of Wollaston Lake have been left with no official advocate and virtually no political power. In northern Saskatchewan, as in almost every region of Canada, the final authority has remained in the hands of non-native institutions.

Even the legislation that is supposed to protect the threatened land from environmental damage is little help for the aboriginal people. The environmental reports—thick volumes written in highly technical language—come pouring into the offices of the Chipewyan band councillors to satisfy the official requirements for environmental approval. But they pile up in stacks on the floor, unread, because the Indians cannot afford to hire a specialist to analyse the reports. In the history of the Wollaston Lake band, only a handful of band members have ever completed high school, so for all practical purposes the environmental reports from the uranium companies are incomprehensible. And without money to hire experts, the Chipewyan cannot challenge the companies.

"The companies put a book on the table and away they go," says Jean Marie Tsannie, a Chipewyan band councillor at Wollaston Lake. "We don't have the education to go through all these environmental books. We can't do anything—they can start the mines without the permission of the people."

Individually, each uranium mine can satisfy the province's environmental requirements. But some experts are worried about the cumulative effect of six uranium mines in the same small corner of northeastern Saskatchewan. "Down the road, there could be a nasty surprise," says Stella Swanson, a senior scientist at the Saskatchewan Research Council.

Already, testing has found high levels of ammonia in the effluent from the uranium mines in northern Saskatchewan. Ammonia can asphyxiate fish and damage their growth and reproduction, so there is a possibility that the ammonia could affect the fish in Wollaston Lake when the new mines are all operational. "One would suspect there could be problems," Swanson says.

But it is not only the fish that could be threatened by the environmental effects of the uranium mines. Dr. Dermot McLoughlin, a radiologist at Chedoke-McMaster Hospitals in Hamilton, Ontario, who has visited Wollaston Lake to conduct preliminary work for the testing of wildlife in the region, believes that the moose and other animals in the area should be tested for radium and uranium. Some people have reported seeing moose drinking from the Rabbit Lake tailings pond, where the uranium waste is dumped. "Because of the very high grade of uranium ore in that region, even if there are small amounts getting into the water and the wildlife, it could eventually get into people's food," Dr. McLoughlin says.

Throughout the 1970s and 1980s, the native people of northern Saskatchewan voiced their opposition to the uranium mining. In 1977, for example, the chiefs of the northern Saskatchewan Indian bands told the Cluff Lake Board of Inquiry that they would oppose any expansion of the uranium mining industry until their hunting and fishing rights were guaranteed. Their opposition was ignored. By 1985, the people of Wollaston Lake had become so frustrated that they resorted to civil disobedience. They organized a blockade of traffic on the gravel road that links the Rabbit Lake uranium mine to its markets in the south. After blocking the road for three days, the Indians were faced with the threat of arrests by the RCMP. They ended the futile blockade and soon became resigned to their fate. Mary Ann Kkailther, a Chipewyan woman who helped organize the blockade in 1985, has given up her attempts to fight the uranium mining. "There's nothing we can do about it," she says.

When the uranium companies held meetings at Wollaston Lake in 1988 to describe their latest plans for new mines, the Chipewyan and Métis hardly bothered to register their opposition. "Everybody's heard the same thing over and over," says Terri Daniels, administrator for the Métis community at Wollaston Lake. "They knew it didn't matter what they said to the company. Sometimes I think that the companies think we're animals in the north. They don't ask the animals for permission, so why would they ask us?"

Once development has occurred, native people have no choice but to try to adapt to the new economy that has been imposed on them. Yet it is difficult for Indians and Métis to gain employment in the mines or the hydro stations, which require highly trained staff for technical jobs. They are caught between the unfulfilled promise of the wage economy and the damaged traditions of the native subsistence economy.

Dennis Powder, a twenty-seven-year-old Cree who lives at the Indian reserve of La Ronge in northern Saskatchewan, recalls the uranium- and gold-mining companies promising that half of their jobs would go to northerners. "I went to all the meetings for all the mines," he says. "I'm a welder, but I can't even get a job. They say I need more experience." In his bid for a mining job, Powder completed a one-year training course in welding. "All I got was congratulations," he says. Unable to find a job in the mines, he is now driving a taxi in La Ronge for an average income of $23 per day. His brother took a six-week course in diamond drilling, but he too was unable to land a job in the mines.

Despite the promises made in the late 1970s, that at least 50 percent of their employees would be northerners, today the uranium companies acknowledge that only about 25 percent of the 1,500 employees at the three existing uranium mines come from the north. And only about half of the northerners in the mines are native people. "People are asking what happened to all the jobs that were promised," says Mary Ann Kkailther.

For many people at Wollaston Lake, the cash income from a temporary job is attractive, but native people are usually given low-skill, low-status jobs and it isn't long before they return to the traplines and hunting grounds. William Hansen, a trapper at Wollaston Lake, worked at the Rabbit Lake uranium mine for several months in 1985. After a lifetime of moving freely on his trapline and on the lake, he found it difficult to adjust to the restrictions of a mining job. "We were in the same place all day. We're not used to that. It was very tough—shovelling rocks all day." Even the food was foreign to him. Accustomed to eating fish, he did not like the steak that was served to the miners. "A lot of us couldn't stand the grub. It was strange."

In 1981 a consultant's report commissioned by the federal and provincial governments to help plan the future of Wollaston Lake concluded that the native people "have not participated in the wealth generated by the mining activity." Seven years later, little had changed. A 1988 consultant's report said the employment created by the uranium mines had been "disappointing".

The havoc wreaked by hydro flooding and other forms of northern development has not been restricted to Indian and Métis communities in Manitoba and Saskatchewan. Throughout the twentieth century, but especially after the Second World War, native communities have been assaulted by northern industrial development. As non-native Canadians have sought greater prosperity by exploiting northern resources, aboriginal people have watched their traditional economy disintegrate in the wake of hydro dams, uranium mines, oil wells, logging operations, pulp mills, and mineral exploration. When the damage has come to public attention, it is usually presented as an isolated event, an unfortunate accidental side effect. Yet the evidence shows it is neither an accident nor an isolated occurrence. And there is a clear pattern in almost every case—a pattern of official denials, lengthy delays in compensation, a weakened or destroyed native economy, mounting dependence on welfare, and a terrible toll of violence and anger in the affected communities.

In 1958, hydro dams flooded almost 1,600 hectares of the Whitedog reserve, damaging traplines at Whitedog and the nearby Grassy Narrows reserve in northern Ontario. Then, from 1962 to 1970, a pulp mill dumped 9,000 kilograms of mercury into the English-Wabigoon river system, poisoning the fish. Dozens of Ojibways at Grassy Narrows, who relied on fish as a staple in their diet, ended up with dangerous levels of mercury in their blood and symptoms of mercury poisoning such as tremors, tunnel vision, impaired hearing, and slow reflexes. For several years, politicians assured the Indians that their fears were exaggerated. The provincial government suppressed the results of the mercury tests. Warning signs were pulled down. But the Indians were eventually forced to stop fishing, and their commercial fishery was completely wiped out.

Alcoholism and crime, which had been minor problems at Grassy Narrows in the early 1960s, soon reached epidemic proportions. By the late 1970s, a survey found that two-thirds of the adults on the reserve were heavy drinkers, and half of the children in Grade 2 and Grade 3 were sniffing gasoline regularly. The suicide rate soared, and three-quarters of all deaths were caused by violence. Not until 1985 were the Ojibways compensated for the destruction of their way of life. The owners of the pulp mill agreed to pay $11.75 million in compensation, while the federal and provincial governments provided $4.92 million, and Ontario Hydro gave $1.5 million to the Whitedog band to compensate for the flooding.

The litany goes on. In 1952, the Carrier Indians of Cheslatta Lake in northern British Columbia saw their reserve disappear under water as a power dam was constructed to provide energy for a giant aluminum smelter at Kitimat. Their graveyards were flooded and the bones of their ancestors floated away. They lost fishing stations, trapping cabins, and hunting trails. "Now my people depend on welfare and alcohol," the chief of the Cheslatta band said. A decade later, a dozen Sekani Indian villages in northern British Columbia were submerged under eighty metres of water when the W. A. C. Bennett Dam was constructed. Although the province made arrangements to help the white farmers who would be affected by the flooding, it ignored the 125 families in the Sekani band. A government report in 1962 quoted only one Indian. "By the time the water comes, I find some other place," the Indian was reported as saying. That seemed to satisfy the planners.

The federal government transferred the Sekani reserve into the possession of the province. The Sekani houses were burned down, the villages were bulldozed, and most of the Sekani were dumped into the territory of another Indian band. In the late 1960s, after several years of misery, the band migrated back to Ingenika Point, the only remaining habitable corner of their homeland. Because they did not officially have a reserve, the federal government gave them virtually nothing. They lived in one-room shacks made of logs salvaged from the hydro reservoir and carried buckets of water up a steep hill from the reservoir. The water soon became contaminated with salmonella. The Sekani became so desperate that they threatened to blockade the roads. "We're refugees on our own land," band chief Gordon Pierre said. In 1987, under pressure from the media, a provincial Cabinet minister flew to Ingenika Point and admitted that the living conditions were the worst he had ever seen in British Columbia. Eventually a morsel of compensation was provided—the houses were repaired and a deep well was drilled to provide drinking water.

In northern Quebec, a Cree band near the town of Chibougamau has been shunted from site to site since 1951 to make room for copper- and gold-mining and logging operations. The dislocation began when the Cree were uprooted because the sand on their island was required for the construction of a road to a mine. Every other piece of nearby land was owned by mining companies, so they had to move to a swampy point on a lake. In 1962 the band moved out of the swamp to a spot about two kilometres away and asked Ottawa to recognize this new site as a reserve. But in 1970 the Indian Affairs Department announced that the band was too small to warrant a reserve. To save money, the department decided to merge the Cree with another band. They were told that they would not receive any federal assistance unless they joined the Mistassini band, about eighty kilometres from their traditional hunting grounds. They were warned that they should abandon their homes because their lake water was unfit to drink, and they were informed that a mining company had purchased and staked out the land on which the Cree had hunted for generations.

Seeing no alternative, the Cree reluctantly moved away. Their homes were torn down, and even the building where they held their religious services was demolished. They scattered into six isolated campsites, where they were regarded as squatters on provincial land.

By 1986, they were living in one-room shacks with plastic sheets for roofs, and their children were falling ill because they had to drink contaminated water from stagnant lakes. Ottawa promised to establish a separate reserve for the band, but by 1988 the Cree were still landless because of delays in negotiations between the federal and provincial governments. "It's pathetic," a Quebec negotiator admitted. "They've been kicked around since the first prospector came in. Whenever they settled in at a lake, some prospector came in and found copper or gold."

For the past hundred years, governments have used the same strategies to deal with native people. James Waldram, an anthropologist who has studied hydro developments on Indian land in western Canada, points out the similarities between the Indian treaties of the nineteenth century and the wholesale removal of native communities to make way for resource development in the twentieth century. The Indian treaties were negotiated in the 1870s to remove natives from the path of railways and agriculture, while the compensation agreements were negotiated in the 1960s and 1970s to move Indians away from modern industrial projects. Waldram points out that the nineteenth-century treaties were often violated or disregarded by governments after they were signed. He warns that, in the same way, compensation agreements could be broken after the hydro projects have proceeded.

When the Indian treaties were signed a century ago, federal negotiators promised that the government would fulfil the treaties for "as long as the sun shines and the rivers flow". Ironically, as Waldram reminds us, many of the rivers are not flowing any more. They have been blocked by hydro dams.

The victimization of aboriginal people whose interests conflict with the goals of resource developers is not unique to Canada. The aboriginal people of Australia have seen their land expropriated for mining developments since the 1950s. In Norway, the Sami people chained themselves to a mountainside in 1980 in an effort to stop a hydro project that threatened to destroy their way of life. In the Amazon region of Brazil, thousands of indigenous people have suffered from oil exploration, hydro flooding, gold mining, logging, rubber extraction, sugar plantations, and cattle ranches. In the Philippines, hydro projects have jeopardized the ancestral lands of 85,000 tribal people. Large-scale logging operations in Malaysia have severely damaged the hunting and gathering economy of the nomadic Penan people.

In most countries, indigenous people were historically given the most barren and marginal land available. "These lands are now found to contain valuable minerals and resources," the World Council of Indigenous Peoples said in a report to an international conference in 1981. "Indigenous peoples are increasingly being seen as a nuisance to governments and transnational corporations. To promote corporate investments, the indigenous people must be removed or silenced to make room for mines, dams, plantations and factories. Indigenous nations today are suffering economically more than ever before and are not in control of sufficient resources to protect their interests and maintain their traditional forms of life."

The world council summarized the problem in one brief sentence: "An Indian without land is a dead Indian."

Since the late 1960s, Canada's aboriginal people have begun to resist the destruction of their land. Their leaders have become better educated in the ways of the white man, and they have gained enough expertise and government funding to launch court challenges, hire consultants and lawyers, use the media, and organize blockades and demonstrations. As a result, governments have finally been forced to provide millions of dollars in compensation for hydro flooding. They have been compelled to establish training programs and job quotas to help native people get jobs at the sites of mining operations and hydro projects.

In 1966, when Manitoba announced plans for another massive hydro development in the north, native leaders were already aware of the damage inflicted on the Moose Lake and Chemawawin Cree by the Grand Rapids hydro dam. The new project, a diversion of water from the Churchill River into the Nelson River, would flood the homes of hundred of Indians and Métis in the community of South Indian Lake. The project would also wreak havoc on the traplines of the Cree reserves of Nelson House, Cross Lake, Norway House, York Landing, and Split Lake. The native people responded quickly by hiring lawyers to defend themselves. In the social climate of the late 1960s, public support for the Indians was widespread. Hearings were held in 1968 and 1969, and enormous crowds attended. A parade of native and non-native witnesses, ranging from scientists to housewives, spoke out against the hydro project.

In 1969 the people of South Indian Lake went to court to seek an injunction to block the hydro project. The government immediately introduced legislation that would effectively kill the lawsuit and authorize the project to proceed. In the midst of the furious public debate that ensued, a provincial election was called, and the Conservative government was defeated by Ed Schreyer and the NDP. Ten weeks after his election, Schreyer announced that the project was being cancelled.

However, the premier soon unveiled a different version of the hydro project, in which half of the homes in South Indian Lake would still be flooded and hundreds of square kilometres of forests would be submerged. The NDP government became as obstinate as the previous government. Schreyer told the Indians that the project could not be halted because too much money had already been spent on it.

In 1972, the Indians went to court in another bid for an injunction, but they were severely hampered by a lack of money for legal expenses. When the province adopted a divide-and-conquer strategy, offering $1,000 in compensation to each trapper at South Indian Lake, many of the trappers, living in poverty, accepted the money. The lawsuit was abandoned in 1974. By then, the hydro project had been completed and the floodwaters were gradually rising. Fishing locations and traplines were destroyed. Most of the native residents were forced to abandon their homes and move to higher ground. As Schreyer himself admitted, the community of South Indian Lake was "slowly dying".

In 1979, a provincial inquiry concluded that the Manitoba government and Manitoba Hydro had adopted a stance of "confrontation, hostility and procrastination" as well as "a lack of frankness" in their dealings with the people of South Indian Lake and the other five native communities. The inquiry found that Manitoba Hydro knew it had no legal right to flood Indian lands. And it concluded that the provincial government had been in a conflict of interest because it had become an advocate for Manitoba Hydro at the expense of the native communities. South Indian Lake, which once had a thriving economy based on commercial fishing and trapping, today has an 85 percent unemployment rate. The floodwaters have brought mercury from the soil into the lake and the fish, posing a long-term threat to the health of the Indians, who now have high levels of mercury in their blood.

Unwilling to accept the position of victim, the five Cree bands affected by the hydro flooding had formed the Northern Flood Committee in 1974 to seek compensation. The Cree gained the support of the federal government and then negotiated a settlement with the province. The Northern Flood Agreement, signed in 1977, guaranteed compensation for damage to fishing and trapping. In the end, the bands obtained promises of compensation worth hundreds of millions of dollars from the provincial government, Manitoba Hydro, and the federal government. Their organized stand on the hydro project allowed the Cree bands to achieve a better outcome than the Moose Lake and Chemawawin Indians who suffered from the disastrous results of the Grand Rapids hydro project. But the bulk of the compensation was not provided until twenty years after the hydro project was launched and, as always, the money could never replace the land and the way of life that had been destroyed.

During the 1970s and 1980s, land claims became a crucial element in native resistance to industrial development as native people realized they needed a power base to help them control the pace of development in their traditional hunting and trapping territories. Successful land claims could give them the resources they needed to improve their economic future. The Cree of James Bay, led by Billy Diamond, and the Cree of Lubicon Lake, led by Bernard Ominayak, were among the most prominent of those who launched land claims to help protect their traditional territory. In both cases, the Cree bands were ignored in the early stages of industrial development. In both cases, they adopted a variety of imaginative tactics, eventually forcing government officials to pay attention to their demands.

The Cree of James Bay had never signed a treaty to surrender their land. Their hunting and trapping economy had survived for centuries because they saw the wilderness as a garden, a vast fertile land to be tended and harvested and protected. But in the spring of 1971, the Cree were shocked to hear a brief news item on the radio, announcing that the Quebec government was planning to flood their land to create the massive James Bay hydro project.

The government did not bother to consult the Cree. Indeed, the Cree were not even shown the details of the plan until nine months after the announcement. But the Indians were determined to resist the destruction of their territory. Led by Billy Diamond, the shrewd and aggressive chief of the Rupert House band, they organized their eight villages into a united front against Quebec's $6 billion "Project of the Century". When the Cree were given a stack of government brochures on the project, they burned them in a gesture of defiance. To further dramatize their plight, Billy Diamond arranged for the Montreal media to tour the Cree villages. Then he turned to the courts, launching a legal challenge in a calculated bid to block the hydro project. Diamond told his followers that the Cree would "turn the white man's laws onto himself."

After seven months in the courtroom, the Cree emerged in 1973 with a temporary injunction to block the development. The injunction was suspended a week later, but the temporary Indian victory had shocked the provincial government into serious negotiations. By 1975, the Cree had negotiated Canada's first comprehensive land claim settlement. They received $150 million in compensation, along with extensive land rights for hunting, fishing, and trapping.

The Cree of Lubicon Lake, like the James Bay Cree, had never signed a treaty. They were overlooked when federal commissioners were negotiating treaties with Indian bands in northern Alberta in the nineteenth century. In 1939, after they petitioned for a reserve, Ottawa promised to provide one square mile for every band member. The reserve was officially approved and mapped in 1940, but the land was never transferred. Two years later, a federal official flew to Lubicon Lake and arbitrarily removed seventy-five people from the band's membership. Then he declared that the band was too small to warrant a reserve.

In 1980, dozens of oil companies began to bulldoze the band's hunting and trapping grounds. The forest was cleared to make room for pipelines, roads, oil wells, and trailer camps. One trapper woke up to find a road bulldozed to within three metres of his front door. Traplines were destroyed by slashing crews. Snare sticks and poles were chopped down. Trapping equipment was dug up and used as road markers. Indian trails were barred with "No Trespassing" signs. Hundreds of seismic lines were cut through the wilderness. "Hope this will not cause you any problems," one company said in a letter to a trapper at Lubicon Lake. The Indians were stunned. The oil companies and the provincial government were soon earning $1.3 million in daily revenue from four hundred oil wells in the Lubicon area. By 1989, an estimated $5 billion in oil revenue had been obtained from the Lubicon land.

Until the oil invasion, the Cree had maintained a life of self-sufficiency by hunting and trapping. Only 10 percent of the band members were on welfare. But in the early 1980s, as the oil companies roared into the Lubicon land, the native economy went into a steep decline. The Cree had taken an average of two hundred moose each year before the oil development, but they could find only three in 1984. The total value of hunting and trapping fell to one-tenth of its traditional levels. By the mid-1980s, an estimated 90 percent of the band members were dependent on welfare. There were twenty-two violent alcohol-related deaths among the Lubicon in an eighteen-month period. In 1987, more than forty band members fell sick with tuberculosis—a disease caused by overcrowding and inadequate diet.

After an investigation, the World Council of Churches warned of "genocidal consequences" among the Lubicon Cree. A federal investigator, former justice minister Davie Fulton, reached a similar conclusion. "Their need was urgent, their situation was desperate and worsening daily, and their best efforts along the line of negotiation were producing no results," Fulton wrote in his report. But the Alberta government refused to halt the oil development or transfer any land to the Lubicon people.

Like their counterparts at James Bay, the Lubicon Cree tried to use the courts to protect their homeland. When they sought an injunction against the oil development, however, their request was denied. And when they used the courts to pursue their claim for a 234-square-kilometre reserve, they encountered nothing but delays.

The Lubicon band, on the brink of disintegration, declared that they would no longer recognize the authority of the Canadian court system. Led by their stubborn and tenacious chief, Bernard Ominayak, the Cree set up barricades on roads entering their land in October 1988. For the first time, the oil companies were prevented from entering the area. Five days later, the RCMP tore down the barricades and arrested fifteen of the Indians. They also arrested a dozen Lubicon supporters, including two Quakers and two West Germans. But the blockade had succeeded in increasing the pressure on the provincial government. Two days later, the Alberta government agreed to provide a reserve of 204.5 square kilometres.

By early 1989, however, the Cree had reached a deadlock in their negotiations with the federal government for funding to help establish the new reserve. Oil wells continued to pump oil from the Lubicon land, and the fate of the Lubicon people was still uncertain.

As hydro dams and oil companies encroached on aboriginal land, native leaders realized that they could not gain control of their traditional homelands without filing land claims. The increasing number of land claims was also sparked by other factors: the arrival of a new generation of university-educated Indian leaders, the rise of native political consciousness, the cultural revival among aboriginal people, and their growing understanding of the differences between European and native concepts of land ownership. According to the native view, land must be controlled collectively by the community to ensure long-term stewardship of its resources. This view is incompatible with the European notion of private ownership, which often leads to short-term exploitation of the land.

In some cases, land claims were the result of honest disagreements over the interpretation of vaguely worded nineteenth-century treaties. Indian leaders tended to interpret the treaties broadly, looking at how the spirit of the treaties would have been understood by the chiefs who signed them. Government officials tended to take a narrow, legalistic view.

In many cases, oral promises were made to the Indians by the white officials who negotiated the treaties. These spoken promises were never recorded in the treaties, which had usually been drafted in advance. Yet the Indian chiefs would never have signed the treaties without the oral promises. Land claims are a way of asserting the validity of those spoken promises, which were remembered by Indian elders and passed down by word of mouth to the current generation of Indian leaders.

Some treaties were arbitrarily extended to cover Indian bands that had never signed a treaty. In other cases, native people were simply cheated out of their land. Treaties were ignored, reserves were never created, and some white settlers stole land from Indian reserves. A number of treaty obligations, especially in the Prairies, have never been fulfilled by the federal and provincial governments. Indian bands in Saskatchewan, for example, are still waiting for 1.1 million acres of land to which they are entitled under the treaties of the 1870s. In other cases, land grabs were authorized by official inquiries. In 1915, a commission in British Columbia allowed the government to take 47,000 acres of valuable land from Indian reserves and replace it with 87,000 acres of much poorer land. The Indians were not compensated for the land grab until the 1980s.

In some regions of Canada—including Labrador, Quebec, British Columbia, and the Yukon and Northwest Territories—the land was never officially surrendered by treaty. The federal government, assuming that the Indians had no aboriginal title anywhere in those regions, allowed settlers and industrialists to invade the land. But the native people believe that they must have some legal right to the land they live on, since they have been using it since time immemorial. "Our interpretation is that we didn't give up any rights whatsoever," says William Erasmus, president of the Dene Nation in the Northwest Territories. "The only thing we did was that we acknowledged that other people were coming on to our land, so we had our hands open and said, 'Yes, we have lots of land; come on our land.' We didn't say, however, that we were going to give up our right to make our own decisions over our own lives, to have our institutions so that we can continue to survive as a unique people."

Indian land rights were confirmed as early as 1763, when King George III issued a Royal Proclamation declaring that the Indians should not be "molested or disturbed" in any of their homelands which were not specifically purchased by the Europeans. Unless the land was clearly ceded to the Europeans, it was reserved for the Indians.

A century later, the Nishga Indians of northwestern British Columbia were astonished to discover that the colonial government believed Indians had no right to their land. In the 1880s, the Nishgas took their case to the governor general, Lord Dufferin, who criticized the British Columbia government for suppressing their rights. But the province continued to insist that the Indian land rights had been extinguished. "We cannot understand it," Chief David McKay told a royal commission in 1887. "They have never bought it from us or our forefathers. They have never fought and conquered our people and taken the land that way...."

The leaders of the Nishga Indians travelled to London in 1906 and 1909 to seek justice. They met Prime Minister Wilfrid Laurier twice, and they created the Nishga Land Committee to lobby politicians and government officials. In 1915, the officials finally responded by giving the Nishgas a token land grant—an estimated 0.5 percent of the land in their former territory.

For fifty years, the Nishgas continued to fight. They submitted briefs to Parliament in 1926 and 1959. And in 1968 they hired Thomas Berger—a talented lawyer who later became the head of the Mackenzie Valley Pipeline inquiry—to launch a court action affirming that the aboriginal title of the Nishgas had never been extinguished.

The political climate was poor. The weight of the federal government was tilted against the Indians. In a major policy paper in 1969, the government announced that aboriginal land claims and other aboriginal rights were too "general and undefined" to be accepted. Prime Minister Pierre Trudeau, who was strongly opposed to Indian land claims, summarized his government's position: "We say we won't recognize aboriginal rights. What can we do to redeem the past? If we think of restoring aboriginal rights to the Indians, well what about the French who were defeated at the Plains of Abraham? Shouldn't we restore rights to them?"

Nor was Trudeau willing to recognize Indian treaty rights. "We must be all equal under the laws and we must not sign treaties amongst ourselves," Trudeau said. "I don't think that we should encourage Indians to feel these treaties should last forever within Canada…. They should become Canadians as all other Canadians."

Indian leaders fiercely opposed Trudeau's vision of an assimilated culture. The Nishgas persisted with their court action, and in 1973 the Supreme Court of Canada issued a landmark ruling. Six of the judges agreed that the ancestors of the Nishgas had aboriginal title to the land. Three of the six judges said that the aboriginal title had been extinguished in the nineteenth century, but the three remaining judges ruled that the aboriginal title continued to exist today.

The tie was broken by a seventh judge, who ruled against the Nishgas on a technicality. However, the Supreme Court decision had a dramatic effect on the federal government. For the first time, the concept of aboriginal title had been recognized by the highest court in the land. "Well, it looks like you've got more rights than I thought," Trudeau told an assembly of native groups.

Six months after the Supreme Court decision, the federal government revised its policy on aboriginal rights and announced that it was prepared to accept land claims from Indian groups in regions where no treaty had been signed. Since then, Canadian aboriginal groups have filed thirty-three comprehensive land claims in regions where native title had not previously been settled. In each case, they argued that they had never surrendered their land. Ottawa has begun negotiating six of these claims, and it has agreed to negotiate a further fifteen.

Several hundred Indian land claims have been filed in Canada since the 1970s, but only a few dozen of these have been resolved. Most are specific claims, relating to an unfulfilled treaty promise or the loss of land from a reserve. Only one comprehensive claim—the James Bay land claim in northern Quebec—has produced a final settlement. In many cases, the government has simply rejected a claim outright—without explanation, without even producing a legal opinion to support the decision. When this happens, the courts are the only recourse for the Indian bands. Because of the time and money required for a court challenge, however, few Indian groups can afford to pursue this course of action.

Indian land claims are most strongly opposed in British Columbia, where the government refuses to negotiate at all, arguing that settlements might bankrupt the province. Thomas Berger is among those who have strongly criticized the province's policy. "Any government that, in the 1980s for political gain, seeks to turn the populace against the native people and their claims will occupy a lonely and unforgiving place in the history of our country," he has written.

In the Canadian North, significant progress has been made toward a resolution of two of the largest comprehensive land claims in Canadian history. In both cases, the federal government and native groups have signed agreements-in-principle. In one of the claims, about 6,500 Indians in the Yukon have negotiated a settlement that will give them $232 million and about 41,000 square kilometres of land—about 9 percent of the total area of the Yukon. The Indians are guaranteed representation on a wildlife management board and a land-use planning board, and they will also gain rights to oil, gas, and other minerals in most of the land. It took fifteen years of negotiations to produce the agreement between the government and the thirteen Indian bands in the Yukon.

In the second comprehensive claim settlement, about 15,000 Dene and Métis in the Northwest Territories will receive approximately $500 million over a twenty-year period, as well as about 180,000 square kilometres of land. In a further 1.2 million square kilometres of land, they will receive special rights such as a percentage of royalties from resource developments, participation on a wildlife management board and a land-use planning board, and guaranteed rights to hunt, fish, and trap in the area. The details of the settlement are still to be negotiated, but when it is finalized the Dene and Métis will be among the largest non-government landowners in North America.

The Bear Island Indians of Lake Temagami in northern Ontario have been less fortunate. Although they have never signed a treaty to surrender their land, in 1850, government negotiators persuaded an Indian leader from southern Ontario to sign a treaty on behalf of the band. For the equivalent of $25, the Bear Island Indians lost their land without even participating in or being aware of the surrender. The Indians ended up with a tiny reserve of only 2.5 square kilometres.

The federal government offered to give the Indians a much larger reserve in 1885, but the Ontario government refused to provide the land for the reserve. The Indians believe the province was already planning to lease or sell the land to logging and mining companies.

The eight hundred members of the Bear Island band have been trying to negotiate a land claim settlement for more than 110 years. While the land claim was virtually ignored, an estimated $2.7 billion worth of timber and minerals have been extracted from the Indian homeland. In 1973, the band took drastic action, issuing a legal caution on 10,000 square kilometres of forests and lakes in its territory. The caution, based on the Indian claim of ownership of the land, effectively froze many kinds of development in the area. The Ontario government took the band to court, and in 1984 the Supreme Court of Ontario ruled against the Indians. The case was appealed. In early 1989, the Ontario Court of Appeal dealt a crushing blow to the concept of aboriginal rights. The court ruled that under the 1850 treaty, the land had been legally taken away from the Bear Island Indians, even though they had never signed the treaty. The court also ruled that a government could extinguish aboriginal land title merely by declaring it extinguished— even if a proper treaty was never signed—and that the Crown could legally take Indian land without communicating with the Indians in the area. It also ruled that the Royal Proclamation of 1763—with all its guarantees for Indian rights—was null and void as a result of another law, passed in 1774.

The Supreme Court of Canada will ultimately decide the fate of the Bear Island land claim. Until then, a cloud of uncertainty lingers over the question of aboriginal land title in Canada. And a growing number of native leaders are beginning to lose faith in the court system—the same system that was employed so skilfully by Billy Diamond and other leaders in the 1970s.

The recognition of native claims to a larger land base is crucial to the future of aboriginal self-government and economic development. Without land claim settlements, Indian reserves will be limited to their present size—too small, in most cases, to permit any realistic plan for economic development—and self-government will be a mere façade. "Without land, without resources, there is no self-sufficiency; and without being self-sufficient, there is no Indian government," the Association of Iroquois and Allied Nations said in 1983.

In the Cree villages of northern Quebec, the James Bay Agreement was just the beginning of the fight for economic independence. In 1984 the James Bay Cree persuaded Ottawa to pass legislation giving them an unprecedented form of self-government. As the first Indians to be exempted from the Indian Act, they gained control of the planning and administration of almost all government services in their region, including health programs, economic development corporations, housing, education, and water and sewage services.

However, the federal government still retains some control over the annual flow of funds to the James Bay Cree. Throughout the 1970s and 1980s, they have been forced to fight for the money to which they are legally entitled, while funds have been delayed or withheld because of federal Treasury Board decisions. It took a deadly epidemic of gastroenteritis in 1980 to persuade Ottawa to begin providing the money required for proper water and sanitation services.

Even so, the James Bay and Northern Quebec Agreement remains a model for comprehensive land claims and self-government. No other Indian band or tribal group in Canada has gained such a level of control over its own affairs.

In recent years, the federal government has backed away from the James Bay model of self-government, preferring to give Indian bands a set of diluted powers similar to those of municipalities. In 1986, for instance, the Sechelt band in British Columbia was given a mild form of municipal-style self-government. Other bands have been given "alternative funding arrangements"—a pale imitation of the principle of self-government.

In 1983, a special committee of the House of Commons recommended an amendment to the Constitution to entrench the right of Indians to self-government and urged Ottawa to settle Indian land claims as soon as possible. "Prospects for economic development would improve if the land base were expanded, claims were settled, and the control of resources on Indian lands were transferred to Indian First Nations," the committee said. "The assets now controlled by Indian governments are not sufficient to support those governments."

The committee also concluded that the federal Indian Act is "antiquated" and "completely unacceptable as a blueprint for the future." Oscar Lathlin, chief of The Pas band in northwestern Manitoba, agrees. He has watched the Indian Act cause frustrating delays in his band's business plans. When the band tried to lease parts of its land to car dealers and gas stations, almost two years passed before all the required approvals were received from the Indian Affairs minister. Because Indian bands are not considered to be legal entities, Lathlin had to get a loan guarantee from the Indian Affairs minister whenever his band wanted to borrow from a bank. "It's a heck of a way to do business," says Lathlin. "Compared to the average non-Indian businessman, we're at a disadvantage."

Because of the Indian Act and the restrictions it imposes, Indian bands are hampered by a great deal of legal uncertainty whenever they try to sign contracts, borrow money, purchase land, or launch lawsuits. They cannot even acquire legal title to the land they purchase. "The uncertainty permeates all dealings between bands and employees, suppliers, contractors, financial institutions and governments," a Halifax law firm said in a 1982 report. Even the Indian Affairs Department has admitted that the Indian Act "often leads to interminable technical complications to accomplish the simplest act."

Oscar Lathlin has helped his band grow from a $250,000 annual budget in 1968 to a $17 million budget today, and his band controls

$21 million in assets, including a 21,000-square-metre shopping mall. But he knows his people could be further advanced if they were not restricted by the regulations of the Indian Affairs Department. "It controls too much," the chief says. "The minister has such sweeping powers over Indian land and Indian people from the day you're born to the day you die." The Indian Affairs Department should be dissolved, he says, and native-controlled financial institutions should be created to help Indians gain access to capital.

Economic power, once obtained, can give Indian bands enough clout to protect their traditional economy from the ravages of industry. Lathlin is already planning for the day when his band will purchase 10 or 15 percent of the logging company in The Pas. That would allow the band to influence the company's cutting areas, in order to ensure the survival of hunting grounds and traplines. Until the Indians own a stake in the logging company, the loggers will simply ignore the hunters and trappers.

In his efforts to combine a modern economy with the traditional hunting and trapping economy of his people, Oscar Lathlin is challenging the conventional wisdom about northern economic development, which assumes that the native economy is doomed to failure. The Cluff Lake Board of Inquiry, which approved the expansion of northern Saskatchewan's uranium industry in 1977, was one of many official bodies that accepted the conventional view. "The intrusion of the twentieth century into all parts of Canada is inexorable and the accompanying force of industrial expansion in its diverse and sometimes subtle forms is irresistible," the inquiry concluded. "The important fact remains: the northerners are clearly moving toward a lifestyle which entails technology, modernity and industrialization."

Some observers, however, have questioned the value of this new lifestyle. Thomas Berger, who headed the Mackenzie Valley Pipeline Inquiry from 1974 to 1977, travelled to every village and settlement in the Mackenzie Valley and the Western Arctic and listened to 283 days of testimony from 1,700 witnesses. Berger concluded that the traditional native economy must be preserved and strengthened—even if that means a delay for the inexorable march of resource exploitation in the north. "We have always undervalued northern native culture," he wrote, "and we have tended to underestimate the vitality of the native economy. We have been committed to the view that the economic future of the North lay in large-scale industrial development. We have generated, especially in northern business, an atmosphere of expectancy about industrial development. Although there has always been a native economy in the North, based on the bush and the barrens, we have for a decade or more followed policies by which it could only be weakened or even destroyed. We have assumed that the native economy is moribund and that the native people should therefore be induced to enter industrial wage employment."

The pipeline companies had told the Berger inquiry that hunting and fishing were relatively insignificant for northern native people. Yet Berger's own eyes told him that the companies were wrong. Everywhere he travelled, he saw native people eating moose, caribou, muskox, dried whale meat, whitefish, trout, and Arctic char. Testimony by native people and other experts confirmed that this food was still an important part of the diet and lifestyle of native northerners.

In their close relationship with the land, native people can be compared to Canada's family farmers, who have been stewards of the land for generations. The federal and provincial governments have always recognized the value of family farming: they have introduced dozens of programs to support agriculture and they have subsidized farmers and protected them from low prices and droughts. Commercial fishermen on the Atlantic and Pacific coasts have been supported by government programs and by extended unemployment insurance benefits in the off-season. Yet native hunters and trappers have been told to abandon their lifestyle and make way for industrial development.

Berger warned that the unfettered growth of industrial development and resource exploitation in northern Canada will lead to unemployment, welfare dependency, alcoholism, sickness, crime, and violence among native people. "All of the evidence indicates that an increase in industrial wage employment and disposable income among the native people in the North brings with it a dramatic increase in violent death and injuries. I am persuaded that the incidence of these disorders is closely bound up with the rapid expansion of the industrial system and with its persistent intrusion into every part of the native people's lives."

He also concluded that the economic benefits of northern resource development are less than what some people assume. "The fact is that large-scale projects based on non-renewable resources have rarely provided permanent employment for any significant number of native people. There is abundant reason to doubt that a pipeline would provide meaningful and ongoing employment to many native people.... The extension of the industrial system creates unemployment as well as employment."

Berger recommended a ten-year moratorium on the construction of the Mackenzie Valley pipeline. He also recommended steps to strengthen and modernize the traditional native economy. "Productivity must be improved and the native economy must be expanded so that more people can be gainfully employed in it," he said. The preservation and modernization of the native economy would be cheaper than the massive cost of industrial development in the North. "Huge subsidies of the magnitude provided to the non-renewable resource industries would not be necessary."

Even before the Berger inquiry, northern native leaders such as Georges Erasmus of the Dene Nation were advocating steps to strengthen and modernize the traditional native economy. When the concept has been given a chance, it has worked. The government of the Northwest Territories, for example, has provided funds for outpost camps to support hunters and trappers. It has also helped pay the cost of airplane transportation for native people who participate in the traditional community hunt each fall.

In the past, Dene hunters from communities near Great Slave Lake would have to canoe hundreds of kilometres and trudge along dozens of portages to meet the caribou that migrate south in August and September. Then they would have to haul the meat back home. Now, with the air transportation subsidies, they can find the caribou more quickly and carry more meat back to their communities.

In northern Saskatchewan and Manitoba, as in other regions of Canada, provincial governments have invested huge sums of money in subsidies and tax breaks for uranium mines, hydro projects, and other forms of industrial development. Even a fraction of that money, invested in programs to support the traditional economy, could strengthen native communities immeasurably. "If any government paid as much attention to the traditional economy as they paid to these boom-town phenomenons—the mining exploration, the oil exploration—and if the same tax advantages and benefits went into it, we believe it would be very successful," Erasmus says.

Native leaders have lobbied for other policy changes to help support the traditional subsistence economy. For example, they have persuaded some oil and mining companies to give their employees rotating job duties and seasonal time off so that they can take part in hunting and trapping. "It's been reasonably successful," says Erasmus. "People can spend more time on the land, instead of this nonsense of only getting two weeks a year. Indigenous people can live in their own communities and follow their traditional economy and then get back into the organized work force for perhaps six weeks at a time."

The strengthening and modernization of the traditional native economy is becoming more crucial as new threats emerge. In the 1980s, a concerted effort by anti-trapping activists has led to a decline in European demand for furs, weakening the price of most furs caught by Canada's native people and sharply reducing their incomes. "Enthusiasts for animal rights have now joined the missionaries, bureaucrats and entrepreneurs in their rejection of the subsistence economy," Thomas Berger wrote in 1988.

There are other threats too. Sports hunters have invaded the traditional hunting grounds of Indian bands in many regions of Canada. Logging and mining roads have allowed sports hunters to drive their vehicles deep into native hunting territories. A study by Hugh Brody found that the sports hunters killed 3,625 moose in the hunting territories of seven Indian bands in northeastern British Columbia in a single year. In some of the traditional native hunting grounds, sports hunters have killed many more animals than the Indians have.

In Labrador, the Innu people are deafened by the supersonic roar of bombing practice runs and low-level training flights by military jets from a NATO base at Goose Bay. The intense noise has disrupted the migratory patterns of caribou, thus endangering the traditional Innu hunting economy. Geese, fish, and fur-bearing animals are also affected by the aircraft.

Provincial wildlife regulations are another threat to the native economy. A number of court decisions have upheld the right of Indians to hunt and fish freely, but the provinces have continued to enforce strict limits. Indians have traditionally hunted to build up a food supply for the winter and to provide food for children and elderly people who cannot hunt. Yet they are charged when they exceed an arbitrary limit of fish or animals. Indian hunters in northern Manitoba, for example, have been fined and had their guns seized when they exceeded the provincial bag limit of six ducks a day. Others have been charged with hunting out of season, despite their treaty guarantees. Native fishermen have seen their nets seized because they did not obtain the required licences and permits. On the salmon rivers of British Columbia, Indians have come to blows with provincial fisheries officers who are determined to enforce fishing limits.

Industrial development, however, still presents the biggest danger to the aboriginal economy. But native leaders do not pretend that they can halt development forever. They simply want to achieve a balance between the native economy and the industrial economy.

The Cree of James Bay have accomplished the balancing act by purchasing an airline and establishing a canoe-building factory on their land to supplement their still-active economy of hunting and trapping. Hunters and trappers at James Bay are also supported by an Income Security Program, which the Quebec government agreed to establish as part of the settlement with the James Bay Cree. The program guarantees a minimum cash income for full-time hunters and their families and an extra allowance for every day the hunter spends in the bush. The program pays for the cost of airplanes to fly the Cree hunters and trappers into remote areas where wildlife is plentiful. And it encourages them to remain active in the native economy even if there is a cyclical downturn in the supply of animals and birds.

Every other hydro project in Canada has led to a decline in hunting by Indian people, but in northern Quebec the Income Security Program has succeeded in strengthening the native economy. By 1981, there were nine hundred full-time Cree hunters at James Bay, compared to a total of fewer than six hundred in 1971. While every other hydro project in Canada has led to an increase in welfare dependency, the James Bay welfare caseload was actually reduced by two-thirds from 1971 to 1981. The Income Security Program is a model for other Indian communities across Canada. "Compared to unemployment or welfare, it is not only cheaper, but it enables people to remain productive, doing something that gives them a sense of achievement and personal worth," observed Richard Salisbury, an anthropologist who has studied the James Bay Cree.

The Cree of Lubicon Lake have a similar plan. They are proposing the creation of a $500,000 trust fund to support the income of their trappers, along with a wildlife management system to ensure the stability of the moose population. At the same time, they are planning an economic development project that would include a cattle farm, a vocational training centre, an eight-unit motel, a gravel pit and gravel-crushing operation, a concrete-making plant, a berry farm, a slaughter house, a gas station, and a grocery store. They are also hoping to establish a capital fund to provide money for the start-up of new businesses by Lubicon band members.

The Lubicon people are aiming to establish a diversified economy. "We'd like to keep hunting forever, if possible," Chief Bernard Ominayak says. "We're trying to preserve it as much as we can. But we're trying to balance everything, so that we're not dependent on just one thing."

To strike that difficult balance between the traditional economy and the modern economy, Canada's native people need to control their own land. In their vision of the future, the land is still the central element—just as it has been central to their way of life for centuries. Without a land base, they will be unable to modernize their economy, and their traditional way of life will be doomed. Land will always be the key to survival for aboriginal people. "Being an Indian means…saying the land is an old friend and an old friend your father knew, your grandfather knew, indeed your people always have known," Richard Nerysoo of Fort McPherson told the Berger inquiry. "If our land is destroyed, we too are destroyed. If your people ever take our land, you will be taking our life."

CHAPTER SIX

Foreign Justice: Native People and the Law

The teenaged girl held a rock in her hand as she stared silently at the two small airplanes on the darkened airstrip at Gods Lake Narrows. Then, methodically, she began to smash their windows. By the time she had finished, she had done $42,000 worth of damage to the aircraft. With the same determination, she demolished four of the airstrip's runway lights, broke the windows of two nearby buildings, and trashed the interior of the community firehall. Then she went home to wait for the RCMP.

"What took you so long?" she asked the police officers when they arrived. She was waiting impatiently to be flown south to the youth detention centre in Winnipeg.

For a bored teenager, a remote northern reserve like Gods Lake Narrows in northeastern Manitoba is a prison. There is nothing to do. There are no jobs and few recreation programs. Tantalizing images of middle-class urban life, beamed into native homes by satellite television, contrast with a day-to-day life of poverty and isolation. Many northern Indian reserves have no permanent roads to connect them to the rest of the world. In winter, temporary roads are built across the frozen lakes to allow trucks to deliver supplies from Winnipeg, but these routes are too treacherous for ordinary cars. During the rest of the year, airplanes are the only link to the outside world. The prison

141

door can be unlocked, but it costs money. At Gods Lake Narrows, the cost of a return plane ticket to Thompson, the nearest northern city, is $184 — too expensive for a native teenager.

The isolation seems like an insurmountable barrier—until the teenagers see the RCMP escorting prisoners out of the reserve by airplane. Weeks later, the prisoners come back with stories about the recreational programs and regular meals at Winnipeg's youth detention centre. Listening to the stories, the teenagers decide to do whatever they can to get sent to the detention centre. For them, it is a logical decision. In a strange way, a trip to the detention centre is a form of upward mobility. The reformatory is more attractive than life on the reserve.

Most of the crimes are break-ins, assaults, or vandalism sprees. They are always very public. By vandalizing a conspicuous public building—a school, a nursing station, or an airport—native teenagers can ensure that their crime is quickly detected. Often they don't even bother to steal anything from the buildings they break into. They leave valuable property untouched. Sometimes they carve their names into the walls to make sure the police know who to arrest. "They just keep walking around and wait until the band constable comes and picks them up," explains Ira Andrews, a teenager at Gods Lake Narrows. The crimes are easily solved. "If we don't catch them, they come to us and turn themselves in," says Steve Gourdeau, an RCMP constable at the Shamattawa reserve.

The RCMP officers do not blame the teenagers. The problem, the police agree, is the lack of employment and recreation for Indian youths at the northern reserves. "They wake up in the morning and they have absolutely nothing to look forward to," Constable Gourdeau says. "People have to understand what it would be like to wake up in the morning and have absolutely nothing to do. And it's forever. Weekends don't mean anything. Mondays don't mean anything. It's just another day. The drinking, the crime, and the violence come from the fact that there's nothing to do."

Tony Trout, an alcohol and drug counsellor at Gods Lake Narrows, estimates that 30 percent of the reserve's teenagers are prepared to commit criminal offences to escape the reserve. Another band official, Lawrence Okemow, remembers talking to a teenager who had committed a minor crime at a nearby reserve. "He was crying because the RCMP wouldn't take him out," Okemow says.

Vandalism and petty crime and assaults become methods of escape and outlets for pent-up frustrations. "It's like when you put a bunch of wolves in a pen and starve them," says Jeff Brightnose, a young Indian at the Cross Lake reserve in northern Manitoba. "They start fighting with each other."

As hunting and trapping fall into decline, often because of hydro flooding and industrial developments which destroy the traditional way of life, native youths are increasingly left idle. Education is beginning to fill the gap as Indian bands gain control of their own schools, but too many reserves are still hampered by poor-quality federal schools which ignore native culture. When education cannot engage the attention of native youths, communities must rely on wage employment and recreational facilities to keep their young people out of trouble. Yet unemployment remains at 80 to 90 percent at most remote northern reserves. And many native communities cannot afford the cost of sports complexes or recreation centres.

Stan Sinclair, a Métis from the native community of Moose Lake in northwestern Manitoba, has been in trouble with the law for sixteen of his twenty-six years. Jail, he says, is better than the overcrowded houses of Moose Lake, where there is no running water and there are few jobs or recreational opportunities. "I don't feel anything any more when I go to court. It's just routine now.... We have nothing to look forward to when we wake up in the morning. We get frustrated and scared. We don't give a damn what happens to anybody any more because nobody gives a damn about us. The only thing we know is to cause trouble and go to jail, where you have three meals a day and a place to sleep and a TV to look at."

Across Canada, the crime rate tends to be highest in native communities where the unemployment rate is highest, and it tends to decline where recreational programs are provided. In 1987, the crime rate dropped by 17.4 percent in four native communities in northern Manitoba after a sports and recreation program was established there. Organized by University of Manitoba professor Neil Winther, this program—the Northern Fly-In Sports Camp—was financed largely by donations from community groups and individuals. Even as the crime rate was declining among the 1,600 young people in the four native communities where the sports camp was available, crime increased by 10.6 percent in the twenty-six northern communities that did not have the program.

While native teenagers often go to jail by choice, adult Indians are more likely to be imprisoned for reasons they cannot control. Sometimes poverty forces people to commit offences simply to survive. One thirty-four-year-old native woman, for example, was sentenced to a three-month jail term for stealing a jar of relish and $9. She was a single mother, trying to raise three children, one of whom was only five months old. At her sentencing, the judge called her a menace to society and a bad example for her children. "Judges have never experienced what it is like to be poor," the woman told an interviewer later.

Another native woman, Cindy Fobister, was overcome by tears when she told a similar story to the Manitoba aboriginal justice inquiry in 1988. She described how she broke into a store after she found herself without enough money to buy diapers and food for her baby. "We ran out of food," she told the inquiry. "Everyone has to eat." For her efforts to feed her infant child, Cindy Fobister was sentenced to four months in jail. When she is released from prison, she will have a criminal record and her job prospects will be poor. "I've done some thinking and I'm almost certain I'll have to resort to the same thing again," she said. "Sometimes I get scared that I won't be able to keep going."

Poverty sends Indians to jail for another reason as well: their inability to pay the fines imposed on them by the courts. When convicted, they are often given a choice of sentences—a jail term or a fine. Most people, confronted with those options, will pay the fine in order to avoid jail. But native people often have no choice in the matter. They are shipped to prison because they cannot afford to pay a court-imposed fine of just a few hundred dollars.

Today several provinces have "fine-option" programs to allow people to perform community work if they cannot afford to pay a fine. In 1987 about 3,700 aboriginal people in Manitoba performed volunteer work as an alternative to paying a fine. Before the program began, most of them would have been sent to jail.

Where fine-option programs exist, they have helped to reduce the native incarceration rate. But half of the Canadian provinces do not have any such program, and even in provinces where a fine-option program is functioning, many natives continue to be sent to jail for defaulting on fines. At one provincial jail in Manitoba, up to 60 percent of the native inmates in 1987 were serving jail terms because they were unable to pay fines.

Poverty also makes it difficult for native people to travel to their court hearings. In the north, judges and lawyers usually travel to an Indian community once or twice a month to dispense justice. But in some northern communities, natives are required to travel hundreds of miles to attend court. They often cannot afford the airfare, so they are arrested and charged with failing to appear in court. That makes it harder for them to get bail, so they are held in custody until their trial.

When their jail term is over and they are released from custody, Indians can rarely afford the cost of airfare to return to their homes on the northern reserves. Many are penniless when they are released from jail. They sleep in the bushes or ditches of cities such as Thompson and Winnipeg, often committing another crime to try to survive.

Robinson Napoakesik, a forty-year-old resident of Shamattawa, knows several people from his reserve who were left homeless in Thompson after they were released from jail. "They have no money and no place to stay and they have no friends in Thompson. When they want to eat, they go to garbage dumps. They survive on garbage. The food is rotten. Sometimes they have to go to hospital for food poisoning. One time, they killed some ravens on the street. They cooked the ravens and made soup out of it. They got sick and they started vomiting."

The mayor of Thompson did not like to see the former prisoners sleeping in the ditches of his city. So he ordered the city's staff to cut down the bushes inside the city limits where the homeless ex-prisoners were congregating.

But that made little difference to the native people. "They just wander around the streets without any food or shelter," says Bennett Redhead, the probation officer at the Shamattawa reserve. "I've seen it with my own eyes. I spent money to buy food and shelter for one of them. Sometimes they shoplift to eat and they get into more trouble. It's not their fault. I would do the same thing if I were in their boots."

*

After their first exposure to the legal system, many aboriginal people soon find themselves on a treadmill of repeated convictions. In comparison to the general population, Indian and Métis people are jailed in shockingly large numbers. About 10 percent of Manitoba's population is Indian or Métis, yet almost 60 percent of the prisoners in Manitoba's provincial jails are native. Among aboriginal women and youths, the lock-up rate is even higher: about 70 percent of the women in Manitoba's provincial jails and about 75 percent of the juveniles in Winnipeg's youth detention centre are native.

Elsewhere in Canada, the pattern is similar. In Newfoundland and New Brunswick, the native incarceration rate is four to six times worse than the provincial average. In British Columbia and Alberta, natives represent 20 to 30 percent of the prison population, even though they represent just 5 percent of the total population. In Saskatchewan, 10 percent of the population is Indian or Métis, yet more than 60 percent of the Saskatchewan jail population is native.

Consider the city of Prince Albert in northern Saskatchewan. Locking up Indian and Métis people is one of the town's biggest industries. The town has three jails, and all of them are filled with natives. There is a federal penitentiary, where half of the prisoners are native. There is a provincial correctional centre, where 75 percent of the inmates are native. And there is a women's jail, where 85 percent of the inmates are native.

These statistics are bad enough, but there are signs that the native incarceration rate is growing worse. Across Canada, the proportion of Indian and Métis prisoners in federal jails has more than doubled in the past three decades, and the number of native prisoners is increasing much faster than the number of non-native prisoners. Within a few years, natives will represent 80 percent of the prison population in Saskatchewan, according to one provincial official.

One statistic, above all others, captures the full meaning of the great lock-up of aboriginal people in this country. It has been calculated that an ordinary Indian boy in Saskatchewan who turned sixteen in 1976 had a 70 percent probability of being thrown into jail by the age of twenty-five. "Prison has become, for young native men, the promise of a just society which high school and college represents for the rest of us," a committee of the Canadian Bar Association concluded in 1988. "Placed in a historical context, the prison has become for many young native people the contemporary equivalent of what the Indian residential school represented for their parents."

From the courts to the jails, the Indian is faced with a foreign justice system that consistently puts aboriginal people at a disadvantage. "He will probably appear before a white judge, be defended and prosecuted by white lawyers, and if he goes to jail he'll be supervised by white guards," says Al Chartrand, president of Native Clan Organization, which provides parole services to natives in Winnipeg. "The justice system is often seen as a white man's weapon—a heavy hand that enforces his laws. It is them and us...the white man's law."

The unequal treatment can begin with the first contact between an Indian and a police officer, who is usually white. Most of the country's Indian reserves are still policed by the RCMP or the provincial police forces, which employ only a tiny handful of Indian officers. In 1988, for instance, just 26 of the 4,450 members of the Ontario Provincial Police were native. And the policing on most Indian reserves is ultimately controlled by senior officials in the regional headquarters of the RCMP or the provincial police. If a band in northern Manitoba wants an extra police officer on its reserve to battle a crime wave, it must plead for help from the RCMP, knowing that the final decision will probably be made by a superintendent in Winnipeg.

Although some bands have auxiliary police forces or band constables who enforce bylaws and investigate minor crimes, these native law enforcers have limited authority. They cannot investigate serious crimes and they are not permitted to carry firearms. The low status of their positions is reinforced by the fact that they are poorly paid—as little as $17,000 in annual salary. They are expected to provide their own vehicles and pay for their own gasoline. The band constable program, financed by the Indian Affairs Department, is so seriously underfunded that many constables do not have uniforms, offices, communications equipment, or jail cells in which to hold suspects.

The federal government has also financed a Special Constable program which allows Indians to join the RCMP after taking a short training course. Although hundreds of Indian constables have been recruited under this program, they do not have the same powers as a regular RCMP officer, and they report to RCMP superiors, not to a band council. The regular police officers often use the special constables merely as translators and intermediaries in their dealings with the Indian communities.

In urban centres, an equally low proportion of native people are employed as law enforcers. Only 19 of the 12,093 municipal police officers in Ontario are native. In Thunder Bay, almost 10 percent of the population is Indian or Métis, yet there is only one native constable among the city's 200 police officers. Just 9 of the 1,140 police officers in Winnipeg are native, and there are only two native police officers in Vancouver, two in Calgary, and seven in Regina. There has never been an Indian on the municipal police force in Sydney, Nova Scotia.

Confronted by white police officers who are controlled by outside institutions, aboriginal people tend to be mistrustful of the police. Their suspicions are probably well founded. Some studies suggest that natives are at a greater risk of arrest than white Canadians—partly because they are more visible than non-natives, partly because they are more likely to be transient or homeless, and partly because police officers often have negative attitudes toward Indian and Métis people.

The police exercise a great deal of discretion in deciding whom to arrest and charge. A police officer's decision to charge someone with public drunkenness, for example, is not simply determined by the person's behaviour or by the amount of alcohol he has consumed. "It depends on where the police are, and on what they and others perceive to be acceptable or unacceptable alcohol-related behavior," a University of Regina study concluded.

"It depends, for example, on whether or not a hotel owner or manager asks someone who is drunk to leave or calls the police. And it depends on whether the police decide to come. All of these influences on arrest rates probably discriminate against people who are poor, unemployed, transient, and native. They are not protected by preferential status and authority when they drink in public places. They often have no other places to go but where their exposure to arrest is high."

A study by Professor James Harding of the University of Regina, which looked at the arrest rate for public drunkenness, found that 30 percent of the Indians arrested for drunkenness were charged and sent to court. By contrast, only 11 percent of non-natives arrested for drunkenness were charged.

Municipal police often prefer to patrol inner-city neighbourhoods and downtown streets where Indians tend to congregate. They know they can eventually find somebody to lay a charge against if they stay in those neighbourhoods long enough. "A native person is much more likely to be checked by police or stopped," says Terry Thompson, an assistant deputy-minister in the Saskatchewan Justice Department. He cited one case in which a judge agreed that the police had reasonable and probable grounds to stop and question any Indian who is riding a new ten-speed bicycle. The police and the judge assumed that an Indian could not afford to buy a new bicycle, so the bike would have to be stolen.

A report by the Alberta Attorney-General's Department in 1978 concluded that RCMP officers, especially the younger and newly appointed ones, are often too hasty in making arrests and laying charges against Indians. According to the report, police frequently stop and search Indians without explanation.

Murray Sinclair, a young Indian lawyer who was later to become one of two judges appointed to the Manitoba aboriginal justice inquiry, told a conference in 1984 that native people are easy prey for the police because they are more likely to be convicted than non-natives. The police measure their efficiency by their conviction rate, Sinclair noted. "The court system focuses on Indian people as an easy target," he told the conference.

Four years later, when Sinclair was appointed to the Manitoba bench as an associate chief judge in the provincial court, he was asked whether he still believed that the justice system is weighted against Indians. He made it clear that he had no regrets about his previous comments. "I don't doubt for a moment that the questions of enforcement—discretion in processing charges and selecting areas of the city in which to enforce laws—lead to over-representation from those [Indian] communities in court," Sinclair told a Winnipeg newspaper. "If the City of Winnipeg police concentrated their efforts of enforcement in River Heights or Tuxedo or St. James, the crime statistics for those areas would go up dramatically."

If there was a single incident that symbolized the strained relationship between native people and the police, it was the J. J. Harper case in Winnipeg. At about 2:30 on the morning of March 9, 1988, John

Joseph Harper was strolling home along Logan Avenue after drinking a few coffee-and-whiskeys at a Winnipeg tavern. Harper, the father of three children, was a well-known Indian leader who headed the Island Lake Tribal Council. He was alone on the street until, without any warning, he saw a Winnipeg police constable approaching him.

At first, Harper simply ignored the officer. He was minding his own business, after all, and he knew he had no legal obligation to talk to the constable. The police officer asked Harper to show some identification. Harper refused. The constable repeated the demand, but Harper again refused to stop. He walked away from the police officer. The constable grabbed Harper's arm and spun him around. A few minutes later, J. J. Harper was dead. He had bled to death with a police bullet in his chest.

Lawyers and native groups are still debating exactly what happened in those brief moments after the police officer grabbed Harper's arm. All we have is the constable's version of the incident. The police officer testified that Harper pushed him to the ground and reached for the constable's gun. There was a struggle for the gun, and the constable's finger somehow ended up on the trigger of the revolver. The gun went off, and Harper was dead. At the inquest, a provincial judge accepted the officer's version of the events, but Indian groups denounced the judge's decision.

The death of J. J. Harper and the subsequent inquest raised some troubling questions about police officers and the justice system. In fact, the Harper case was one of the major reasons for Manitoba's decision to launch an official inquiry into the justice system and its treatment of native people. The major questions surrounding the Harper case remain unanswered, however.

For example: Why did the constable approach J. J. Harper and grab his arm? The police officer was searching for a twenty-two-year-old suspect in a car theft, yet Harper was thirty-six. The constable knew that the suspect would probably be running away from the scene, yet Harper was calmly walking down the street. The constable knew that a young native suspect had already been taken into custody, but he decided to stop Harper anyway. The constable testified that he thought Harper fit the suspect's description better than the young man who was already in custody. The young man in custody, however, was the real car thief. "It's almost as if it's a crime to be an Indian walking late at night," said Louis Stevenson, chief of the Peguis band and spokesman for the Assembly of Manitoba Chiefs.

Native groups were also angered by the fact that the Winnipeg police department had exonerated the constable within thirty-six hours of the shooting. Even before daylight had broken on the morning of Harper's death, the police had already hosed down the scene of the shooting, making it virtually impossible for others to investigate the incident. The police made no attempt to obtain fingerprints from the constable's gun to check the accuracy of his story, and they made only a token search of the area. Their investigation was so lax that they failed to notice Harper's smashed, blood-spattered glasses lying on the ground near the scene of the shooting. (The glasses were later found by a newspaper reporter.) When the brief investigation was over, the Winnipeg police chief announced that the constable was innocent, and the mayor of Winnipeg immediately agreed that the police officer had done no wrong. Later, the judge at the inquest said the police had been "a bit hasty" in their investigation.

The inquest heard testimony from two native youths who were present at the scene of the death. The youths said they heard police officers cursing Indians and making disparaging remarks about native people, but the judge rejected their testimony, declaring that they were "not credible". After the inquest, native groups said it appeared that the testimony of white police officers had more weight than the testimony of natives.

The judge's report on the Harper case was curious. The judge confirmed that aboriginal people feel harassed by the police, and he agreed that the police officer's decision to question J. J. Harper "could easily be perceived as yet another instance of police harassment." He observed that Winnipeg's natives have an "utter distrust" of the police and even recommended that the Winnipeg police "vigorously pursue a program of recruiting natives" to ease the tension between the police and the native population. At the same time, however, he described that sense of harassment as merely "a perception" by natives, implying that it had no basis in reality. Native leaders are convinced that there would not be such a widespread feeling of harassment unless there were facts and personal experiences to support it.

Aboriginal groups had expected little from the judge. "There's a lot of cynicism and bitterness," one Indian leader said. After the ruling, the bitterness increased. "We have long suspected that, in the white courts, an Indian's testimony is worth nothing and a white man's testimony is pure gold," said Ken Wood, chief of the St. Theresa Point Indian band in northeastern Manitoba.

"There's almost no value placed on an Indian life," said Louis Stevenson. "It appears there isn't any justice for us."

If native people suffer because of the racial attitudes of police officers, the court system does little to improve their chances of seeing justice done. At the Shamattawa reserve in northern Manitoba, the court proceedings are typical of the system of justice for Indian and Métis defendants across Canada.

At eleven o'clock on a September morning at Shamattawa, lawyers and court officials are milling around the entrance to the Leonard Miles Memorial Centre, talking intensely among themselves and holding brief discussions with the Indians. Today is court day. Twice a month, a travelling judge and his court officials are flown into the reserve, where they set up a temporary courtroom in the drop-in centre. The same judge and the same officials are flown into Indian reserves across northern Manitoba to preside over court proceedings in the region's remote communities.

A typical docket at Shamattawa might include twenty-five adults and thirty juveniles. The juveniles are often locked up in a youth detention centre in Winnipeg until their case is scheduled to be heard in Shamattawa. Then a float plane picks them up in Winnipeg and flies northward. The small airplane splashes down onto the river at Shamattawa and the handcuffed juveniles are taken into the drop-in centre to await their brief trial.

The court was supposed to begin at 10:00 A.M., but things are behind schedule. When the half-dozen juveniles arrived from Winnipeg, one young girl managed to escape from her police escort. Now the RCMP are searching for her in the bush.

At 11:30, the officials decide to begin the court proceedings without the escapee. The chairs and tables have been cleared away from the middle of the drop-in centre, and a couple of battered tables are rearranged to form a rough setting for the trials. The drop-in centre is crowded with spectators—Indian men and women who sit quietly along the walls. The middle-aged judge, wearing a tie and a black and red robe, enters the room. "All rise," the clerk tells the Indians. "Please take your hats off. There will be no talking or smoking."

One by one, the names of the defendants are read aloud by the clerk. Many are absent. Warrants are issued for their arrest. An official explains that two of the absent defendants are members of the search party looking for the young escapee.

The judge, after telling one woman to appear in court in Thompson on October 14, asks her if she knows where the court is located. Another man has been remanded four times already. The judge asks an official to explain why a legal aid lawyer has not talked to the man yet.

One of the first trials involves a large, soft-spoken man who works as the manager of the drop-in centre. He has been charged with assault. Early one morning, he discovered that the gas tank of his Honda all-terrain vehicle had been slashed and gasoline had been stolen from it. When he learned the name of the youth who had broken into the vehicle, he walked to the youth's house and entered it. The youth's mother swore at him, and he lost his temper and punched her. His lawyer describes it as "a momentary lapse" by someone who had no previous criminal record. When the defence lawyer has finished speaking, the Crown announces that it is dropping the charge against the man because the information was not drawn up properly.

A mother of four children has been charged with firing a rifle in the air. Her lawyer describes her household as "one of the better homes in the community." There are problems only when she falls into drinking binges, the lawyer says. He says the woman recognizes her drinking problem and is willing to enter a counselling program. The woman's household is a stable family unit, and she has committed no criminal offences for the past ten years, the lawyer says.

The judge tells the woman that she is guilty of a serious offence. Firing a rifle when highly intoxicated is "a dangerous combination", which could lead to deaths, he says. The judge puts her on supervised probation for one year and orders her to attend an alcohol counselling program.

By 12:30, the RCMP are still searching for the runaway girl. A large spider is crawling across the grimy floor of the drop-in centre. The judge is complaining about the lack of security at this location. He wants to hold court hearings at the new school building, where security can be tighter and there would be less chance of people escaping custody. The school principal is reluctant. He does not want his school associated with the system of courts and punishment.

The judge listens to a lawyer describing a youth who was found drunk in the middle of the night. The police found him carrying a plank of wood and muttering about revenge for something. The judge gives him a $150 fine for breach of probation. The judge asks him to estimate how long it will take to pay the fine. "Two months," he replies. He is given until mid-November to pay the $150.

And so it goes. By early afternoon, it is all over. The juveniles in handcuffs are marched off to the airplane. They are laughing. Behind them, a parade of giggling children follow the handcuffed teenagers. Court day is over.

Whether a case is heard in the temporary courtroom of a northern reserve or the regular court building of a big city, aboriginal defendants soon become alienated from the justice system. Because of language barriers, cultural differences, and economic misfortune, Indian and Métis people are less likely to receive a fair hearing. The problems begin before the case reaches the courtroom. Since most native defendants cannot afford to hire a lawyer, they must rely on legal aid lawyers and duty counsel, who are swamped with work and often see their native clients only a few minutes before a case is heard. In such a short period of time, it is impossible to ensure that the defendants understand all of their options and rights. Nor is it possible for the lawyer to learn enough about the case to give the judge a full explanation of the defendant's side of the story.

On the northern Indian reserves, justice is dispensed by a travelling court party. The judge, Crown prosecutor, legal aid lawyer, and court staff all travel together, flying into a reserve in the morning and flying out in the afternoon. With as many as forty cases to be handled in a single day, the prosecutor and the judge have to rush through the cases at break-neck speed. One judge in northern Quebec, after hearing 186 cases in a week, called the travelling court system "a mockery" and "a circus".

The judges and lawyers have no time to meet the community leaders to try to understand their concerns. As a result, the courts are perceived as an alien and arbitrary system, imposed by outsiders. "They are always in too much of a hurry when they arrive and leave," said Alan Ross, chief of the Norway House band in northern Manitoba. "Even spending a night in our community and talking with our people might help."

Canada's justice system is founded on the European tradition of adversarial justice, which concentrates on placing blame and assessing guilt. Each case is resolved by a form of retribution or revenge against the offender—which is completely foreign to the native tradition of justice. Before the arrival of Europeans in North America, native societies had no jails or prisons. Offences were resolved by a form of conciliation between the victim and the offender, aimed at restoring peace and harmony in the community.

Because of this philosophical difference, and because they do not understand their rights in the Canadian justice system, aboriginal people tend to be baffled and intimidated by the courts. They plead guilty because they are anxious to end their ordeal as quickly as possible. "Generally, native people perceive that being charged is the same as being found guilty," a federal Justice Department study concluded. Misunderstanding is made worse by the fact that English is an unfamiliar tongue for many natives, and legal jargon is incomprehensible. Indians usually do not retain a lawyer before answering questions from the police, and they tend to incriminate themselves by cooperating in police questioning. By the time the interrogation is over, they have given the police an airtight confession.

During the Manitoba aboriginal justice inquiry in 1988 and 1989, native inmates said they pleaded guilty because their legal aid lawyers advised them to do so—even if they were innocent. A study of 230 native inmates in Canadian jails found that 75 percent of them had entered guilty pleas. Almost one-third of the inmates said they did not understand their sentences or the sentencing process. Many said they were advised to plead guilty. "We know there are a horrendous number of Indian people who plead guilty and get convicted for crimes for which they were improperly charged," Murray Sinclair said in 1984.

Bernie Francis, a former native courtworker in Nova Scotia, cited a case in which a Micmac woman pleaded guilty to arson without understanding what the word meant. In fact, the fire at her house was accidental, but she had not understood the charge. Although Micmac is still the daily language for many Indians in Nova Scotia, interpreters are rarely provided. Micmacs often misunderstood the word "guilty" because there was no such word in the Micmac language, Francis said. The closest translation is the Micmac word for "blame." When they are asked whether they are guilty, some Micmacs answer "Yes" because they think they are being asked whether they are being blamed for the offence.

To help aboriginal people understand their rights in the justice system, some provinces have introduced native courtworker and native court communicator programs. However, the funding for these programs has been cut back in recent years, and Saskatchewan, Nova Scotia, New Brunswick, and Prince Edward Island have eliminated their programs altogether. The program in Saskatchewan had been saving about 250 native people from jail terms each year, according to one estimate, yet it was killed by budget cuts. In other provinces, the programs are underfunded and understaffed. A report in Manitoba found that court communicators often don't have time to visit courts and remand centres where they are needed. Most Indians have never heard of the court communicator program, so they are unlikely to benefit from it.

Even after they are sent to prison, Indian and Métis people continue to be victimized by the justice system. Because they are unfamiliar with the parole release program, they tend to waive their right to parole hearings. When they do apply for parole, they are sometimes rejected because they are perceived as having lower job skills and a lack of definite plans for the future. In 1987, only 18 percent of Canada's native inmates were released on full parole, compared to 42 percent of the general inmate population. Indian and Métis parolees are also more likely to have their paroles revoked for technical violations, even when they have not committed any new criminal offence.

Native alienation from the Canadian justice system is worsened by the almost total absence of Indians and Métis among the key decision makers and authority figures within the system. Just as there is a lack of native police officers in Canada, there is an equally serious shortage of native judges and lawyers. Only a handful of native judges have been appointed to Canada's provincial courts, and there are no Indian or Métis judges on the superior courts anywhere in the country. Only 0.25 percent of Canada's 45,000 lawyers are Indian or Métis.

In northwestern Manitoba, fewer than 10 percent of jury members are native, yet more than half of the local population is native. In the town of Sydney, where the wrongful conviction of Donald Marshall took place, no Indian has ever been selected for a jury. In some provinces, juries are selected from names in telephone books or city directories—yet Indian and Métis people are still seriously underrepresented because many do not have telephones.

The predominance of white lawyers and judges in Canadian courts means, at best, that Indian cultural values and living conditions are rarely taken into account when a case is decided. At worst, the white monopoly can lead to biased attitudes at the upper levels of the justice system. A judge in British Columbia, hearing a lawyer argue that his Indian clients might have difficulty finding transportation to a trial in a town sixty kilometres away, made this comment: "If there is a drink party in Terrace, everybody can get a lift." In 1982, one of Manitoba's highest-ranking judges said in a courtroom: "If I had to strike from the record the evidence of drunken Indians that I had heard over the past 25 years, there wouldn't be much left." The judge was criticized by the Manitoba Human Rights Commission, but the Canadian Judicial Council rejected a complaint about him.

Discrimination can affect the sentencing of convicted natives as well. Several studies have found that aboriginal people are less likely to receive non-custodial sentences such as probation. When a jail term is imposed for a serious offence, natives tend to receive longer sentences than non-natives, according to a study of sentencing in Edmonton.

A study of capital murder cases from 1926 to 1957 (when capital punishment was in effect) found that Indians were much more likely to be executed than other Canadians. While the risk of execution for an English Canadian who killed a white person was 21 percent, an Indian who killed a white person in the same circumstances had a 96 percent risk of execution. Kenneth Avio, a professor at the University of Victoria who conducted the study, found memos from Indian Affairs bureaucrats recommending that Indian offenders be executed because native people needed "special deterrence".

Because of the gross underrepresentation of aboriginal people in the administration of justice in Canada, justice has become a one-sided relationship for natives. They are the accused and the inmates, but almost never the decision makers. "To them, justice means arrests, criminal charges, fines and often jail," says Donald Purich, director of the Native Law Centre at the University of Saskatchewan. "We cannot afford to have one segment of our society always in the prisoner's box and never having a role to play in administering justice."

In a logging town in northern Manitoba in 1971, a nineteen-year-old Cree Indian girl named Helen Betty Osborne was brutally murdered. In that same year, a Micmac Indian named Donald Marshall was sent to a Nova Scotia jail for a murder he did not commit. For eleven years, Marshall was wrongly imprisoned, while the real killer—a white man named Roy Ebsary—went free. Meanwhile, during the same period of time, the white men who were involved in the killing of Betty Osborne remained free in western Canada. Both the Osborne and the Marshall cases were blatant miscarriages of justice with ugly racist overtones.

On the night of November 12, 1971, four young men were drinking heavily and driving around the frontier town of The Pas in northwestern Manitoba. They wanted sex, and they were looking for a compliant Indian girl. Cruising for native girls was common in The Pas—natives were thought to be "easy" and less likely to complain. When they spotted Betty Osborne walking along a street, the men tried to persuade her to join them for a "party." She refused, but they grabbed her and forced her into the car. As they drove through the town and the surrounding wilderness, Betty Osborne's clothes were ripped off and she was sexually assaulted. She struggled to resist the attack, but her arms were pinned to her sides by one of the men while another man assaulted her. The two other men continued drinking as they watched the assault.

The next day, Osborne's naked body was discovered in a secluded area of bush and forest, north of The Pas. She had been stabbed fifty-six times with a screwdriver. Her chest and back were covered with stab wounds, and her skull had been cracked by a vicious blow from the screwdriver.

Lee Colgan, one of the four men in the car, soon began talking about the murder. He described the slaying to friends, acquaintances, people in stores, fellow workers, and even people he had just met. He described it to a local sheriff and to a civilian employee of the RCMP, but nobody contacted the police to report Colgan's confessions.

At a party in 1972, a crowd of people laughed as they heard Dwayne Johnston describe the murder. He had been among the four men in the car that night. "Do you know what it feels like to kill someone?" he asked his friends at the party. "It feels great." He made stabbing motions with his hand as he boasted about the killing of Betty Osborne. "I picked up a screwdriver and I stabbed her and I stabbed her and I stabbed her," Johnston told the crowd.

Still nobody went to the police. By this time, the police had found clues pointing to the four men, but they could not prove the guilt of the killer or killers unless they found witnesses who would testify that they had heard Colgan or Johnston confessing their involvement in the murder. Dozens of townspeople could have provided the crucial testimony, but none came forward.

Friends of Colgan and Johnston, including a prominent lawyer in The Pas, helped to protect the four men. One friend threatened to kill a witness who had heard Colgan describe the murder. Another helped one of the men avoid an RCMP lie-detector test. The prominent lawyer arranged to represent all four men, even though that was a violation of the rules of the legal profession. He told the men to remain silent.

The case was finally cracked open in 1985 with a simple technique: the police placed an ad in the local newspaper, asking the people of The Pas for information about the murder of Betty Osborne. One of the responses came from a woman who had heard Johnston bragging about the murder at the party in 1972. Fourteen years of silence had finally been broken.

Colgan and Johnston were arrested in 1986. A few months later, Colgan struck a deal with the Crown. In return for complete immunity from all charges related to the murder of Betty Osborne, he agreed to testify for the Crown at the trial of Johnston and Jim Houghton, one of the other men who had been in the car. The fourth man in the car, Norman Manger, was not charged with anything. He said he was too drunk to remember any details of the night of Osborne's death.

At the trial in 1987, Colgan testified that Johnston had taken Osborne out of the car when they reached a secluded spot in the bush. There were banging noises, and Houghton got out of the car, Colgan testified. Shortly afterward, Johnston returned to the car to get a screwdriver. Johnston and Houghton remained outside with the Indian woman as the other two men continued drinking in the warmth of the car. Then they returned to the car, and the four men drove off together. The trial heard evidence about footprints in the snow which suggested that two men had dragged Osborne's body into the bush after the murder.

At the end of the trial, it was an all-white jury that considered the evidence. The region's population was heavily native, and 20 of the 104 prospective jurors had been Indian or Métis, but all of the natives were rejected by the lawyers. In the end, the jury decided to convict Dwayne Johnston and let Jim Houghton go free.

On the night of May 28, 1971, less than six months before the murder of Betty Osborne in The Pas, seventeen-year-old Donald Marshall was strolling through Wentworth Park in Sydney, Nova Scotia. Marshall and a teenaged buddy, Sandy Seale, decided to ask for money from two men who were returning from a beer-drinking session in a Sydney tavern. One of the men was Roy Ebsary, a grizzled war veteran with a penchant for knives. After a confrontation and a scuffle, Ebsary stabbed Seale viciously and slashed Marshall. Seale died the following day.

Although the Sydney police could not find any physical evidence to connect Donald Marshall with the stabbing, they immediately made him their prime suspect. Their case against Marshall rested on three teenaged witnesses who eventually agreed to testify against Marshall. Years later, all three witnesses admitted that the Sydney police had coerced them into giving their testimony. One fourteen-year-old boy had been told by the police that he might receive a jail term if he refused to give the story that the police wanted.

None of the three witnesses had seen the stabbing, but after hours of grilling, two of them agreed to testify that they had seen Marshall kill Seale. The third witness agreed to testify that she had seen Marshall alone with a man who looked like Seale on the night of the stabbing. Each of the three witnesses had given different versions of the incident during earlier questioning, but they revised their stories under strong pressure from the police. After obtaining these revised statements, the police arrested Donald Marshall and charged him with murder.

At the murder trial in November 1971, the prosecutor refused to allow the defence to see a key portion of his evidence—the original police statements by the three key witnesses. These statements, which contradicted the later testimony of the three witnesses, would have been invaluable to the defence lawyer. By refusing to show them to the defence, the prosecutor was going against the basic ethics of the legal profession, which require the Crown to disclose all evidence to the defence.

In a courtroom corridor, near the end of Marshall's trial, one of the key witnesses told the Crown and defence lawyers that he had lied on the witness stand. He admitted that he had never seen Marshall stab Sandy Seale. But when the prosecutor told the witness that he could be charged with perjury if he changed his testimony, the witness decided to continue testifying that he had seen Marshall stab Seale.

On the afternoon of November 5, 1971, after four hours of deliberations, a jury of twelve white men convicted Donald Marshall of murder. He was sentenced to life in prison.

Ten days later, a man named Jimmy MacNeill went to the Sydney police. He had been Roy Ebsary's companion on the night of Sandy Seale's death. He told the police how Ebsary had stabbed Seale and how he had washed the blood from the knife at his home a few minutes later. MacNeill's description of Ebsary was remarkably similar to Marshall's description of the killer. But the police did not question Marshall again or search for a knife at Ebsary's home. Instead they questioned Ebsary and accepted his denials, then closed their books on the case.

Marshall spent eleven years behind bars. Only a stroke of blind luck led to his vindication. An acquaintance of Marshall, who had once lived at Roy Ebsary's house, heard Ebsary boast of stabbing a man in Wentworth Park in 1971. The acquaintance visited Marshall in prison and mentioned Ebsary's claim. Marshall contacted his lawyer, and soon the RCMP were reinvestigating the case. When the RCMP approached the three key witnesses from the 1971 trial, the witnesses admitted they had given false evidence.

In the spring of 1982, the case was referred to the Nova Scotia Court of Appeal, where, for the first time, a court heard the truth from the witnesses. The Crown prosecutor acknowledged that Marshall should be acquitted.

However, the prosecutor also asked the court to exonerate the Sydney police on the grounds that the credibility of the criminal justice system might otherwise be damaged by Marshall's acquittal. "It seems reasonable to assume that the public will suspect that there is something wrong with the system if a man can be convicted of a murder he did not commit," the prosecutor told the court. The five judges on the Court of Appeal accepted this argument and ruled that Marshall's conviction was largely due to his "evasive" statements during the 1971 trial. They said that Marshall had "triggered" the death of Sandy Seale by trying to rob Ebsary and MacNeill. "Any miscarriage of justice is...more apparent than real," the judges declared. In effect, they were declaring that the justice system and the police were innocent. The real culprit, they seemed to be saying, was Donald Marshall.

The Marshall and Osborne cases demonstrated that the flaws in the justice system are part of a more widespread problem of racism in white society. The Marshall case revealed patterns of bias and prejudice among judges, lawyers, prosecutors, and police officers. The Osborne case showed that natives were treated more harshly by the police than non-natives. Both cases uncovered a long history of racism among whites who lived near Indian reserves. And in each case, the killers were influenced by racism. According to testimony at provincial inquiries, Roy Ebsary disliked Indians and Dwayne Johnston had an intense hatred of native people.

In Manitoba and Nova Scotia, the justice system failed to proceed with charges against white men who were connected with the murders. In the Marshall case, the police ignored evidence that pointed directly to Roy Ebsary. In the Osborne case, charges of sexual assault or unlawful confinement could have been laid against at least one of the three men who walked free after the 1987 trial. All three men had remained silent and helped the killer escape justice, and at least two of them had made no attempt to prevent the assault or the murder, yet they were left unpunished.

The history of discrimination and prejudice in The Pas can be traced back to the early days of the twentieth century. In those days, many Indians lived in The Pas on the south side of the Saskatchewan River. But when the railway arrived and the town became an important stop on the route to Hudson Bay, the Indian land suddenly became valuable. Soon the Indians were forced to move to the less profitable side of the river, where they still live today.

Six years before the murder of Betty Osborne, two researchers conducted a survey of racial attitudes in The Pas. Almost 75 percent of the town's residents showed some prejudice against Indians, and 10 percent displayed extreme prejudice, the survey found. Most of those surveyed said that Indians were shiftless and undependable. Almost half said the average Indian had "complete disregard for the common standards of personal decency."

As recently as the early 1970s, blatant forms of racism were practised routinely and openly by merchants and other residents of The Pas. Natives could not get service in restaurants unless they were accompanied by a white person. If they walked into a store, they were watched and followed by storekeepers who refused to serve them. The high school cafeteria was divided into two sections, and the native students were not allowed to eat with the non-natives. All the native students were placed in vocational training classes, which prevented them from entering university. And the town's movie theatre was strictly segregated. "We weren't allowed to sit in the centre of the theatre—we had to sit on the side," a native woman remembers.

Racial slurs and violence against natives were common. "When you met a white person in the street, the Indian felt that he had to get out of the way," recalls Frank Whitehead, a councillor in the Indian band at The Pas. In the mid-1970s, tensions arose when the white merchants went to court to try to block the Indian band's construction of an $8.2-million shopping mall on reserve land.

Testimony at the Manitoba aboriginal justice inquiry in 1989 revealed that the RCMP had concentrated on interrogating native youths in the days following the Osborne murder, even though none of the natives was likely suspects because none of them had a car—and a car would have been necessary to transport Osborne to the isolated murder scene. The RCMP did not ask permission to question the underage natives. Sometimes they did not even identify themselves as police officers. In one case, according to testimony at the inquiry, plainclothes RCMP officers took a native teenager to a lonely back road and assaulted her when she refused to answer their questions. By comparison, Lee Colgan and Dwayne Johnston were represented by lawyers who refused to let their clients be interviewed by the police.

Many natives in The Pas can still sense the racism in the community today. About a dozen Indian residents formed an anti-racism committee in 1987 to discuss racial incidents they had experienced. The aboriginal justice inquiry heard a litany of complaints about police brutality against Indians and a series of unexplained deaths of Indians in

The Pas that did not seem to be taken seriously by the justice system. "Things have never really changed," said Oscar Lathlin, chief of The Pas band.

A provincial inquiry into the jailing of Donald Marshall found that racist attitudes toward Indians were as deeply ingrained in Sydney as they were in The Pas. Early in 1982, an RCMP investigator discussed the Marshall case with Marshall's lawyer, Stephen Aronson, who said there had been a "redneck atmosphere" in Sydney in 1971. At first, the RCMP officer refused to believe it. But by mid-April of 1982, he had talked to lawyers, doctors, merchants, and educators who had lived in Sydney in the early 1970s. "I learned that, in fact, Mr. Aronson was right," the RCMP officer told the Marshall inquiry. "There was a rednecked atmosphere." The jury's decision to convict Donald Marshall was partly a result of "the mood of the City of Sydney at the time," he said.

The inquiry was told that some Sydney police officers referred to the Micmacs as "broken arrows" and "wagon burners". Two witnesses recalled an incident in which the police stopped a group of white girls who were walking down a street with several Micmac youths. The police contacted their parents and warned them that their daughters were "walking with the Indians" and keeping "very bad company".

Evidence at the provincial inquiry made it clear that the Micmacs were effectively blocked from participating in the major public institutions in Sydney. Not a single witness could recall any Micmacs ever being employed by the City of Sydney, the Sydney police department, the Sydney fire department, or the Sydney court system. Nor could anyone recall any Micmac lawyers, teachers, or city councillors in Sydney. Perhaps most remarkably, no witness could recall any Micmacs serving on a jury in Sydney. For many years, most Indians were excluded because jurors had to be landowners. Yet even after that requirement was dropped, no Micmacs were chosen to sit on Sydney juries.

Most significant in the Marshall case, however, were the racist attitudes expressed by people in positions of legal authority. Donald MacNeil, the Crown prosecutor at Marshall's trial in 1971, was once censured by the Nova Scotia Human Rights Commission for remarks he had made about Micmacs from the Eskasoni reserve near Sydney. During a trial, MacNeil said judges ought to take drastic action against law breakers at the Eskasoni reserve because Indians needed to be taught to respect the law. In 1970, after investigating the comments, the Human Rights Commission concluded: "MacNeil's statements were inappropriate and tended to be prejudiced in suggesting discriminatory treatment of Eskasoni residents before the courts and supporting such treatment in the general community." Seventeen years later, witnesses at the Marshall inquiry testified that MacNeil "didn't like Indians."

Stephen Aronson recalled the remarks of a prosecutor at a trial in Nova Scotia in the late 1970s. The prosecutor, referring to the Micmacs at a nearby reserve, said derisively: "They're all on welfare." When he wanted the Indian defendants in the trial to remain in the region, he told them: "Don't go potato-picking down in Maine." The same kind of prejudice was displayed in a report by a prison official at Dorchester Penitentiary, where Marshall spent several years of his sentence. The report said: "Marshall is the typical young Indian lad that seems to lose control of his senses while indulging in intoxicating liquors."

Bernie Francis, a former native courtworker, described several racial remarks made by Crown prosecutor Lewis Matheson, who was the junior prosecutor at Marshall's murder trial in 1971. Francis said Matheson suggested that a fence be built around one of the Micmac reserves "so that the Indians couldn't get out to come to Sydney to cause problems." He said Matheson also asked Indians why they couldn't stay on their reserves instead of "upsetting the peace and quiet" in Sydney. Matheson admitted he might have made those statements. "I may've made such a statement in jest or in frustration, yes," he told the inquiry.

Felix Cacchione, a former lawyer for Donald Marshall, told the inquiry that a senior provincial official had advised him not to push hard for compensation for Marshall. He said the official, Robert Anderson, told him: "Felix, don't get your balls caught in a vice over an Indian." Anderson was the director of criminal prosecutions in the Attorney-General's department at the time. At the inquiry, Anderson did not question the accuracy of Cacchione's testimony. "It sounds like something I might say," he said.

Lewis Matheson and Robert Anderson are both working as judges in Nova Scotia today. Matheson is a provincial court judge and Anderson is a county court judge.

Even at the highest levels of the Nova Scotia government, there were disturbing attitudes. George MacDonald, the lawyer for the Marshall inquiry, said the Attorney-General's department had given every benefit of the doubt to two former Cabinet ministers who were investigated by police in the early 1980s. By contrast, the department refused to take the Marshall case seriously and was not interested in being fair to Marshall, he said. The department "simply did not care very much about Donald Marshall, and was not prepared to make any special effort on his behalf."

In both the Marshall case and the Osborne case, racism had drastic effects on the lives of native people. It led to the death of an innocent Indian woman in The Pas, and it destroyed the life of a wrongly convicted Indian man in Sydney. Under the pressure of constant public scrutiny and court appearances from 1982 to 1988, Marshall sometimes went on drinking binges. He felt as if he was still on trial. A psychologist described him as anxiety-ridden, wasted, fatigued, and emotionally distraught: "a self-conscious and mistrustful individual" who perceives the world as "hostile and threatening".

The revelations in the cases of Betty Osborne and J. J. Harper provoked a political controversy in Manitoba. In 1988, after an intense period of protest rallies and backroom lobbying, Indian leaders persuaded the Manitoba government to appoint a formal inquiry into the justice system and its treatment of aboriginal people. The inquiry was headed by two judges—Justice A. C. Hamilton of the Manitoba Court of Queen's Bench and Judge Murray Sinclair of the Manitoba provincial court.

As a child in the 1950s, Murray Sinclair had sometimes strolled through the farmland near the junction of Netley Creek and the Red River, just north of the town of Selkirk. His grandfather, Jim Sinclair, would point to the former boundaries of the old St. Peter's reserve—the place where Chief Peguis and his descendants had lived for a century until they were forced to give up their land to make room for European settlers.

Jim Sinclair's family had refused to leave the reserve, and the government eventually allowed the Ojibway family to keep a six-hectare farm at St. Peter's. In return, they had to enfranchise themselves and give up their legal status as Indians. Murray Sinclair lost his Ojibway language when he was required to speak English at a provincial elementary school. But he knew who he was, and he always remembered the injustice that was done to his forefathers at St. Peter's. After graduating from law school, he worked as legal counsel for a number of Indian and Métis organizations. He also worked on a study documenting the illegal takeover of the St. Peter's reserve and the forced relocation of the Peguis band. An elder gave him an Ojibway name—*Mezanaygeezhik*, which meant "images in the sky". To complete the journey back to his roots, Sinclair applied for membership in the Peguis band. He wanted to regain the Indian status that had been stripped from his grandfather.

Sinclair became a provincial judge in early 1988, and he joined the aboriginal justice inquiry a few weeks later. From September 1988 to April 1989, Sinclair and Hamilton listened to more than eight hundred witnesses in about fifty communities around Manitoba. They travelled by truck, car, small aircraft, motorboat, snowmobile-powered toboggan, school bus, and dogsled. They slept in nursing stations, tiny hotels, and Roman Catholic missions. They ate caribou meat and bannock. They helped lug heavy equipment from planes to buses. Several times they were stranded at remote airstrips, waiting in freezing winter weather for people who sometimes never showed up.

Most of the hearings began with a prayer in Cree or Ojibway. Then the judges would listen patiently to anyone who wanted to describe his or her experiences in the justice system. They kept the hearings as informal as possible, allowing the Indians and Métis to talk about virtually anything that was important to them. There was no time limit on the presentations. Many of the witnesses spoke through interpreters.

In the northern reserves, the judges wore sweaters and jeans and moccasins as they sat behind a plain wooden table. Sinclair, a large man with long braided hair and a soft voice, was thirty-seven years old. Hamilton, a veteran of the family courts who had never seen a remote Indian reserve before the hearings began, was sixty-two. They expect to release their final report in the spring of 1990, after reviewing the Osborne and Harper cases.

Manitoba's native people had been defendants and suspects in the justice system for decades, but the provincial inquiry gave them their first chance to voice their feelings about the process of courts and jails.

Eight months of testimony at the inquiry confirmed the existence of many problems in the system. Aboriginal people testified that they had pleaded guilty to criminal charges because of fear or confusion, that they had experienced prejudice and discrimination from judicial officials, and that they felt alienated from a foreign system of justice.

The problems began at the highest levels of the court system. Testimony indicated that one provincial judge was often drunk or hung over as he pronounced sentence on native people. A witness said he sometimes drank with the judge and then was sentenced by the judge for alcohol-related offences. One night Indians found a judge passed out, completely drunk, outside a local hotel. "It was like it was okay for him to do that when he was just dealing with a bunch of Indians, but I doubt he would go to court drunk in the city," a witness said.

The inquiry was told that some judges refused to visit one northern reserve because it had no indoor washrooms. The band was forced to use its welfare funds to cover the cost of flying its defendants to the nearest city. Welfare recipients had to cut back on food purchases to pay for the airfare.

At other communities, Indians spent hundreds of dollars to fly to court hearings far away from their home reserves, only to have their cases remanded again and again. One man testified that his family spent $5,000 on airfare in a two-year period, during which time their son was remanded twenty-four times. When they tried to save money by travelling by snowmobile to the court, the son had to be treated for frostbite. In southern Manitoba, meanwhile, court proceedings were always held in white communities—even when the vast majority of cases involved natives.

The inquiry heard sharp criticism of the bail system. In some cases, Indians had to wait in jail for six months because they could not afford bail that was set at only a few hundred dollars. To a low-income native person, $500 might as well be $5 million, a lawyer told the inquiry.

Some of the most shocking testimony was provoked by the behaviour of the police. An Indian chief who once served in the RCMP said his former partner used to tell him: "Let's go shoot us another Indian." The inquiry was told about one incident in which police officers ordered two native youths up against a wall and searched them because they were sitting in a friend's convertible car. They assumed that the youths had stolen the car. "They said there's no way two Indian kids could own a car like that, it was too expensive," a witness told the inquiry.

Dozens of unexplained or suspicious deaths had occurred in northern Indian communities. The police either failed to investigate the deaths properly or failed to inform relatives about the results of their investigations, natives testified.

In another case, an armed Indian was shot in the back by an RCMP officer after a stand-off. The RCMP made no effort to negotiate with the Indian, communicate with him by telephone, bring in a relative to talk to him, or follow standard police procedures for resolving such incidents without bloodshed, the dead man's sister told the inquiry. At an inquest, the presiding judge would not allow the family to question the training and tactics of the RCMP, the sister said.

Some native leaders were hopeful that the Manitoba inquiry would produce solutions to the problems of the justice system. Others, however, were cynical and pessimistic. The Manitoba inquiry made it clear that the white-dominated justice system has led to enormous anger and frustration among Indian and Métis people. "We have become an object in an assembly line that, more often than not, ends up in a correctional institution," Chief Oscar Lathlin told the inquiry.

Ed Anderson, chief of the Fairford band, gave perhaps the most eloquent condemnation of the justice system. "If medicine was like justice, we would only administer it during the post-mortem," he said. "And then ask, 'How did they die?' Not, 'How can we live?'"

The Manitoba inquiry was just one of several public investigations into the treatment of natives by the justice system in the late 1980s. An inquiry into policing in Ontario, for example, heard testimony from native people who said the police often ignored serious crimes against Indians. One Indian travelled more than five hundred kilometres from a remote community in northern Ontario to tell the panel that the police had refused to investigate the deaths of three men in his area. "If they were white men it would be different," the Indian said. Another witness described seeing a police baton with four words etched onto it: "For Indians, hold here."

In southern Alberta, a judicial inquiry was appointed to investigate the deaths of five Blood Indians. The inquiry, which began in the spring of 1989, followed years of deteriorating relations between the

Blood Indians and the local RCMP. The inquiry heard testimony from a former Indian special constable who said he had endured a steady stream of racist remarks and derisive jokes from RCMP officers.

Public inquiries can expose the injustices experienced by aboriginal people, but they are only the first step in a gradual process of change. Some native leaders—like Chief Pascall Bighetty of the Mathias Colomb band at Pukatawagan in northern Manitoba—have become impatient at the slow progress. In the mid-1980s, Bighetty was angered by the lack of native control over the judicial decisions in his community. He felt that the sentences imposed by the provincial judges were too lenient. Bighetty believed that the judges were ignoring the wishes of his 1,400 band members, who wanted tougher jail sentences to battle a rising crime rate at Pukatawagan. "Northern courts have become a farce," the chief declared in 1986.

As his frustration mounted, Bighetty warned that he might prohibit the provincial judges from entering his community. A senior provincial official scoffed at the threat and accused the Indians of "grandstanding". That was the last straw for Pascall Bighetty. "The ban is on," the chief announced. "Any provincial judge, official or lawyer who sets foot in our community will be charged with trespassing." The people of Pukatawagan had the legal right to keep outsiders off their reserve, so the monthly court proceedings were shifted to Lynn Lake, the nearest town.

Pascall Bighetty, who had earned a political science degree from Brandon University in 1982, had a reputation for decisive action. In the 1970s, when he was first elected as chief, Pukatawagan had one of the highest murder rates in North America. The new chief responded by gathering as many rifles as he could find and dumping them in the river. The murder rate soon declined, but crime was still a problem in 1986.

Bighetty proposed that the administration of justice on twenty-five northern reserves be turned over to three tribal councils, which would then be responsible for hiring judges, court officials, and probation workers. Under his proposal, the native-controlled courts would have the power to impose stronger sentences. For example, they would have the authority to banish bootleggers and other offenders from the community. Banishment is a traditional native punishment, aimed at protecting the communities from habitual offenders.

The ban on provincial judges, which continued for more than six months, was finally lifted in early 1987 when the judges agreed to some modest reforms. They promised that court communicators and paralegal workers would arrive at Pukatawagan a day before each monthly court sitting to talk to the Indians and to ensure a smoother functioning of the court proceedings the next day. The bigger issues, however, were not resolved. Pascall Bighetty is still waiting for the introduction of a justice system fully controlled by native people.

A wide range of native groups and Indian leaders have called for a tribal court system, such as the one proposed by Pascall Bighetty, which would give Indian people the right to resolve cases in their own communities. One of the most intriguing proposals, submitted by the Interlake Tribal Council in central Manitoba, calls for the establishment of a Native Harmony and Restoration Centre to replace the courts and jails for native people in the Interlake region. Under this system, disputes between band members would be resolved peacefully by a mediator who could arrange restitution for the victim or counselling for the offender. Contracts would be written between the victim and the offender to ensure compliance.

For serious offences in which the RCMP has laid charges, the Harmony and Restoration Centre would seek a delay in the case while it tried to arrange a reconciliation between the victim and offender. A council of elders would be the final arbitration body on the reserve if no settlement could be reached. If there was still no reconciliation and the offender was convicted in the criminal courts, he could choose to be sent to the Harmony and Restoration Centre, where he would be allowed to set his own program of daily routines, counselling, and self-policing. The offender's family would be allowed to stay with the offender at the harmony centre, and the offender's home community would sign a contract agreeing to support the family throughout the process.

Every band or tribal council has its own concept of native-controlled justice, but the same basic philosophy operates in all cases: the notion that an offender has hurt the entire community, not just an individual victim. When the community is involved in dispensing justice, the offender soon realizes that he is in danger of losing his place in the community if he continues to break the law. In native society, that is the ultimate punishment.

There will, of course, be strong resistance to the idea of Indian self-government in the justice system. Justice Minister Douglas Lewis has already expressed misgivings about the idea, suggesting that it would be too expensive and would encourage other groups to make similar demands. But the idea of a tribal court system has been supported by many prominent legal experts. A committee of the Canadian Bar Association has thrown its weight behind the concept of a native-controlled justice system, and legal aid officials in Manitoba and spokesmen for the John Howard Society have publicly advocated a form of Indian self-government in the justice system.

In the meantime, native-controlled police forces and judicial institutions have been successfully established on a number of reserves across Canada. The Cree Indians of Split Lake in northern Manitoba have had their own system of peacekeepers for as long as the elders can remember. Today, the peace officers are elected from the community for a two-year term, and almost every band member gets a chance to serve as a peace officer at some point. It is a natural outgrowth of a traditional form of peacemaking, going back centuries in native society.

The ten peace officers at Split Lake prevent crime by patrolling the community and resolving conflicts before they result in violence. The band has passed a bylaw prohibiting alcohol on the reserve, and the peace officers enforce it by searching vehicles that enter the reserve. Because they are chosen by the community, the peace officers are respected, and Split Lake has one of the lowest crime rates of any Indian community in Manitoba. The RCMP sit idle in their trailer on the reserve. In some months, not a single offence is reported. The band's chief, Larry Beardy, says the crime rate is "close to non-existent." In fact, he wants the RCMP to leave the community because there is not enough crime to keep them busy.

In 1987, the Louis Bull band became the first Indian band in Alberta to gain full policing powers. The band's police force, supervised by a six-member police commission and funded almost entirely by the band at a cost of $500,000 annually, has the same authority as municipal police departments in large cities such as Edmonton. Members of the force police the reserve twenty-four hours a day, seven days a week and have the right to carry handguns. The responsibility for criminal investigations has been transferred from the RCMP to the Louis Bull band.

The Mohawks of Kahnawake, just outside Montreal, have established their own police force and court system. With funds from the federal government and revenue from local court fines, the community has hired nineteen peacekeepers, eighteen volunteer conservation officers, three justices of the peace, and a prosecuting attorney. The Mohawk court has the power to deal with minor offences such as assault, break-and-enter, and provincial traffic offences. And the Mohawks are seeking to extend the court's authority to cover more serious offences within their territory. According to a sociologist who has studied the community, the Kahnawake justice system is successful because it is sensitive to local personalities and traditions. For example, the Mohawk court might be aware that the best way to deal with one offender is to remand him in the custody of his uncle, rather than to incarcerate him.

In northern Manitoba, the St. Theresa Point band has established its own youth court system. The native-controlled court sends juveniles to get counselling from elders and others in the community. The juvenile crime rate has declined in St. Theresa Point since the youth courts were created.

Several native communities in Ontario and Manitoba have established justice committees to assist judges in sentencing their people. The justice committees include elders and other community leaders who are consulted by the judge before each sentencing. They recommend sentences such as community work, restitution, curfews, or bans from social activities. The judges normally accept the recommendation, and the native community feels it has some control over judicial decisions for its people. The system has helped reduce the crime rate at Indian communities such as Christian Island in Ontario.

There have also been successes outside Canada. Tribal courts have been established in aboriginal communities in Australia and the western United States. Peacemaker courts in Arizona and New Mexico have been functioning for a century. The Navajo Indians of New Mexico have their own judges, appeal courts, and criminal code. Their peacemaker courts resolve disputes by drawing on traditional values to negotiate a solution.

Even in the prisons, aboriginal people are recognizing the strength of their traditional culture. Native inmates at several Canadian jails and penitentiaries have revived their spiritual heritage by persuading prison officials to allow sweetgrass and sweat lodge ceremonies within the prison walls. "It gives me the strength to go on, because there were times when I thought about suicide," said one native inmate at the Regina Correctional Centre.

In some cases, prison officials have restricted these spiritual ceremonies or ordered security searches of the medicine bundles that contain a prisoner's spiritual belongings. In 1988, a parliamentary committee reported that some Canadian prison officials look at the spiritual revival "with cynicism and disdain." The committee recommended that Canadian prisons should provide enough resources to support the native cultural revival, since native spirituality has helped to rehabilitate aboriginal inmates.

In the same way, native self-government could help restore justice to the Canadian legal system. For centuries, aboriginal people had their own cultural traditions for resolving conflicts and disputes, but Canadian governments have always suppressed them. Now native people are pleading for a chance to revive their philosophy of justice. In places like Split Lake and Kahnawake, the traditional system has worked. Aboriginal leaders say it is time for a more ambitious revival of the traditions of native justice. The faces of the people in the jails show that the alternative has failed.

"The offender is not born in the Indian—the Indian is born into a system which offends," Chief Louis Stevenson told the Manitoba aboriginal justice inquiry in 1988. "In a free and democratic society, this system was to be 'just' for everyone. It was 'just' for the probation officers, because it gave them a livelihood. It was 'just' for the police officers because it gave them a sense of duty to lock up Indian people. It was 'just' for officers of the Crown, so they would close their files after another Indian is incarcerated. It was 'just' for the personnel of the jails.... The justice system thrives in this country, and the commodity that provides the fuel is Indian people."

CHAPTER SEVEN

Alkali Lake: Resisting Alcohol

The Dog Creek Road follows the path of the old Cariboo Trail, the route blazed by the gold seekers of the 1860s in British Columbia's interior. Heading southwest from Williams Lake, a lumber town on Highway 97, the Dog Creek Road winds through the forest, past narrow logging trails and cattle ranches carved precariously out of the wilderness. The landscape soon becomes more rugged, the road turns to gravel, and the potholes get worse. The road begins to snake along ridges and the sides of hills. Then the forest disappears from sight and the road emerges at the top of a valley.

Below is a miniature paradise—a collection of log cabins and colourful bungalows nestled at the bottom of the valley, surrounded by hills covered with pines and sagebrush. This is the Shuswap Indian village of Alkali Lake.

Behind the picture-postcard beauty of the scene lies a history that is not so pretty. Alkali Lake is an artificial community, built a century ago to surround a white man's church. Today the houses are overcrowded and the Shuswap people are hobbled by poverty. More than four hundred Shuswap Indians live on the Alkali Lake reserve, two families crammed into almost every house. Since the 1940s, Alkali Lake has endured a nightmare of alcoholism and brutal violence. Now it is a symbol of hope. The people of Alkali Lake have achieved sobriety,

175

and they have become the inspiration for hundreds of other Indian communities across Canada. But the shadows of the past are never far away. This is a village where the laughter of a child is soon followed by the tears of a man or a woman. In the evening, at counselling sessions and support groups, they cry openly as memories of the past come flooding back.

For centuries, the Shuswap were a semi-nomadic hunting and gathering people, fishing salmon from the Fraser River and hunting deer, elk, cariboo, and moose. In 1808, the explorer Simon Fraser became the first white man to enter their territory. Fraser was followed by more explorers and fur traders, and within thirty years the Shuswap were selling furs at nearby trading posts. Almost immediately, the traders introduced the Indians to alcohol. It was the beginning of a 150-year struggle.

During the gold rush of 1858 to 1870, when saloons and roadhouses opened all along the Cariboo Trail, drunkenness among the Shuswap became a serious problem. Then the gold rush ended and alcohol abuse soon diminished. For the rest of the nineteenth century and the early years of the twentieth century, drinking at Alkali Lake was relatively moderate, but in the middle of the twentieth century, alcohol made a deadly comeback.

Liquor consumption began to rise around 1940, after the death of Chief Sxoxomic, a strict and tough-minded leader who had been chief of the Alkali Lake band for several decades. Sxoxomic had imposed harsh penalties on anyone who was found drinking in the community, but after his death, there was a breakdown in social control on the reserve. The new chief was unable to command the same respect as his predecessor.

Meanwhile, liquor was being sold openly by a merchant at a neighbouring ranch. Then, in 1951, amendments to the Indian Act made it legal for Indians to drink alcohol in licensed taverns, and a new provincial law passed in 1962 allowed Indians to purchase liquor outside bars. The motivation behind the new legislation was good. Canadians were beginning to realize that Indians were entitled to the same rights as white people, and these changes in the law stemmed from the new attitude. However, the sudden accessibility of liquor was more than many Indian communities could cope with.

Alkali Lake and other Indian communities were also susceptible to alcohol abuse because a high rate of unemployment and a growing dependence on welfare were leading to apathy and despair. Provincial game laws and fishing regulations, combined with the increasing amount of logging and farming in the area, made it harder for the Indians to hunt and fish. The Shuswap people were further weakened by the devastating effects of a Roman Catholic residential school near Williams Lake, where their children were sent. A trial in 1989 revealed that a Catholic priest at the residential school had committed dozens of sexual assaults on Indian children at the school in the 1950s and 1960s. Many of the traumatized victims turned to self-destructive behaviour—including alcohol abuse.

All of these pressures contributed to the increasing alcoholism at Alkali Lake, and by the late 1960s, drinking had reached frightening levels on the reserve. Outsiders called it "Alcohol Lake". There were drinking parties every weekend, often lasting for several days. All of the adults—and many of the children—were drinking heavily. Violence, child abuse, suicides, and accidental deaths were rampant, and funerals were held every month—sometimes every week—for victims of alcohol abuse. Alcohol could not be purchased legally on the reserve, but taxis and buses brought liquor regularly from Williams Lake. Bootleggers and homebrew makers ensured that the reserve had a constant supply of alcohol. Even the band councillors were bootlegging liquor to adults and children. "Every weekend you saw people walking around this whole reserve, people holding bottles and jugs and hollering," one band member recalls.

"We have a graveyard full of people who have died because of alcohol," another band member says. "Even now I cry when I remember the hurts that were caused by alcoholism."

Francis Johnson, one of thirteen children in a Shuswap family at Alkali Lake, lived through the worst of this era. His father and mother were both heavy drinkers. "My first memory is of hearing my Dad sing," he wrote in a memoir of the Alkali Lake saga from the 1950s to the 1980s. "It really hurt to see him in a drunken condition. He would continue to sing and sing until he passed out. It really tore my heart out."

When the father was drunk, the children and their mother were kicked and beaten with a broom. Francis was often so frightened that he would hide under his bed all night.

"Many times our parents left us children alone when they went to town. When they went in the bar, we would spend hours waiting in the truck, not knowing when they would be back.... Many times we went to bed hungry and without knowing when our parents would get back."

His mother would send the children to the store to buy malt and yeast. "Sometimes I would think that she was going to make bread, but really I knew that it was to make homebrew," he remembers. "I used to hate what would happen when the drinking began."

Often the children would throw away the homebrew after their parents blacked out, and as they grew older they tried to stay away from home when their parents were drinking. Francis remembers staying at a neighbour's house and watching the drinking parties grow worse across the street at his parents' place. No matter what they did, however, the drinking continued to increase. And soon the children were experimenting with alcohol themselves.

In 1963, on New Year's Eve, Francis watched his parents head off to town. Within a few days, the boy learned that his mother had died after she was beaten by his father. "I could not describe the feeling I had, and yet like a brave little boy I hid my feelings.... Inside I was all lost and torn apart."

Francis finished high school and found part-time jobs for a while. He was an angry man, fighting and drinking and getting into car accidents. Alkali Lake had reached the absolute bottom of its downward slide. "Many of the women were beaten up and it was common to see them with black eyes or puffed up faces following the weekend. Some were even hospitalized. Girls were raped and even gang-rape was usual.... The people's spirit was almost dead. Everything revolved around drinking."

Francis Johnson's rage kept boiling to the surface. One day he asked his father if it was true that he had killed his mother. His father denied it, but the denial made Francis even angrier. Later, when he was drunk, Francis tried to avenge his mother's death by attacking his father. "I was very angry and kept on hitting him until his nose bled.... My younger brother heard about it and came after me. He hit me pretty hard with a rock on the face. It made me feel very sad to fight him...."

Francis drank to escape. "It gave me a sense of false security and serenity," he remembers. "For many years when I woke up in the morning I would feel nauseated and be afraid to face the day ahead. I would look for a drink to get courage to face the day."

But the liquor could not provide a complete escape, and he began to contemplate suicide. Voices told him to drown himself in the river. He climbed to the top of a mountain with a rifle, intending to shoot himself. He came across a beaver and shot it—then realized it was the last shell in his gun. "I believe that the beaver offered its life for mine."

In 1971, the Shuswap of Alkali Lake held an emergency meeting. Anyone who was drunk was not permitted to attend. The band members knew that radical action was necessary. Dissatisfied with their chief because of his failure to end the alcoholism, they wanted stronger leadership to turn their community around. They voted to abandon the old system of hereditary chiefs and establish a new system of elected chiefs. But the heavy drinking continued. The bootleggers still reigned in the village.

One of the bootleggers at Alkali Lake was a young Shuswap man named Andy Chelsea, who could usually be found in the middle of the drinking parties. Sometimes when he was drunk he would beat his wife, Phyllis, who was also a heavy drinker. After years of drinking, Andy's kidneys started to give out. "I was dying from alcohol," he recalls. "I was constantly in and out of the hospital. I didn't care. As soon as I got out, I went right back to the bars."

One day in the summer of 1972, something happened to the Chelseas—something that changed the course of history at Alkali Lake. It was a Friday afternoon, and Andy and Phyllis Chelsea were planning a weekend drinking spree. Phyllis stopped at her mother's place to pick up her seven-year-old daughter, Ivy. But this time, Ivy refused to come. She had seen her parents in drunken fights, and she knew what alcohol did to them. "You and Daddy drink too much," Ivy Chelsea told her mother.

Phyllis was stunned. Rejected by her own daughter, she realized she had to do something drastic. She did not want to be hated by her daughter. She poured her bottle of liquor down the sink. From that day on, Phyllis no longer drank. She was the first at Alkali Lake to become sober.

Her husband kept drinking. But one morning, a few months later, Andy Chelsea was standing by the side of a road when he noticed a group of hungry children with bruised faces, walking to school after their parents had been on an all-night drinking binge. He asked the ragged children if they had been given anything to eat that morning. They said no. Andy decided to quit drinking.

For a year, the Chelseas were the only sober adults at Alkali Lake. Andy went to the same spot every day, watching the hungry children walk to school. It gave him the motivation to stay sober.

At the end of the first year, the Chelseas held a Christmas party, inviting anyone who was willing to stay sober while the festivities lasted. Only a few children showed up. But then, as the Chelseas served a hot meal to the children, a woman arrived and announced that she wanted to quit drinking. Andy and Phyllis gave her Christmas presents. She said it was the best Christmas she had ever had.

The sobriety of Andy and Phyllis Chelsea soon earned them the respect of the other band members. In September 1973, Andy Chelsea was elected chief of the Alkali Lake band. From this new position of strength, Andy and Phyllis launched a bold campaign against alcohol.

Their first target was the bootleggers. "The bootleggers would never refuse anyone," Andy Chelsea recalls. "If you had the money, they'd sell it to you. It didn't matter if you were an old man or a young kid."

With the cooperation of the local RCMP, the Chelseas organized a sting. They marked a number of $5 and $10 bills, then called in a sympathetic band member and asked him to use one of the bills to buy a bottle of liquor. When the man returned with the bottle, they asked for the name of the bootlegger who had sold it to him. They made several more purchases and then called the police. The RCMP searched the bootleggers' houses, found the marked bills, and arrested seven people.

It was a tough campaign, sparing nobody—not even Andy Chelsea's mother, who was one of the suspected bootleggers. Her home was raided by the RCMP on the instructions of Andy and Phyllis. With this, the Shuswap people saw that their chief was prepared to take action against anyone in the community who trafficked in liquor.

In his next move, Andy confronted the driver of the Dog Creek Stage—the bus that regularly brought liquor to Alkali Lake from Williams Lake. It was bringing thousands of dollars worth of liquor to the village in a single trip. The chief told the bus driver that he would not be permitted to enter Alkali Lake again.

Phyllis, meanwhile, had turned her attention to the social assistance cheques that were the main source of income at Alkali Lake. A bureaucrat in the Williams Lake office of the Indian Affairs Department was simply mailing the monthly welfare cheques without visiting the reserve. Most of the band members were taking their welfare cheques and immediately cashing them at the store at the nearby ranch, where they could buy liquor. When the Chelseas pointed out that the welfare money was being spent on liquor, the federal bureaucrat just shrugged.

So the Chelseas persuaded the Indian Affairs Department to allow Phyllis to become the welfare supervisor, with the authority to distribute the monthly cheques. Instead of just doling out the cheques, however, Phyllis established a system of food and clothing vouchers. Band members were given vouchers that could be used only to obtain food or clothing. Phyllis and another band member set up a grocery store on the reserve. The vouchers were redeemable at the new grocery store or at a department store in Williams Lake that had agreed to accept them.

This move angered many band members, but the Chelseas persisted, and within a month two bootleggers decided to stop selling liquor. As a reward, they were permitted to receive cheques instead of vouchers. The same offer encouraged others to stop bootlegging and drinking.

Elizabeth Furniss, a University of British Columbia anthropology student who has documented the Alkali Lake sobriety movement more thoroughly than any other scholar, has concluded that the strength and determination of Andy and Phyllis Chelsea were "crucial to the movement's survival" in its early years. One of their most effective tactics was the strategy of confrontation, Furniss says.

After an incident of alcohol-related violence or child neglect, Andy and Phyllis would confront the person involved. In a low-key conversation, they would point out how the person's drinking was hurting others. If the drinking continued, the Chelseas would make it clear that they were willing to order the band member off the reserve or call in the provincial authorities to seize his children. Several children were in fact apprehended and placed with foster parents in Alkali Lake. When a band member assaulted his wife or his father, the Chelseas made it clear that he would be arrested unless he stopped drinking. Band employees who were stealing to support their drinking were given the choice of entering a treatment program or facing charges of theft.

On several occasions, bitter fights broke out between Andy Chelsea and drunken band members who resented his tough actions, and threats were even made against his life. In one incident, a pair of band members confronted the chief with a gun. Andy refused to be intimidated.

One of Andy Chelsea's strongest opponents was a priest at the Catholic church at Alkali Lake, who was himself a heavy drinker and an occasional bootlegger. The priest encouraged the band members to resist the chief's reforms and even attempted to organize a meeting of band members to remove Andy from his office. But the meeting never took place. Andy approached the priest outside the church and gave him an hour to leave the reserve permanently. The priest went.

Throughout 1973, alcohol remained a deadly plague at Alkali Lake. During one three-month period, there were nine deaths linked to alcohol abuse on the reserve. By 1974, only two band members had joined the Chelseas in abandoning alcohol, but Andy was re-elected as chief by acclamation. Two years later, he was elected again. By then, almost half of the band members were sober.

The Chelseas organized "Alcohol Awareness" meetings, where band members could give each other moral support as they tried to quit drinking, and they kept up an informal network of social contacts with band members who were struggling with alcohol. They visited their homes, encouraging the band members by sharing stories of their own efforts to stop drinking.

"When we felt like having a drink, a few of us would get together and stay up the whole night talking," says Fred Johnson, a band member who quit drinking and eventually became the principal of the Alkali Lake school. "We learned to hang onto each other during the hard times."

Dozens of band members began to attend special treatment programs for alcoholism, most choosing six-week programs at treatment centres in Alberta and British Columbia. Three of the most popular treatment centres—Poundmaker's Lodge, the Bonnyville Indian and Métis Rehabilitation Centre in Alberta, and the Round Lake Treatment Centre near Vernon, B.C.—were native-controlled centres that emphasized native cultural traditions such as sweat lodges and sweetgrass ceremonies to help their clients gain strength and pride. They incorporated the standard alcohol treatment methods, but they also brought in elders to help counsel their clients on native spirituality. The techniques of the native-controlled treatment centres were summarized by their guiding philosophy: "Culture is treatment; all healing is spiritual; the community is a treatment centre; we are all counsellors."

While band members were attending the treatment programs, their homes were painted and repaired by a team of volunteers from the community, so that they could return to a happier environment when the treatment had ended. Cards and letters were sent from Alkali Lake to the people at the treatment centres to boost their spirits. Whenever possible, the band provided jobs for the graduates of the treatment programs when they returned to the reserve.

By the late 1970s, the social pressures against the drinkers were tremendous. Band members felt isolated if they continued drinking. They didn't want to be feel excluded from the community, so they rushed to sign up for treatment courses.

The Chelseas' leadership and the community's support were vital to the success of the battle against alcohol, but each band member ultimately had to make a personal decision to kick the drinking habit. One band member, who had become hooked on alcohol at the age of thirteen, remembers drinking for ten days straight at the worst point of his life. He drank until he was throwing up blood and his fingers were stiffening into claws from the alcohol's effect on his nervous system. "Somehow deep in my mind I knew that death was coming," he told Elizabeth Furniss. "There was people sobering up, and you watch and watch, and they aren't suffering like I was suffering, and what happens is you say, 'Well, I wouldn't mind being like that.'"

Following a confrontation with Andy Chelsea in 1976, the man decided to enroll in a treatment program. He has been sober ever since.

After a series of failed suicide attempts, Francis Johnson was still drinking heavily and suffering from a deep depression. One night in 1974, alone in his bedroom, he found a nylon rope and put it around his neck. "I pulled and pulled and still I failed to end my misery," he remembers. Then, as he pulled the rope, the image of the devil appeared before his eyes. He was terrified. "I said to myself that I wanted to live, and that was the turning point of my life."

In March 1975, after more than a year of sporadic sobriety, Francis Johnson quit drinking permanently. That was in the early days of the Alkali Lake sobriety movement. "Many people used to ridicule me because I had quit drinking. On one occasion, three men held me down and tried to pour wine into my mouth. I struggled with all my might and kept my mouth shut while they just poured it on my face.... It used to hurt to see my brothers and sisters drinking. When I went into our home I would sometimes catch a glimpse of them as they hid their booze."

Francis disciplined himself to resist the temptations of alcohol. As the sobriety movement progressed and shifted into its next stages, he started to discover his roots. "I had to begin learning about my culture and to understand what being Indian was all about. At the beginning I was confused, because there were not many people that I could turn to. Not many people or elders on the reserve were visibly practising their cultural beliefs.... I slowly learned to respect my culture and its rituals."

For a century, the elders of Alkali Lake had struggled to keep their culture alive. But by the time the alcohol epidemic spread through the reserve, the Shuswap spiritual beliefs had slipped away. "In my drinking days, we used to laugh at the elders and their customs," school principal Fred Johnson recalls. "We figured we didn't need them in modern society. The language was gone, the culture was gone. I never knew how to be an Indian. I didn't know who I was."

After the sobriety movement began, two band members went to Alberta and saw traditional Indian dancing for the first time. They decided to form a dance group in Alkali Lake and asked Fred Johnson if he could do the singing. "I didn't know how to sing, so I went to the elders and I asked them to teach me some songs. They told me I had to make a drum, so I made a drum. Slowly I started to learn. I went to the elders with my drum, and they taught me the songs of the Shuswap people. They told us about the sweat lodge and fasting. They said, when you are singing, you need to fast for two days and learn about yourself and pray. It took about five years for us to learn, but now our young people are getting strong."

Francis Johnson was one of the young band members who was introduced to the sweat lodge. The sweat lodge is one of North America's oldest religious ceremonies. It is a traditional native ritual of cleansing and purification, conducted around a firepit of hot stones in the humid darkness inside a lodge built from willow poles and canvas. "I was like a little child, I did not know what to do," Francis remembers. "People used to tell me to sing and I would feel confused because I did not know any songs. Gradually many people were sent to help us understand the sacred sweat lodge as it should be understood. I learned how to sing some of the songs. I also learned to sing around the drum and enjoy it as much as Indian dancing."

The community invited a Shuswap medicine man to visit Alkali Lake to help the people revive their traditional dances and spiritual rites: pow-wow dancing, sweetgrass and pipe ceremonies, drumming, daily prayer ceremonies, sage burning, and sweat lodges. Some band members fasted on mountaintops and on sacred grounds. There was always an implicit rule for these cultural events: anyone who wanted to participate had to be sober. These were traditional spiritual activities, to which alcohol was foreign.

At the Alkali Lake school, the children are learning the Shuswap language. They sit on the floor of a small room with a skylight and a log roof supported by wooden poles, constructed in the style of a traditional Shuswap "winter house". A respected elder, Celina Harry, talks to the Grade 2 and Grade 3 children in their ancient language. At the beginning of the class, she asks: "How are you?" The children, shouting in Shuswap, reply that they are fine. She asks them if it is a good day. "Yes, the day is good," the children say in Shuswap.

On the walls of the room are posters listing the Shuswap names for the four seasons and the four winds. Flawlessly, the class recites the names of animals and plants from a chart of pictures.

The revival of the Shuswap language is a crucial element in the rejuvenation of Alkali Lake. The language classes began in 1974 after the band gained control of its school.

Phyllis Chelsea was the first teacher of the Shuswap language classes. It was a big step forward for her. As a child, she had spent ten years at a residential school, where her life was controlled by nuns and priests. "I didn't have an identity," she recalls. "I was ashamed to be an Indian. It's only recently that Indian people are proud of who they are. Now they're learning about their tribe. I never heard about that when I was a teenager. I didn't know that I was Shuswap."

The dropout rate has declined drastically at Alkali Lake in the past fifteen years. The school brings in Indian lawyers and other successful native professionals to talk to the students about university and careers. Indian teenagers from other reserves in British Columbia often spend a year or two at the Alkali Lake school as part of a program to help them experience life in a sober community. "The kids really enjoy school now," says Fred Johnson, the principal. "They'd spend all day in school if they had the chance."

Today, more than 90 percent of the band members are sober. Sobriety has become the fundamental value of the people of Alkali Lake. There is a strong sense of pride and community spirit in the Shuswap village.

But many of the younger band members at Alkali Lake are still bitter about the suffering they experienced when their parents were abusing alcohol. "They were eight or nine years old when they saw all this drinking and fighting," says Ken Johnson, an alcohol counsellor at Alkali Lake. "Now it's payback time. They're saying, we might as well pay back our parents for what they did to us."

More than a dozen youths at Alkali Lake still require treatment for alcohol abuse, Ken Johnson estimates. Even the sober adults are sometimes described as "dry drunks"—a condition that Johnson knows from personal experience. "It means you're sober but you still act like you're drunk. The biggest problem is that some people aren't doing anything with their sobriety. They think that's enough. But the old ideas are still there. Some say they feel like going back to drinking again. The kids can feel that."

In his own case, Johnson felt a lot of anger remaining inside him, even after he stopped drinking. "I was throwing frying pans and slapping my sister. I said, why am I doing this? I'm sober, but I'm still acting this way. The anger and hurt was still stuffed in me."

Eventually he eased his turbulent emotions by going to a regular Alcoholics Anonymous meeting and attending a weekly Men's Sharing

Session with a dozen other Indian men. But he often cries as he talks with the band members about the legacy of their alcoholism.

In the meantime, Indian leaders from across North America are making the pilgrimage to Alkali Lake to learn how the village achieved its dramatic turnaround. In 1985 more than a thousand native people and addiction counsellors from Canada and the United States came to the reserve to attend an international conference on alcohol abuse. Experts have studied the community to analyse its success. "This is perhaps one of the most important movements in the Indian community in the last twenty or thirty years," said a University of Washington psychiatrist who has watched the Alkali Lake revival.

Andy and Phyllis Chelsea and other band members have accepted invitations to travel across North America to spread their message of hope and inspiration. They also produced a video to dramatize the story of Alkali Lake—a video that has helped several native communities win the war against alcohol.

Theresa Strawberry, chief of the O'Chiese band of western Alberta in the early 1980s, saw the video when she was undergoing treatment at a native-controlled alcohol treatment centre near Edmonton. It inspired her to launch a campaign for sobriety at the O'Chiese reserve. When she returned home in 1986, she announced that the fight against alcoholism would be her top priority.

The chief and her council passed a resolution requiring all council members to seek treatment for their alcoholism within six months of their election to council. Band employees were required to attend an alcohol treatment program as a condition of their employment. And the band asked its elders to help revive the sweat lodge, the sweetgrass and pipe ceremonies, and the traditional prayers.

Meanwhile, the band's child welfare workers arranged for ten mothers to enter an alcohol treatment program. Support groups and lifeskills classes were established for band members, and a counsellor was made available every day at O'Chiese for alcohol counselling and home visits. There were weekly "aftercare" sessions to support those who had completed a treatment program. Sober dances and sports nights were organized to provide an alternative to drinking, especially during holidays such as Christmas and Thanksgiving.

By 1988, three-quarters of the band members had completed an alcohol treatment program. People as young as sixteen and as old as sixty-two had entered treatment. The community of O'Chiese had begun a new era.

Andy and Phyllis Chelsea are hoping for even more success stories like this one. When they talk to native communities, their message is simple: alcoholism can, indeed, be defeated. Their goal is to establish sobriety on every Indian reserve in Canada by the end of this century.

Hundreds of years ago, when European fur traders first came into contact with North American Indians, they concluded that the Indians must have a defect that made them particularly susceptible to alcoholism. They assumed there was a physical difference between Indians and Caucasians that predisposed the Indians to addiction and drunken behaviour when liquor was consumed in any quantity. This mistaken belief, based on an assumption of racial inferiority, was widely held among whites throughout the nineteenth and twentieth centuries. One historian, Robert Pinkerton, told his readers in 1931 that liquor "has an entirely different effect on an Indian than on a white man.... Mayhem becomes the mildest of his desires."

In the twentieth century, this racial myth was cloaked in the authority of medical science. As recently as 1971, the writers of an article in the *Canadian Medical Association Journal* alleged that Indians had a lower tolerance for alcohol because of special characteristics in their metabolism. Many other white authorities adopted the same racial theory, even in the 1960s and 1970s.

The myth of genetic inferiority was effectively demolished by a study published in the *New England Journal of Medicine* in 1976. The study found no significant differences in the alcohol metabolisms of Indians and whites—and it discovered no other physical traits that might affect their relative tolerance of alcohol. Most experts now admit there is no evidence that Indians are genetically susceptible to liquor. The lingering myth, in fact, may simply have been a convenient way for white society to disavow any responsibility for alcohol abuse among native people.

To understand the relationship between alcohol and Canada's native people, one must begin by looking at the traffickers—the white entrepreneurs who introduced liquor into Indian communities and deliberately encouraged the Indians to become addicted. Before the arrival of the European fur traders, alcohol was virtually unknown among Canadian Indians. But by the 1790s the Indians were caught in a brutal fur-trading war between the Hudson's Bay Company and the North West Company—both of which were using liquor as their primary weapon.

The fur traders had discovered that alcohol was the perfect trading commodity to maximize their profits. Rum and brandy were relatively easy to transport: in concentrated form, they were much less bulky than other trade goods. Since the booze was addictive and quickly consumed, the Indians would keep returning to the bush to trap more animals to serve as the currency for their liquor supply. It guaranteed that the Indians would make regular trips to the trading posts. And it weakened their bargaining ability. "They undergo every hardship and fatigue to procure a Skinfull of this delicious beverage," an early fur trader named Duncan McGillivray wrote in his journal.

The disastrous effects of alcohol swept across the continent, bringing death and devastation to the Indians. "Every night is filled with clamors, brawls, and fatal accidents," a French Jesuit wrote during the early years of missionaries at Indian villages in New France. Alcohol was "so common here, and causes such disorders, that it sometimes seems as if all the people of the village had become insane."

The traders took advantage of the fact that the Indians had no experience with alcohol and no social taboos against its consumption. Lacking any experience with the long-term dangers of alcohol addiction, they had no feelings of guilt or anxiety to restrain their drinking.

Among some tribes, there was a cultural tradition of consuming all food and drink at one sitting. It was considered impolite to leave food untouched. When alcohol became available, it was consumed in the same way. This led to a pattern of binge drinking among the Indians—a pattern that was reinforced by the fact that alcohol was not always available to them. When the Indians emerged from the bush to sell their furs at the trading posts, they could obtain a large quantity of liquor for the first time in months and sometimes drank the entire supply of liquor immediately. This tendency towards spree drinking has persisted even today in many northern reserves where the supply of alcohol is irregular because it has to be flown or smuggled in.

In the late 1780s, the Hudson's Bay Company complained that its rival fur traders at the North West Company were "going through the

Barren Ground with Rum, like so many ravenous Wolves, seeking whom ever they may devour." In a petition to the British colonial authorities, a Hudson's Bay official said: "It grieves us to see a body of Indians destroyed by a set of Men, merely for self Interest, doing all in their Power to Destroy Posterity."

But within a few years the Hudson's Bay Company had resorted to the same tactics as its rivals. Realizing that they could obtain two beaver pelts in exchange for a pint of diluted brandy, the HBC fur traders were soon giving the Indians more than 900,000 litres of liquor each year. "The unrestrained use of liquor in the Canadian fur trade ranks as one of history's more malevolent crimes against humanity," writes Peter C. Newman in his chronicle of the Hudson's Bay Company. "The traders of both companies debauched a civilization, leaving in their wake a dispirited people and nearly destroying a once-proud culture."

In the 1860s and 1870s, American traders moved into the Canadian Prairies and made enormous profits by trading whiskey to the Blackfoot Indians in exchange for buffalo hides. At least twenty-six whiskey forts were established in southern Alberta from 1869 to 1874, and others were established in the southwestern corner of what is now known as Saskatchewan. By keeping the Indians addicted and desperate, the American traffickers could obtain an entire buffalo robe in exchange for a single cup of whiskey.

The first of the whiskey forts was the notorious Fort Whoop-Up, established in 1869 near the present-day site of Lethbridge. Within its first six months of operation, the traders made a profit of $50,000. In one winter alone, seventy Indians died as a direct result of alcohol from Fort Whoop-Up. Some of the Blackfoot chiefs became convinced that the liquor would cause the complete extinction of the Indians. Indeed, the whiskey traders and other white men of that period seemed bent on destroying the entire Indian race. One visitor to Fort Whoop-Up said the whiskey traders "were a great benefit" because "they keep the Indians poor, and kill directly or indirectly more Indians…than the entire regular army did in ten years."

A missionary, Father Scollen, watched the Blackfoot fall into ruin after the whiskey forts were established. "It was painful to me to see the state of poverty to which they had been reduced," he wrote. "Formerly

they had been the most opulent Indians in the country; now they were
clothed in rags and without guns."

In the 1830s, just a few decades before the arrival of the whiskey
traders, the Blackfoot Indians had enjoyed their greatest prosperity.
Their hunting grounds were vast and their population reached more
than 16,000. But by the 1870s the Blackfoot were decimated by
whiskey and epidemics of smallpox and other diseases. "Surviving
relatives went more for the use of alcohol, they endeavoured to drown
their grief in the poisonous beverage," wrote Father Scollen. "They
sold their robes and horses by the hundreds for it, and then began
killing one another so that in a short time they were divided into small
parties, afraid to meet."

Not until the second half of the twentieth century did the Blackfoot
population return to the level it was at before the arrival of the whiskey
traders.

In the eyes of many city-dwelling Canadians today, an Indian is a street
drunk in the downtown core. "That is the first and only way most white
people see Indians," says Cree playwright Tomson Highway. "That's
our national image. In fact, the average white Canadian has seen that
visual more frequently than they've seen a beaver. To my mind, you
might as well put an Indian drunk on the Canadian nickel."

How accurate is that image? Many native leaders believe it is exaggerated. Indians tend to be public in their drinking—they drink openly,
without embarrassment or concealment. That leaves them vulnerable
to stereotypes and speculative theories. White people, on the other
hand, often drink in private, behind closed doors, where neighbours
cannot watch. Drunken Indians are also remembered more than white
drunks because they belong to a visible minority, and because they fit
into the preconceived notion that Indians are drunkards.

There is little systematic evidence to prove that the level of alcohol
consumption is much greater among Indians than among whites in
similar circumstances. The percentage of Indians who enter alcohol
treatment programs is certainly larger than the percentage of whites
who enter such programs—but that might merely indicate a greater
willingness to be treated. There is usually a lot of drinking on the
average northern Indian reserve, but how much drinking is there in a
nearby mining town where the residents are mostly white? We do not

know, because the mining towns are less likely to be studied. Statistics are hard to obtain because white drinkers often prefer to keep their addiction a private matter. Without such statistical comparisons, it is perhaps unfair to assume that native alcohol abuse is far worse than the level of abuse among whites in comparable situations.

Nevertheless, there can be no doubt that alcohol is a serious problem in native communities. Many native leaders regard alcohol as their number one problem. Recent studies have estimated that alcohol is abused by about 45 percent of New Brunswick Indians, about 38 percent of Saskatchewan Indians, and 50 to 60 percent of northern Manitoba natives. In other regions the pattern is similar.

Drinking problems among Canadian Indians increased in the mid-twentieth century as a result of events that took place during and after the Second World War. Until the war, Indians had lived in isolation from the rest of Canada's population. But in the battlegrounds of Europe, natives fought side by side with whites. In Canada, military training bases were established in remote locations—often near Indian reserves. Native women travelled to the cities to work in munitions factories. As contacts between natives and whites began to increase, many Indians were exposed to alcohol for the first time.

After the war, the federal government started building a network of social programs. For the Indian communities, these new housing and welfare programs brought in a regular flow of money for the first time. Suddenly there was enough cash to purchase commodities from outside the reserves. When new legislation in the 1950s and 1960s allowed Indians to purchase liquor, much of the newly available cash was spent on alcohol.

More important, however, the government's new social programs helped create a state of dependence in the native communities. The Indian population was growing rapidly—too rapidly for most reserves, which were small and had a fixed size. The traditional self-sufficient economy of hunting and trapping fell into decline as a result of hydro projects, mines, logging, industrial development, and expanding white settlements. Indians lost their pride when they could not support their families without a welfare cheque.

At the same time, traditional native cultural values were undermined and replaced by the values of the cash economy and a rapidly indus-trializing society. Native communities were torn between two cultures with conflicting expectations. Aboriginal people suffered from what is often called "anomie"—a state of powerlessness and hopelessness which arises when traditional values are broken and challenged by new ones. According to native alcohol experts, such as Maggie Hodgson of Edmonton's Nechi Institute, the high rate of Indian alcoholism is largely a result of this phenomenon. Indians drank to ease the pain and frustration of a life of conflicting value systems and dependence on outside institutions for economic survival.

"What we are talking about is the grief over a significant loss—the loss of our languages, our culture," says Bea Shawanda of the National Native Association of Treatment Directors. "We are acting out that grief through the violence and the alcoholism."

The residential schools were one of the biggest reasons for the loss of cultural values. Some residential schools had been established as early as the nineteenth century, but their fastest growth came in the 1920s and 1930s. By the time of the Second World War, as the first and second generations of residential school survivors became adults and parents, the alienating effects of the residential schools were at their height.

"Coming out of the residential school, you're not trained for anything," says Joe Aleck, who was sent to a Catholic residential school in Mission, B.C., from 1942 to 1952. "You go back to the reserve, and you're depressed because you're between two worlds. You don't know how to fish or hunt. You've forgotten what you learnt from your parents and grandparents. Your language is forgotten. Your self-esteem is so low because your language and culture have been knocked down. So people just say, the heck with it. You just sort of give up. You head to town and you turn to alcohol."

Studies of individual native communities have confirmed that the rise of alcohol abuse has coincided with cultural breakdown and a growing dependence on government programs. Paul Driben and Robert Trudeau, who studied the Ojibways of the Fort Hope band in northern Ontario, discovered that alcoholism increased in direct proportion to the rise in federal spending on welfare, social assistance, family benefits, short-term make-work projects, and failed economic development schemes in the community. By 1975, almost 90 percent of the disposable income of Fort Hope band members came from government programs. The Ojibways referred to the federal officials as *shuniah-ogama*, which literally meant "money-boss". As their dependence grew, alcohol consumption and violence rose dramatically. By the late 1970s, teachers had fled the community in fear of the drunken violence, and dozens of band members were being arrested for alcohol-related offences.

Anastasia Shkilnyk, in her study of the Grassy Narrows reserve in northwestern Ontario, found that alcohol abuse was worst among those Ojibways who were dependent on welfare. She concluded that the alcoholism had increased rapidly in the years after the reserve was relocated by government edict in the 1960s and the community was devastated by mercury poisoning which ended their traditional way of life. Shkilnyk said the Grassy Narrows community had suffered a "psychic trauma" because of the loss of their independence and their traditional culture. "Their tribal institutions, customs, beliefs and values simply ceased to be relevant or useful in the new circumstances," she wrote. The federal government had imposed "an entirely different and incompatible way of life" on the people of Grassy Narrows. In the mid-1970s, three-quarters of all deaths at Grassy Narrows resulted from violence induced by alcohol or drugs.

Alcohol abuse tends to decline when a band succeeds in reviving its traditional way of life, when the jobless rate is reduced, when education levels are improved—in short, when a sense of community is restored and collective values are developed again. A province-wide study in Saskatchewan, for example, found that 54 percent of Indian welfare recipients were abusing alcohol, while only 25 percent of the Indians employed full-time were heavy drinkers. A study of Indians in the city of North Battleford, Saskatchewan, revealed that alcohol abuse occurred among 43 percent of those with elementary school education and just 17 percent of those with post-secondary education.

In *Maps and Dreams,* his 1981 study of Indians in British Columbia, Hugh Brody pointed out that drunkenness is rarely found among Indians who are following a traditional way of life in the bush. "The effects of colonial pressure, of the frontier, and of the very presence of the white man are escaped in the bush," Brody has written. "When they set out for the bush, to hunt and trap, they do not drink, are not violent."

Some hunters and trappers take their families into the bush whenever they need to escape the drinking and cultural conflicts of the reserve. "The answer to the alcohol problem is to be found in one word—the bush," a resident of one British Columbia reserve told a public hearing.

That is one reason why Thomas Berger, in his inquiry into the Mackenzie Valley pipeline issue in the 1970s, recommended a strengthening of the traditional native economy of hunting and trapping. Drinking is only a minor problem in communities where it is "kept at bay by the enduring vigor of native society and its values," Berger said. "To the extent that the native people are obliged to participate in the type of frontier development that separates them from their traditional life, their chances of containing the problems of alcohol grow worse and worse."

Each year, more than 20,000 potential years of life are lost as a result of the effects of alcohol among Canadian Indians. About three-quarters of all deaths caused by accidents, violence, or poisoning among aboriginal people are linked to alcohol. The vast majority of Indian suicides, homicides, fire fatalities, and other unnatural deaths occur while alcohol is being consumed.

Binge drinking is still common. A survey of Saskatchewan Indians in 1984 showed that 72 percent consumed five or more drinks each time they drank. Among the Indians of northern Manitoba, the average episode of non-stop drinking lasts for three to seven days.

When they cannot find alcohol or cannot afford it, some natives become desperate enough to consume lethal substances. Almost one-quarter of Indians surveyed in Saskatchewan had sometimes consumed non-beverage alcohol such as aftershave or rubbing alcohol. In 1982, three Métis men died in the village of Fishing Lake, Alberta, after swallowing a combination of solvents and duplicating fluid at a drinking party. In 1986, six people died in the Métis community of Peerless Lake, Alberta, when they drank a jug of duplicating fluid.

One of the most frightening consequences of alcohol abuse is its effect on pregnant women and their unborn children. A medical researcher in British Columbia found that 25 percent of all children at one Indian reserve had birth defects as a result of "fetal alcohol syndrome", a condition in which the infants suffer mental retardation or facial abnormalities as a result of heavy alcohol consumption by the mother.

A study of natives in northern Manitoba showed that the typical abuser of alcohol had four or five siblings who shared the same alcohol problem. In about half of the cases, the spouse of the alcoholic was an equally heavy drinker. In 27 percent of the cases, the parents were drinking so heavily that they could not provide proper meals and hygiene required for their children. Half of the children of alcoholic parents in the northern Manitoba study had already begun drinking. "The illness of alcohol has penetrated the entire fabric of the community," the researchers said. "The teenage alcoholic is now a third and fourth generation alcoholic because the untreated alcoholism is now embedded into the community lifestyle."

Governments and churches have been trying to regulate Indian alcohol consumption for more than two hundred years. But these white institutions have consistently preferred a rigid set of mandatory solutions: moral and legal pressure tactics, laws to prohibit Indians from drinking, and strict sanctions against those who touch liquor. By the late 1700s, regulations to limit Indian liquor consumption had already been adopted by the governments of Upper Canada and Lower Canada. A century later the federal Indian Act of 1876 made it illegal for native people to drink or possess alcohol. In 1895 the Catholic church gave "temperance flags" to Indian chiefs who were recruited as presidents of local branches of the "Total Abstinence Society of British Columbia".

None of these efforts succeeded. They were imposed on Indians by outside authorities, and they failed dismally. The 1876 ban on Indian drinking did manage to restrict the supply of alcohol on the reserves, but it did nothing to solve the root causes of native alcohol abuse. It was not until aboriginal people began developing their own treatment methods that any long-term solutions were found.

In the spring of 1968, a horrible car crash near the Brokenhead Indian reserve in southern Manitoba killed eight native people and left thirty-three orphans. The accident was believed to be caused by drunk driving. Angered at the effects of alcohol abuse, Indian and Métis leaders joined forces to create a treatment program. After years of work, the Native Alcoholism Council of Manitoba (NACM) was established in 1972, and a treatment centre was opened in Winnipeg. It was one of the first native-controlled alcohol treatment centres in Canada.

Until the 1970s, a native alcohol abuser who wanted help was obliged to go to a provincial treatment centre, controlled by non-natives and geared toward middle-class whites. Because of the language and cultural barriers at these centres, the failure rate was high.

The native-controlled treatment centres, by contrast, are usually staffed by Indian counsellors who can speak the language of the alcohol abusers. In addition to using the normal tools of alcohol treatment—group therapy, one-to-one counselling, films, discussions about addiction, and lectures on the physical and mental effects of alcohol—the native treatment programs encourage their clients to develop pride in their cultural identity. Many of the centres begin each day with a native prayer or a sweetgrass ceremony. In the classroom, they teach the traditional native culture and spiritual beliefs. Indian elders are often available to talk to the clients about the native way of life.

The treatment counsellors also tell their clients about organizations like Alcoholics Anonymous. But attendance at such programs is not mandatory. Some natives are uncomfortable with Alcoholics Anonymous because of its reliance on personal confessions. In a small, tightly knit native community, an AA program cannot be as anonymous as it is in a large city.

Most native treatment centres have concentrated on four-week programs. However, some native leaders now believe that longer programs are more effective. The Nelson House Medicine Lodge, which was established on a Cree reserve in northern Manitoba in 1989, has become the first in the province to offer a four-month treatment program.

In British Columbia, native leaders have introduced an entirely new concept: mobile treatment. They realized that sending a group of band members away to a treatment centre was sometimes inadequate because the band members could easily begin drinking again when they returned home. So the treatment program was brought into the community. Native counsellors were invited to the reserves to conduct workshops on the effects of alcohol abuse and to revive the native cultural traditions and beliefs. The entire community was transformed into a healing place.

At the Tachie Indian reserve in northern British Columbia, the alcoholism rate in the early 1980s was almost 100 percent. The band tackled the problem by arranging for a group of twenty-six band members to be enrolled in a mobile treatment program on the reserve. Everyone in the community agreed to stop drinking altogether during the treatment period, and they supported those in the program by babysitting their children and cooking food for them. They hunted and fished to provide food for special feasts during the treatment program, including an honour feast to celebrate the successful completion of the program. The band's elders helped the younger members learn the Indian songs and spiritual traditions that had almost died out at the Tachie reserve. Three years later, about 65 percent of the band members were sober.

The mobile treatment program, which has travelled to six reserves in British Columbia, has reduced the alcoholism rate at each community by an average of 50 percent, and it has demonstrated the importance of changing the collective momentum in native communities where alcohol problems exist. Since each community tends to move collectively and share a collective value, the entire community can be swung from alcoholism to sobriety if that momentum can be shifted.

Today, there are thirty native-controlled alcohol treatment centres across Canada. The federal government, which was spending only $8 million annually on Indian alcohol programs in the 1970s, is now spending almost $50 million each year to support the treatment centres and to pay for alcohol counsellors on Indian reserves.

Native-controlled treatment centres have proven to be more effective than provincial programs. A survey in 1986, for example, found that natives who completed the NACM treatment program in Winnipeg were more likely to get jobs or enter job training programs than natives who went through the conventional provincial treatment centres. Of the native clients who entered the NACM program in November 1985, more than 80 percent were still sober a year later.

Despite the growth of federal spending in the past decade, counselling and treatment programs for native alcoholics continue to be underfunded. In Ontario, a 1980 study estimated that the federal and provincial governments were gaining fifteen times more in annual profits from the sale of alcohol to Indians than they were spending in annual support for Indian alcohol treatment and counselling programs. In northern Manitoba, a survey of nine Indian and Métis communities in 1986 found that the average community had 533 alcoholics, yet there were an average of only two counsellors in each community. In Saskatchewan, a 1984 study concluded that Indian communities needed twice as many alcohol counsellors and four times as many alcohol treatment beds as they were then receiving.

After growing rapidly in the 1970s and early 1980s, the federal budget for native alcohol programs has increased at barely the rate of inflation in recent years. Most native treatment centres have long waiting lists. Counsellors, who are paid as little as $17,000 a year, report that they are overloaded with the demand for their services.

Studies in Saskatchewan and Manitoba have concluded that most native alcohol counsellors need much more training. The situation is no better in other parts of Canada. The federal government spends less than $2 million annually on training for native alcohol counsellors across the nation, and many counsellors receive only a two-week training course. Federal officials admit that the lack of training is one of the biggest complaints they receive from native counsellors.

Despite the underfunding and the often inadequate training, the sobriety movement has gained strength across Canada in recent years. In 1974, only one Indian reserve in Alberta had an alcohol treatment program, and only a handful of native counsellors were available in the province. Today, there are forty-four treatment and counselling programs on Alberta Indian reserves, and the Nechi Institute, a native training centre on the outskirts of Edmonton, has trained two thousand Indian alcohol counsellors, many of whom have become chiefs or band administrators in their home communities.

In northern Manitoba, a training course for forty-three Indian leaders was organized in 1988 to help Indians learn the lessons of Alkali Lake. The leaders, who came from ten northern reserves, were encouraged by the Alkali Lake video. "The course was the most powerful dose of medicine ever handed out on this reserve," said Chris McLeod of the Cross Lake band.

In the fall of 1988, a trial in the British Columbia Supreme Court was watched closely by native groups. Gilbert Jordan, a Vancouver barber, was convicted of manslaughter in the death of a woman who had succumbed to alcohol poisoning after an all-night drinking session with him. Evidence at the trial indicated that six other women had died of alcohol poisoning after drinking with the man. The deaths had begun in 1980. Most of the victims were native women.

The Vancouver police finally began to investigate Jordan in 1987. After following him to the cheap hotel rooms where he took skid-row women, they heard him trying to pour vodka down the throat of one woman. He offered $50 to another inebriated woman in an attempt to make her keep drinking. He was arrested shortly afterward.

Native groups were disturbed not only by the details of the case but also by the long delay that preceded the investigation. For seven years, the police assumed that Jordan's victims had simply drunk themselves to death—even though the same man was linked to each one. Natives were convinced that the police had shrugged off the bizarre incidents because the deaths had fit the stereotype of the drunk Indian. It was proof, they believed, that the national image of the alcoholic native is still fixed in the consciousness of white Canadians today.

Others saw the Gilbert Jordan case as a metaphor for the history of Indians and alcohol. "Gilbert Jordan was only doing on a small scale what Canada has been doing on a massive scale to Indian people for the past three hundred years," said Mohawk journalist Brian Maracle.

"Old Man Canada has forced Indian people to drink themselves to death just as surely as if he had held us down, used a funnel and poured the booze down our throat. In my lifetime, tens of thousands of native people have gone to an early grave with alcohol in their blood. Did these people die because of thousands of individual acts of free will? Or were they driven to their deaths by powerful outside forces that gave them no other choice? When your land has been taken, when your language has been degraded, when your spirit has been crushed, when you have been forced to live in squalor, when you face existence without hope, and when you are offered escape through drink...what choice do you really have?"

CHAPTER EIGHT

From Manitoba to Massachusetts: The Lost Generation

It is late in the winter of 1985, and a social worker from the Manitoba Métis Federation is sitting anxiously in an office in Boston, waiting to meet Lisa, the fifteen-year-old daughter of a Métis family from the town of Camperville in northwestern Manitoba. It is a crucial event in Lisa's troubled life. For the first time in twelve years, she will be meeting one of her own people—a Métis from Manitoba. Lisa is so excited that she has spent two hours getting dressed and groomed for the meeting. The social worker knows that this meeting could be a turning point in the life of the young girl.

Then the door opens and Lisa enters the room. "When she came in, it was hard to swallow the lump in my throat," the Métis social worker recalled later. "She looked so much like her dad—her nose and eyes especially. She has long black hair down to her shoulders and a lovely smile. She's a beautiful girl.... Very shy, smiling all the time. What took me aback was her accent. When I look at her, I see a young girl from Camperville, but when she opens her mouth to talk, the resemblance stops."

Lisa's voice, with its thick Boston accent, is the first hint of the turmoil in her young life. It suggests the contradictions that have disturbed her existence since her infancy, when she was removed from her home and taken to a foreign place, thousands of kilometres away. For years, she has been running—from the authorities, from institutions, from adoptive parents and foster parents. Now she wants to stop running and return home.

Lisa was one of the thousands of native Canadian children who were sent to faraway adoptive parents and foster homes in the 1960s and 1970s. During these two decades child welfare agencies sent Indian and Métis children from Manitoba and other provinces to the homes of white middle-class couples in Canada and the United States, on the assumption that these couples would make better parents than low-income families on Indian reserves and in Métis communities. Years later, it became obvious that the policy was a failure.

It was then, with the help of the Boston Indian Council, that officials in Massachusetts and Manitoba made contact with each other to discuss Lisa's future. They talked about a plan to allow her to meet her Métis parents—and perhaps even to return to Manitoba for the first time in twelve years.

"At first she didn't talk to me much, except to look at me and smile," the social worker wrote later in her file notes. "She had a sparkle in her eyes when she spoke of her dad. She talked a blue streak after she got warmed up. She's well-spoken, intelligent, curious, scared...."

Lisa asked what her father did for a living and whether her mother had a job. She wanted to know if her parents were smokers. She was worried because she smoked and she wondered if that would bother them. The social worker had brought photographs of Lisa's parents and her brothers and sisters. After comparing herself to the photographs, Lisa gave the social worker some poems she had written and some tape recordings with messages for her parents. The social worker gave Lisa a copy of her baptismal certificate from a church in Duck Bay, near Camperville, and a letter from the mayor of Camperville, in which the mayor confirmed that Lisa was a Métis. As the young teenager read the letter and the baptismal certificate, she smiled.

Lisa gave the social worker a tour of her bedroom in the juvenile institution where she now lived: it was a typical teenager's room, its walls covered with pictures of Michael Jackson. She showed off one of her school projects—an essay on the Métis. "She wrote about the Métis so proudly," the social worker remembered. "She says the Métis were a tribe of Indians and Louis Riel was killed trying to save them. She's got her Indian history and Métis all mixed up."

Finally, Lisa asked the most difficult question of all. She wanted to know why so many Indian and Métis children were taken away from their parents. The social worker paused and struggled for an answer. "How do you answer a question like that in a few words for her to understand?"

Lisa is not her real name, but her story is true.[1] She was born in the small town of Winnipegosis on November 24, 1969, and for three and a half years she lived with her Métis parents in the nearby town of Camperville, an isolated Métis community on the western shore of Lake Winnipegosis, about 310 kilometres northwest of Winnipeg. Many of its residents work as loggers or fishermen. It is a community of low incomes and widespread dependency on welfare.

In 1973 Lisa was removed from her home because her parents were heavy drinkers who had neglected their children. There is no record of any attempt by provincial social workers to place her in the home of another Métis family. Instead, she was adopted by a couple in Montreal.

The transition was a shock. Her adoptive parents lived in a fashionable neighbourhood of Montreal, in a large house with domestic servants. Her adoptive father was a wealthy businessman and her adoptive mother was an interior decorator. There were many other children in the family, including several who were adopted. Lisa was showered with toys and clothes, and she was sent to a private school. On weekends, her mother took her to art galleries and museums.

At an early age, Lisa began to wander out of the house at night. Soon she was running away more frequently. When her father began locking her bedroom door at night, she escaped through a window. In her night-time wanderings, she pretended that her Métis parents were accompanying her, imagining that her natural mother had beautiful long black hair and was wrapped in an Indian dress. She often spoke to these imaginary figures, asking for their advice on her problems. She invented long and complex stories in which she travelled through

---

[1] A few minor details have been changed to protect her identity.

the woods and talked to animals. Once, when she was feeling sad, she thought she saw her natural mother in a department store in Montreal.

In 1976 the family moved to the United States, and Lisa's parents began to suffer marital and financial difficulties. There were clashes between Lisa and her mother, who threatened to get rid of her. In 1979 they returned to Montreal, where Lisa's father tried to have her placed in another home. When she did anything wrong, the father punished her with beatings.

In the summer of 1981, when Lisa was eleven, her father began to abuse her sexually. She complied with his sexual demands because she was afraid of being beaten. The incidents continued after they moved back to the United States in November 1981. When Lisa eventually described the sexual abuse to some friends at school, the friends told the principal, and Lisa was removed from her adoptive parents.

Social workers were brought into the case, but the parents said they wanted to sever all connections with Lisa because she was "crazy". They would not even let her keep any of her personal belongings or clothing. In May 1982, in a final meeting between a social worker and Lisa's adoptive parents, the parents said they considered Lisa to be "dead" and they would provide no more information or photos.

Lisa was placed in a series of foster homes in a New England state, but she always ended up running away or fighting with the foster parents. A psychiatrist described her as "self-contained, quiet and frightened...prone to over-control her emotions until they reach a certain point, beyond which explosions are likely to occur." At the age of fourteen, she was roaming the streets of Springfield, Massachusetts. "She thought nothing of staying out overnight, sleeping wherever she could," a therapist wrote in a report in January 1984. "She preferred male companionship and was very promiscuous with boys, engaging in sexual activities with several at a time.... She charged boys, and even older men, money for sexual favors."

Within a few months, Lisa had contracted gonorrhea, ringworm, and yeast infections. She admitted that she was working as a prostitute. Later she explained how it had happened: "While I was on the run, I met this guy who took me under his wing and kept me by feeding me and clothing me and taking me places. After a while, he told me I had to pay him back. So he introduced me to the street."

She began to drink heavily. In one incident in Boston, she was arrested and charged with assaulting a police officer. A few months later, she was charged with disorderly conduct after the police found her stopping traffic on a Boston street, intoxicated. She was sent to another series of detention centres, institutions, courts, psychiatrists, social workers, and therapists.

"Lisa has had a chaotic and traumatic childhood that has left her with many scars," one psychologist concluded in 1984. "Lisa sees the world as being fraught with suffering and hardship. Unfortunately this accurately reflects her life experiences. Lisa is overwhelmed by her hardships and misfortunes. She seeks out any type of love and caring that she can get. She tends to act in very self-destructive ways, in part because of her sense of guilt about her childhood. Lisa is suspicious of adult authority and fearful of getting hurt. She becomes involved in dangerous and self-destructive situations and blots out the difficulties in order not to face the possibility of another loss."

One of the psychological tests required Lisa to finish a series of incomplete sentences. One sentence began: "My greatest mistake...." She wrote: "...was my [adoptive] father." Another sentence began: "I wish my father...." She wrote: "...was dead."

Despite the effects of her traumatic childhood, Lisa was an intelligent girl who had "a good intellectual potential," the psychologist said. Other evaluations agreed that she was bright and articulate—a creative girl who enjoyed music, drawing, and writing.

One day, alone in a locked-door institution in Boston, she talked into a tape recorder. "At times, I feel really scared, really nervous," she said. "I feel like I'm alone. It feels like nobody cares for me any more, at times.... I have to realize I can't keep on feeling sorry for myself. I have to think about what I'm going to do in the future.... The past is done with. There's nothing I can do about the past."

In an interview with a psychiatrist in October 1984, Lisa broke down and cried. She said she was hurting inside. "She seemed to be struggling with loneliness and emptiness and a need to reach out to caring people," the psychiatrist said. "She seemed to feel fragmented and her nonchalant attitude was a defence against some overwhelming feelings. She has an extremely confused and complex family history with a great many losses and changes. She has felt abandoned by anyone with whom she has tried to get close." Lisa told the psychiatrist that she felt like a jigsaw puzzle with the pieces falling out.

From the mid-1960s to the early 1980s, an estimated three thousand native children from Manitoba were removed from their homes and adopted by families outside the province. In most cases, the adoptive parents were white and urban. There was a strong demand from these families, so it was easy for the child welfare authorities to place the children in white homes. The Indian and Métis children were submerged in another culture, and their native identity soon disappeared. They became a lost generation.

By the early 1980s, about 40 to 60 percent of all children removed from their natural families in western Canada were Indian or Métis. In the rest of Canada, the percentage was lower—but only because the native population was much lower. In Ontario, only 2 percent of the population was Indian or Métis, but 8 percent of the children in the child welfare system were native. For the country as a whole, aboriginal children were being taken from their families almost five times more frequently than non-native children. By 1980, about 15,000 native children were under the control of child welfare agencies across Canada, and three-quarters of all adopted Indian children were placed in non-native homes.

The strongest demand for children came from the United States, where private agencies were making profits by finding children for middle-class couples. American newspapers carried advertisements from private agencies offering Canadian Indian children for adoption. Some agencies collected as much as $4,000 in fees for delivering a native child to a family in the United States. From the early 1970s until 1982, more than one thousand native children from Manitoba were shipped to the United States.

By the early 1980s, fewer aboriginal children were being sent south of the border, but they still tended to be placed outside the province. In 1981, for example, 55 percent of Manitoba's adopted Indian children were sent to other provinces, while only 7 percent of adopted Caucasian children were placed outside Manitoba.

In many cases, babies were permanently removed from Indian families solely because they had medical problems requiring treatment in a hospital. The federal government often placed the infant in a foster home near the hospital for the duration of the treatment. When it was over, the babies remained in the foster homes—they were never returned to their real parents, even though the parents had not abused or neglected them. In Manitoba alone, seventy-nine children were permanently removed from Indian families in the 1960s and 1970s after they were placed in hospitals for medical treatment.

Indian and Métis communities had virtually no control over the children who were seized from their homes. Until 1976, there was not a single native-controlled child welfare agency in Manitoba. Decisions about the future of native children were made by white social workers and urban-based bureaucrats.

In 1984, as a result of a provincial inquiry into the shocking number of adopted native children, the Manitoba government launched a campaign to help the children return to their home communities. Many of the adoptions had already broken down. The native children had rebelled, running away from their adoptive parents, often turning to drugs and crime. Manitoba officials wrote to child welfare agencies in every state of the United States, asking them to contact the provincial government if they knew any native children from Manitoba who might want to be repatriated to their home community or relatives in the province.

By this time, Lisa was being kept in a locked-door institution in Boston because of her habit of running away. According to her file, she had spent time in seventeen foster homes and institutions in Canada and the United States in the first fifteen years of her life. She had been identified by four different surnames and three different first names. She had been studied by six psychiatrists, and dozens of other professionals were involved in her life. But it was not until 1985 that anyone had thought of contacting her natural parents.

When the new Manitoba policy was announced, Lisa was allowed to meet a social worker from the Boston Indian Council. For the first time, she heard about her Métis parents in Camperville. She was almost overwhelmed with emotion.

A few weeks later, the social worker from the Manitoba Métis Federation arrived in Boston to meet Lisa. This was the crucial meeting—and it was a success. Lisa and the social worker talked for more than three hours.

Within a few days, Lisa's family in Camperville had received their daughter's cassettes from the United States. In amazement, they listened to the scratchy recording of the fifteen-year-old girl with the Boston accent. "I have been trying so hard to find somebody from my family, but nobody was willing to help me," Lisa told them. "I felt like I was lost. Now I am so happy I've found you. I was so happy I was crying. I felt like I was wanted again. I would really love to meet you, really soon."

Her mother wept when she listened to the tape, and her father and grandparents and cousins in Duck Bay were just as emotional when they heard Lisa's voice. They looked at the photos of Lisa and read her poems. Then they made their own tape recordings.

"I'm just looking at your picture and I'm so glad to see what a big girl you are now," her grandmother said in the tape for Lisa. "We were shocked to hear that you were in the States. But we all love you. We hope to see you soon. Don't be astonished if you find that our home is not very much, but there's a lot of love in it."

Lisa's grandfather described how he made his living by fishing on the lake. He promised to take Lisa on a fishing trip. Then her cousins and her brother spoke briefly, and her father said a few words into the tape recorder. "This is your dad," he said. "I'm hoping to meet you.... I don't know what to say."

When the Manitoba government agreed to finance a trip to Boston for Lisa's family in April 1985, Lisa was so excited that she wrote to a provincial bureaucrat to ask the government to change the visit to an earlier date. "I have been waiting a long period of time to meet and see my parents after twelve long years," she wrote. "I have had a hard childhood. It wasn't easy growing up without my biological parents. I tried to have allegiance to my adopted parents. Right now I am trying to condone my adopted father for all he's done. My adopted father was always vindictive towards my brothers and sisters and I. He never had egalitarianism for nobody in my family. My life has been constantly phantasmagoria."

In the early spring of 1985, Lisa's mother and one of her brothers came to Boston to visit her. "I can't put into words how I felt," she recalled later. "It was happiness, excitement and nervousness. I didn't know what to expect or how to act." They spent the weekend together, talking and looking at photos of other family members. "We spent all that time trying to recapture the lost years."

A few weeks later, Lisa returned to Manitoba for the first time since her infancy. She was placed in a special Winnipeg school which specializes in the treatment of sexual abuse victims.

"It was very obvious how much pain Lisa was feeling about the many losses and changes in her life," a social worker wrote after seeing her in Winnipeg in 1985. "Yet there is a side to her that is very compassionate, sensitive and caring." He described the teenager as a "very resilient" loner who is mistrustful of others. "Lisa has acquired particular survival skills which make it possible for her to spring back when she gets knocked down." The social worker said a reunion between Lisa and her natural family might be the experience she needed to recover "a sense of peace".

Lisa was given permission to go to Camperville for short visits. "When I arrived home on the bus, my family was always there to greet me with open arms. I always felt like a new-born baby, being brought home." She found it difficult to adjust to the Métis community, but she still felt she needed to see her family. "I learned a lot of what I had lost. I learned to accept my family and they've learned to accept me."

Lisa asked to be permanently released from the Winnipeg school, but her social worker said she wasn't yet ready. So she kicked the screen out of her bedroom window, tied her bedsheets into a rope, and tried to escape. She fell to the ground and broke her spine in two places. After undergoing surgery and spending several months in a Winnipeg hospital, she returned to a life on the streets. "That's the only way I know how to make a living," she explained. Eventually her family found her and took her back to Camperville.

Today, at the age of nineteen, Lisa is living with her mother in Camperville. She has dropped her adopted name, but she is still trapped between two worlds. She cannot speak the Saulteaux language of her relatives. "I find it hard to cope with everyday life," she says. "I feel like a white person in a native community. It seems like I'm always trying to fit in with my family's life."

She is still angry at the child welfare officials who shipped her to Montreal. "They ruined my life and childhood. I'm a prime example of the system. I lost thirteen years of my childhood."

In the spring of 1989, the Manitoba aboriginal justice inquiry came to Camperville. Before a hushed audience of fifty people, Lisa gave her life story. Then she addressed her family directly. She apologized for her continuing struggle with alcohol. "I'm hoping you'll understand what I've been through," she told her family. "I know it's not your fault. You've given me the world. It's the past I've never dealt with. Now I've come face-to-face with it. My cousin told me it's either my family or my past. That's why I'm here. I just want to thank you."

Perhaps because of her remarkable inner strength and resilience, Lisa survived. But others did not. One of those who did not make it was Richard Cardinal, a Métis from northern Alberta who was removed from his family at the age of four. He was placed in twenty-eight different homes and institutions, including sixteen foster homes, before he finally committed suicide at the age of seventeen. Richard Cardinal's diary revealed that he had been abused horribly in some of the foster homes. In one home, he was beaten with a stick for bed wetting. At another, he was given as little as a bag of raw turnips for a meal. At a third home, he was given a bed only sixty centimetres wide in a flooded basement. He was once forced to remain outside on Christmas Day while the rest of the family celebrated the holiday inside. Over a period of several years, beginning when he was only nine years old, he made several suicide attempts.

Richard Cardinal often talked about his dream of returning to Fort Chipewyan, the home of his natural family. One time he ran away and headed north, but he was taken into custody before he could complete the journey. By 1984, people noticed that he had stopped displaying any emotions. At his sixteenth foster home, he hanged himself from a board nailed between two trees. His brother took his body home to Fort Chipewyan, where he found his final resting place.

Later, an investigation concluded that the Alberta Social Services Department probably gave Richard Cardinal better treatment when it arranged his funeral than it had ever given him in his seventeen years of life.

In the diary that was discovered after his death, the Métis teenager had written: "Love is a very strange thing. I don't think I would be happy with it, but I am depressed and sad without it."

Then there was the case of Cameron Kerley. Born on the Sioux Valley Indian reserve in southwestern Manitoba, he was removed from his family at the age of eight. His father had died in a drunken brawl and his mother was drinking heavily. Cameron was remembered as "a shy, quiet kid who tried very hard to please." In 1975, when he was eleven, the Children's Aid Society of Western Manitoba decided to send Cameron to the home of a bachelor businessman in Wichita, Kansas.

In the 1970s the supply of adoptable children in the United States was beginning to dry up and the U.S. Congress was considering an Indian Child Welfare Act, which would give American Indian tribes the power to control the welfare of their own children. The legislation would allow Indian parents and tribes to intervene in any court decision involving the placement of a native child. Because of the expectation that this bill would soon be law, it was becoming more difficult for U.S. agencies to find a steady supply of Indian children who could be adopted. Since there were no legislative restrictions on the export of Canadian Indian children to the United States, agencies in places such as Kansas were turning to Canadian Indian children to fill the demand.

Meanwhile, the Children's Aid Society in Manitoba stated that the province had a shortage of foster homes and potential adoptive parents. There is some disagreement as to whether the child welfare agency actually made much effort to search for an Indian home in Manitoba before deciding to export Cameron Kerley to Kansas. But there is no doubt that the adoption in Kansas was a disaster.

At first, Cameron progressed well at school in Wichita. But soon he became withdrawn and sullen. Within six months, he was skipping school and running away from home, roaming alone for days at a time. Social workers and school counsellors tried to help him, but he refused to talk.

"I didn't trust them," he recalled in an interview a decade later. "I wasn't able to tell them. I felt helpless. At that point there was nobody I could turn to for help. I was a kid, taken away from home [at Sioux Valley] and put into a situation I didn't ask to be in."

When the truth emerged, native groups in Manitoba said that the American and Canadian child welfare agencies had ignored the signs of trouble. Cameron's adoption had not been legally finalized at the time of his attempts to run away from the Kansas home, yet the agencies refused to reconsider the adoption, despite the obvious difficulties he was experiencing. Cameron was not legally adopted by the Kansas bachelor until 1977.

In March 1977, the teenaged boy finally began to talk to a native counsellor at school. For the first time, he revealed why he was running away so often. His adoptive father was sexually abusing him, sometimes tying him up and refusing to give him supper until he complied with the sexual demands.

The counsellor asked Cameron if he would tell his story in court, but the Indian boy said he was afraid of being beaten by his adoptive father if he testified. The bachelor had often threatened to beat Cameron if he ever revealed the abuse. Because he was unwilling to go to court, Cameron could not be legally removed from the bachelor's home.

Cameron knew he had been born on an Indian reserve in Canada, and he knew Canada was somewhere north of Wichita. In the spring of 1978, he tried to hitch-hike northward, but the police quickly found him and he was placed on probation for six months for "waywardness". His depression grew worse. He lost interest in school and dropped out at the age of seventeen. Then, when he was arrested for burglary, he admitted that he had been drinking and using drugs for years. A few months later, he broke into another house and was charged with aggravated burglary.

In 1983, Cameron finally left his adoptive father's home and began living in a friend's tiny apartment in Wichita. Trying to find out more about his Indian heritage, he visited Indian art exhibits and an Indian museum. He told his friend that everything would be okay if he could return to the Indian reserve where he was born. But his intense anger did not disappear, and in September 1983, after a drinking binge, he returned to the home of his adoptive father, climbed through a window, and killed the man with a baseball bat.

Cameron pleaded guilty to second-degree murder. Two days later, he told his lawyer about the sexual abuse he had suffered from his adoptive father. Despite a plea for leniency, Cameron was sentenced to a jail term of eighteen years to life. Psychiatric reports described him as a "distrustful, suspicious" youth who "tends to see the world as a threatening and rejecting place." His response, the psychiatrists said, was "to withdraw or strike out in anger as a defence against being hurt."

Four months later, Cameron was permitted to seek a review of his sentence. One of his counsellors contacted the Dakota Ojibway Tribal Council, which had established a native-controlled child welfare agency in southwestern Manitoba in 1981. A delegation from the tribal council, including two of Cameron's natural sisters, went to Wichita to try to convince the court to reduce Cameron's sentence. For the first time in ten years, he met members of his natural family. His sisters cried when they saw him, but Cameron's reaction was more restrained. He had no childhood memories of his sisters.

At the sentence-review hearing in Wichita, the tribal council described the culture shock and identity crisis that Indian children often suffer when they are adopted by white urban families. The dislocation can lead to alcoholism, psychiatric problems, and crime, the judge was told. In a letter to the judge, Cameron pleaded for a chance to return to Canada.

In the end, his sentence was reduced only slightly—to fifteen years to life. In 1985 he was transferred to Stoney Mountain Penitentiary north of Winnipeg. It was the first time he had set foot in Canada in a decade.

The Dakota Ojibway Tribal Council believes the Cameron Kerley case was an example of "the absolute worst consequences" of Manitoba's long-standing policy of "export adoptions". According to the council, Cameron was a product of the failure of social agencies and government policies in both Canada and the United States.

Today, Cameron Kerley is serving his sentence at a minimum-security work farm in Manitoba. Twice a month, he is permitted to go on eight-hour unescorted leaves. That does not give him enough time to return to the Sioux Valley reserve, so instead he visits an Indian elder from Sioux Valley who lives in Winnipeg. He still hopes to return to the reserve some day. "I don't remember much about life there," he told a Winnipeg newspaper. "But it's my people there, and I sort of lost touch. I feel drawn back there. It's where my mother and father are buried."

In the late 1970s and early 1980s, Manitoba's native leaders became increasingly angered by the province's child welfare policies. They protested the permanent loss of their children—the disappearance of a generation whose cultural identity had been wiped out. They called it "cultural genocide".

The protests reached a peak in 1982, when newspaper reports revealed that scores of Indian children were still being sent to the United States. Ernie Daniels, chief of the Long Plain band in southern Manitoba, wrote to the executive director of an adoption agency in Louisiana, saying that the director should be "hanged" for the "wholesale bartering" of native children. "I feel very sad and bitter about your bragging that you have placed thirty-six Canadian Indian and Métis children," Daniels told the Louisiana director. "I hope that we will not ever hear of your organization again in relation to our children."

On March 6, 1982, under severe pressure from the media and native leaders, the Manitoba government agreed to impose a moratorium on the export of native children outside the province. A provincial inquiry, headed by family court judge Edwin Kimelman, was appointed to study the fate of Indian and Métis children in the child welfare system.

Judge Kimelman held hearings across Manitoba, in towns and reserves from Roseau River to The Pas. Indian leaders told Kimelman that the adoption of native children by white families had scarred the hearts and minds of their people. Native women begged the judge to help them find their sons and daughters—children who had disappeared into unknown homes after they were seized by child welfare agencies. Indian foster children told Kimelman how they had run away from white foster homes and returned to their home reserves because they felt lonely and unhappy in white families.

Child welfare officials had always scoffed at the Indian leaders who said the native children were victims of "cultural genocide". But to their amazement, Judge Kimelman agreed with the Indian leaders. After reviewing the file of every single native child who had been adopted by an out-of-province family in 1981—a total of ninety-three children—Kimelman said he could state unequivocally that "cultural genocide has been taking place in a systematic, routine manner."

Kimelman also agreed with native leaders who said the provincial child welfare policy was remarkably similar to the old policy of sending native children to residential schools. Indeed, the seizure of Indian children began to escalate just as the residential schools were winding down in the 1960s. In a way, the child welfare system simply replaced the residential school system—producing the same kind of damaging effects on the native culture. It became the new method of colonizing Indian people, after the residential schools were finally discredited.

"When the Indian residential schools were operating, children were forcibly removed from their homes for the duration of the academic year," Kimelman said. "The children were punished if they used their own language, sang their own songs or told their own stories. But at least under that system the children knew who their parents were and they returned home for the summer months. With the closing of the residential schools, rather than providing the resources on reserves to build economic security and providing the services to support responsible parenting, society found it easier and cheaper to remove the children from their homes and apparently fill the market demand for children in Eastern Canada and the United States."

The judge concluded that aboriginal children were "the primary victims" of a policy of "wholesale exportation" to other provinces and the United States. In the ninety-three cases he reviewed, the white-controlled agencies rarely bothered to contact the native child's home community to see if an adoptive family was available there. Instead they took advantage of the demand from non-native families outside the province. "One gets an image of children stacked in foster homes as used cars are stacked on corner lots, just waiting for the right 'buyer' to stroll by," Kimelman said.

Even when the agencies did consider native homes, they tended to use a selection process that made it difficult for native families to adopt native children. Agencies often required parents to have a steady income, a good home, and a separate bedroom for each child—clearly an impossible standard for parents on most northern reserves. "Whole reserves may be left out of the adoption process because they don't have running water," said Tim Maloney, executive director of the new child welfare agency created by the Dakota Ojibway Tribal Council. He said that some agencies seemed to prefer travelling to the United States to look for adoptive parents. "They found it easier to get on a 737 to Louisiana than to take a drive up to Sandy Bay and talk to the chief and council. The Indian people are ready to take care of their children. They simply haven't been asked."

After interviewing staff at every child welfare agency in the province, Kimelman observed that they "seemed abysmally uninformed about native value systems." They were insensitive to the cultural values of native people and did not understand native attitudes toward child rearing. They seemed to be programmed to regard native people "as carriers of the symptoms of social pathology rather than as fully rounded human beings with weaknesses and strengths," the judge said.

Patrick Johnston, who studied the native child welfare system for the Canadian Council on Social Development in the early 1980s, made the same observation. The staff of child welfare agencies tend to be middle-class white people who unconsciously assume that low-income native parents are providing a less adequate home for their children, he said. "We must recognize that some children may have been taken into care not because they were unloved or unwanted or neglected, but because they were poor," Johnston said.

He also suggests that stereotypes about Indian alcohol abuse have influenced the decisions of workers in the child welfare system. "Social workers may be more likely to find alcohol abuse in native families because they are more likely to look for it," Johnston wrote. "And they may use that as an excuse to apprehend more frequently in native than non-native families."

Kimelman concluded that native families are no more likely to abuse or neglect their children than non-native families. "In fact, actual abuse of children is believed to be lower among native families," he said. Even corporal punishment is rarely used in native families. Yet hundreds of Indian and Métis children were removed from their homes without proof of abuse or neglect. Kimelman said there was mounting evidence to suggest that the native children were being seized "because staff of child care agencies and the judicial system have not understood the cultural values and patterns of native people."

For example, agencies often required a native mother to establish her own home before she would be permitted to regain custody of her child. That ignored the native tradition of letting young mothers stay in the homes of their extended families. "The grandparents and aunts and uncles expect the demands and the rewards of raising the new member of the family," Kimelman said. "To insist that the mother remove herself from the supports of her family when she needs them most is unrealistic and cruel."

A native mother might leave an infant child in the care of a relative for an extended period of time. "A worker who did not understand the Indian concept of the child as a member of the total community, rather than as the exclusive property of a single set of parents, might perceive that child to be abandoned when it is, in fact, residing within its own 'family'," Kimelman said.

Native parents also tend to give their children a great deal of independence and freedom. Children are viewed as equal members of the community. "Native children are expected to assume, and are capable of assuming, responsibility for themselves and for others at a much earlier age than children residing in families whose culture is European-based," Kimelman said. Yet a native mother who does not constantly supervise her child "might be viewed by a social worker as negligent," he said.

When their children were seized and taken away, many native parents were never told the whereabouts of the children. Some agencies would not even confirm that the children were still alive. In one case, an agency closed its file permanently after seizing all of a native woman's children. "Should not a child with memories of parents be permitted to maintain contacts with the parents?" Kimelman asked. He noted that some adopted Indian children were never even told that they were legally entitled to certain treaty rights and privileges because of their status as treaty Indians.

Once an agency had decided to seize a native child, there was little chance for the parents to regain the child. To challenge an agency, the native parents would have to go through a lengthy and complex legal process, with frequent court appearances. The process is almost incomprehensible to many Indian parents. "By consenting to a child being made a ward, parents may see themselves as succumbing to the inevitable, as well as avoiding the public humiliation that a contested case would cause them to suffer," Kimelman said.

As part of the Kimelman study, the Manitoba government sought information from hundreds of Indian children who had been placed outside the province or outside their culture. Dozens of letters came back from Indian youths and adoptive parents, and in every case the letters revealed that the adoptions had eventually broken down. The letters told of children who dropped out of school, ran away from home, abused alcohol, became self-destructive, and broke the law. The lives of the aboriginal children were "seriously and permanently impaired," Kimelman said.

One Manitoba study, cited in the final Kimelman report, revealed that most non-native parents who adopted native children had made no attempt to learn anything about native culture. One-quarter never talked to the children about their native roots. Moreover, white parents often find it difficult to teach native children how to defend themselves against racism. Research suggests that "adoptive or foster parents of the dominant society simply cannot prepare children for the prejudice that does exist," Kimelman said.

Officials in Pennsylvania, where many Manitoba native children were sent, reported that 90 percent of the adopted children eventually needed professional treatment because of their problems in adjusting to white homes. Of the thirty native youths who were repatriated to Manitoba by the Dakota Ojibway agency in the mid-1980s, about half had suffered emotional or physical damage from their adoptive families. They had lost their native language and their identity. Today, they are in limbo between two cultures—uncertain of who they are, unsure of where they belong.

After the breakdown of an adoption, native children are often treated by psychiatrists who have little understanding of aboriginal culture. At least nine Canadian native children were locked up in American psychiatric institutions for months or years after they were misdiagnosed by psychiatrists who had decided that the youths were mentally ill. When they were repatriated to Canada, a closer examination found that the children were simply angry or depressed. Their behaviour—assaulting institutional officials or setting fires—was not a result of mental illness. It was caused by the confusion and frustration they felt after they were removed from their homes and sent to a foreign culture. "They were really symptoms of anger or rage, based on their lives being disrupted," said Dr. Rox Wand, medical director of the Manitoba Adolescent Treatment Centre. "Not one of them was mentally ill. But people could not understand them."

Kimelman recommended that efforts be made to repatriate the "exported" native children to their home communities in Manitoba. "Too many native children have been deprived of their cultural heritage," he said. It was as a result of Kimelman's recommendations that Manitoba sent dozens of letters to agencies in the United States, paving the way for children such as Lisa to return home.

"It is a bitter irony that a system that is designed to protect children and support families has served to weaken native family life inestimably," Patrick Johnston has written. "And, in so doing, because the family had traditionally been the primary social unit in native communities, it has also damaged a distinct way of life.... The disproportionately high incarceration rate of native people in prisons and jails is not an unrelated coincidence. Many consider the child welfare system to be a kind of training ground for children who 'graduate' to the juvenile justice system and, finally, to the penal system."

Johnston uses the term "Sixties Scoop" to describe the seizure of thousands of native children by child welfare agencies, beginning in the 1960s. The result, in the long run, was a serious weakening of Indian and Métis society. "In retrospect, the wholesale apprehension of native children during the Sixties Scoop appears to have been a terrible mistake," Johnston concludes. "While some individual children may have benefitted, many did not. Nor did their families. And native culture suffered one of many severe blows. Unfortunately, the damage is still being done. While attitudes may have changed to some extent since the 1960s, native children continue to be represented in the child welfare system at a much greater rate than non-native children."

In the past decade, some progress has been made. In 1984, Manitoba established a clear policy to ensure that child welfare agencies make a thorough effort to find native homes for native children before considering any non-native homes. The Manitoba Métis Federation is now consulted on child welfare decisions for Métis children (although there are still occasional disputes between the federation and the province). And the province now has six Indian-controlled child welfare agencies, covering almost every reserve in Manitoba.

These agencies were established under tripartite agreements between the federal government, the Manitoba government, and the tribal councils of each region. Ottawa provides the funding for the Indian-controlled agencies, the province passes legislation to authorize the agencies (since child welfare is a provincial responsibility), and tribal councils administer the child welfare services. The Indian agencies provide essentially the same services as the white-controlled agencies, but they are tailored to the traditional customs and beliefs of the Indian communities. They have established Indian foster homes, recruited Indian adoptive parents, and set up emergency receiving homes on each reserve.

Across the country, a growing number of Indian bands are now delivering child welfare services on their reserves. In Alberta, 210 native children were placed in native families in 1987, while only 113 native children were placed in white families. At the same time, provincial departments have boosted their hiring of Indian and Métis social workers to help ensure that native children are handled by native staff. And hundreds of adopted native children have returned to their home communities as a result of repatriation policies in several provinces.

As in Manitoba, this progress has been made largely as a result of pressure from Indian and Métis groups themselves. In 1980, for instance, about one thousand people demonstrated outside the Vancouver home of Grace McCarthy, the British Columbia minister of human resources. Many of the demonstrators, who called themselves the Indian Child Caravan, had travelled from remote native communities to join the protest against the huge number of native children who had been removed from their homes and shipped to non-native families throughout the 1960s and 1970s. At the time of the demonstration, almost 40 percent of the children in the British Columbia child welfare system were Indian or Métis—a dramatic rise from the 1950s, when less than 1 percent of the children were native.

Shortly after the protest, Grace McCarthy bowed to the pressure from the Indians and signed an agreement with one of the hardest-hit native communities—the Spallumcheen band. Though it was just a small community of 300 people, the Spallumcheen band had already seen 150 of its children seized by the child welfare system. The 1980 agreement was intended to halt the loss of the band's children. "The Minister of Human Resources agrees to respect the authority of the Spallumcheen Band Council to assume responsibility and control over their own children," the agreement said.

The band passed a bylaw declaring that it had exclusive jurisdiction over any child custody case involving an Indian child from the reserve. With funding from the Indian Affairs Department, the band created a child welfare program to take over the functions normally provided by provincial agencies. "They won't take our children again," said the chief of the band, Wayne Christian. "Our system now keeps the children within the band and gives support and treatment to families."

Since 1980, several other Indian tribal councils and bands have signed child welfare agreements with the British Columbia government. Under these agreements, no child can be placed for adoption in a non-native home without the consent of the band or tribal council. Adoptive homes are sought among the child's extended family and among other band members before any outside adoption is considered. If there is no satisfactory alternative to an adoption in a non-native home, the province requires the adoptive parents to agree to allow the child to maintain contacts with the Indian band. The parents must also agree to make sure that the child knows about his native heritage.

Despite the improvements in British Columbia's child welfare system, it still has some obvious problems. Indian and Métis children continue to account for one-third of all children in the system, and many of them are still being sent to non-native families. In 1986–87, for example, seventy-eight children were apprehended from B.C. Indian families, and fifty-one of those were sent to non-native homes.

In one case in 1987, a British Columbia family court judge ordered a native boy to be placed in a strict Mormon family, even though the boy's aunt wanted to adopt him. The judge admitted that the boy would lose his native identity in the Mormon family. "I didn't detect in the foster mother much knowledge of, or informed sympathy with, or even curiosity about, Indian people and their aspirations," the judge said. However, he decided that the boy's aunt was unsuitable because she was a strong Indian activist who would take the boy to protests and political battles. The aunt could not provide a "stable, quiet structured life" for the boy, the judge ruled.

Although reforms have swept through most of the western provinces, some are lagging far behind. In Saskatchewan, about two-thirds of the children in the provincial child-welfare system are Indian or Métis, yet there are only a handful of native foster homes in the province. Only one region of Saskatchewan has an Indian-controlled child welfare program, and unlike other provinces, Saskatchewan has no legislation or formal policy to encourage the creation of native-controlled agencies. "It's the most backward in Canada," says Harvey

Stalwick, a University of Regina social work professor who has studied child welfare systems across the country.

The suicide of Marlon Pippin in February 1989 was dramatic evidence of the lack of native involvement in Saskatchewan's child welfare services. Born on the Cote reserve in eastern Saskatchewan, the Indian boy was placed in a white foster home when he was five days old. His real name was Marlon Severight, but he was given the surname of his white foster family. Although he occasionally visited his mother on the Indian reserve, he spent most of his time trying to adjust to white society in Regina, where he grew up. He invented stories to explain his brown skin, telling his friends that he was Spanish or Hawaiian.

There were no Indian-controlled child welfare agencies to help Marlon learn to be proud of his native culture. There were no native counsellors to help him accept his true identity. Nor was there any formal policy to encourage connections between Marlon and his cultural roots.

In the fall of 1988 Marlon became depressed and suicidal. He was examined by psychiatrists twice as a result of his suicide attempts, but they said he was just a normal kid. Nobody recognized the symptoms of cultural confusion. And then, on a winter night in early 1989, the Regina police department received a report of a youth armed with a rifle. The SWAT team confronted the youth, firing four bullets at him, two of which hit him on the left hand and in the abdomen. Marlon Pippin pointed his rifle at his forehead and killed himself. He was seventeen years old.

"He was ashamed of who he was," said his mother, Susan Severight, after his death. "He found out that a lot of people don't like Indians. He never wanted to say he was an Indian. He had an identity crisis. Being raised in a white home, he wanted to follow their ways. He wanted to be white, and yet he was an Indian."

"If he had stronger links to his reserve and his family, he might have felt better about himself and felt more confident," said Carole Bryant, president of the Saskatchewan Association of Social Workers. "The Social Services Department has controlled decisions and set policies in isolation from native groups, and it just hasn't worked." After the death of Marlon Pippin, native groups called for a public inquiry into the Saskatchewan government's treatment of aboriginal people.

Of all the Canadian provinces, Manitoba and Alberta have made the most reforms in the child welfare policies that affect native children. New native-controlled agencies have been established and hundreds of children have been repatriated to native communities after their adoptions broke down. However, the new policies and agencies have not always worked smoothly. Unlike the old agencies, which had decades to establish themselves, the new native-controlled agencies were thrown into difficult dilemmas with little experience or training. Their decisions were closely scrutinized by the media and the provincial opposition parties. And they undoubtedly made some mistakes.

The most notorious error involved a fifteen-year-old Indian girl who was repatriated to the Lac Brochet reserve in northern Manitoba in 1986. Removed from her parents for medical reasons, the infant girl was placed in a foster home in a nearby northern town. The white foster parents eventually moved to Alberta, taking the girl with them. Fuelled by a strong sense of injustice, a band-controlled child welfare agency helped the Indian parents try to recover their child.

After a lengthy court battle, the agency persuaded the foster parents to send the girl back to Lac Brochet. She had been living with her foster parents for most of her life, and she wanted to remain with them. Nevertheless, she was forced to return to the isolated northern reserve in 1986. Desperately lonely and frightened and unable to speak the Chipewyan language, she tried unsuccessfully to persuade pilots to fly her back to her foster parents in Alberta. Within a few months, she was sexually assaulted seventeen times by youths on the reserve. When the assaults were discovered, the girl was returned to her foster parents. Her case sparked national publicity.

Opponents of the Indian-controlled agencies have used errors like these to try to discredit the entire concept of native-controlled child welfare programs. But the critics failed to understand that the problems were largely due to a lack of experience and shortage of federal money at the new agencies. Their funding from Ottawa, in fact, was about 25 percent lower than the amount received by provincial agencies.

One of the objectives of the new agencies was to hire people who lived on the reserves. In most cases, these workers had no university education and only a limited amount of training in social work. Training courses were available, but usually at locations outside the reserve—and most of the workers could not attend these courses because they had to look after their own families at home.

Unlike provincial child welfare workers in middle-class communities, the staff of the Indian agencies must also provide more than just child welfare services. They have to help native families cope with overwhelming problems in housing, unemployment, and alcohol abuse. It is a formidable workload, and it continues to burden Indian-controlled agencies today. The solution lies in increased funding to hire more workers and provide training courses on the reserves.

Mistakes were perhaps inevitable in the early years of the Indian-controlled agencies. But there have been enough success stories to justify an expansion of the concept.

In the 1960s, two-thirds of the children removed from Indian families at the Fort Alexander reserve in eastern Manitoba were placed in homes outside the community. But in 1976, the Indian Affairs Department agreed to provide funds for a band-controlled child welfare program at Fort Alexander, making the Ojibway band one of the first in Canada to establish such a program. As the band recruited native foster families within the reserve, the number of children removed from Fort Alexander began to decline. Today, about 95 percent of the children taken into care at Fort Alexander are placed in foster homes on the reserve, where they can maintain connections with their culture, their language, and their people.

In some native communities, provincial authorities have agreed to consult a native-controlled child welfare committee before deciding whether to remove children from any home. In practice, these committees perform many of the functions of full-fledged child welfare agencies. Again, they have proven to be successful. In native communities such as Stoney Creek, British Columbia, and Sandy Bay, Saskatchewan, the creation of the child welfare committees has led to a significant drop in the number of apprehensions of native children.

Native leaders realize there is still a huge task ahead of them. Métis communities, for example, are laying the groundwork for a network of Métis-controlled child welfare agencies in Manitoba. And the Indian-controlled agencies are turning their attention to a new priority: strengthening native families so that their children can remain at home.

In the late 1970s and early 1980s, Lyle Longclaws was one of the Indian leaders who helped created the native-controlled child welfare agencies in Manitoba. "We've got to start preventing children from coming into care," he says. "We need a strong family support movement. We have to keep the family intact." He envisions a system of family counselling and parent support groups, carefully monitored by the child welfare agencies, to help troubled families stay together. Even if a child must be removed from his parents, the counselling and support programs might allow the child to be returned to his family after a few months.

"It's unfortunate that aboriginal children have to come into conflict with the law before they are provided with any support services," Longclaws says. "That's archaic. Why can't they just walk into an agency and say, Look, our family needs help? The key is to heal the family. You can't do any healing unless you spend some time with them and provide a care structure."

Nobody knows how many Indian and Métis children were permanently damaged as a result of their adoption by outside families. Some, like Richard Cardinal and Cameron Kerley, were physically abused. In other cases, native children were left with deep psychological and emotional scars. The child welfare system, like the residential school system, has left a permanent legacy in many of today's native adults—a legacy of pain and confusion.

"They will have seen worlds and life as we can never imagine," says Judge Murray Sinclair. "We cannot hope to truly understand what they have gone through, for we have not lived it as they have. They will try to tell us…. They will want to be hugged and held, but they will not want us to get too close, for we are almost strangers to them. There can be no love in their lives unless we assist them to understand the reasons behind their sense of rage."

Hundreds of adopted native children have already found their way back to the communities where they were born. Yet there are hundreds of other children who are still missing. In the communities of Camperville and Duck Bay, for example, Métis parents are still searching for fifty children who were taken from them. In almost every Indian and Métis community across Canada, there are parents who yearn for their missing children.

Ernie Crey, an Indian from British Columbia, was removed from his alcoholic mother at the age of twelve and taken to a holding cell in a detention centre. Then, after spending three months in an army-style barracks room with twenty other children, he was shipped to a series of white foster homes. At his first foster home, he heard Indian women described as "squaws" and "smoked meat". Gradually he lost his native identity. "I was taught to be ashamed of being Indian," he says. "When I was twelve, I took a soap and brush and tried to rub the brown colour off my skin. I didn't want to be an Indian. There was a lot of tension in me—a lot of anxiety."

At one home, his foster parents were religious fundamentalists who made daily efforts to convert him to Christianity. When he turned seventeen, he was moved to a group home, where he lived in fear of two social workers who sexually abused many of the children. Other members of his family had similar experiences in their foster homes. One was treated virtually as a slave. Another was sexually abused and beaten.

Ernie Crey eventually went to university and earned a degree in social work. He became vice-president of the United Native Nations, a leading aboriginal group in British Columbia. At the age of thirty-seven, he finally succeeded in restoring his connections to the band from which he was removed as a child.

Today he is a prominent activist in the battle to persuade the province to let Indian bands establish their own child welfare policies. He has lobbied for legislation to help ensure that native children are placed in native homes, and he has acted as an advocate for adopted native children. But he still has nightly terrors and anxiety attacks as he has flashbacks to his childhood in the foster homes. "It's post-traumatic stress syndrome—the same psychological and physical problems that people suffered returning from Vietnam," he says. "The damage and the pain that's done to a kid...echoes down through your entire adult life."

Laurence Boucher, a Métis from northern Alberta, was removed from his parents at the age of six. "I don't know why I was taken away," he says. "One day, the welfare car pulled up, and that was the last of the family. It just disintegrated."

Boucher and his brothers and sisters spent time in almost a dozen white foster homes near the town of Lac La Biche in the 1950s and

1960s. Most of the foster parents were farmers. "They had children of their own. I can remember nights when we had to sleep outside in barns while their own children slept inside. And we weren't fed at the table. Food was brought to us, and it wasn't the same food that the children would eat with their parents at the table. I ran away from those places."

At the age of eighteen, Laurence Boucher tried to return to his Métis parents, but his dreams of a joyful reunion were soon shattered. "After twelve years in the white world, I had become alienated from my own people. I'd forgotten my language. I was not the same Laurence that left there at six. My parents were afraid of me because all of a sudden I represented everything that they'd feared. And the thing they feared the most was anything that was white, because it caused them pain and shame. It put fear in their hearts. And so I was rejected."

In a documentary film produced by the National Film Board, Boucher described how he left his parents and moved to Edmonton. "I didn't have an identity. No language. No mother or father. No brothers and sisters. No God, because I had lost Him. I took a razor blade and I tried to take my own life, because I didn't know what else to do."

Laurence Boucher survived. And he has persevered. His dreams today are modest. "Ambition to me means…to find peace and contentment by sharing. That's the value of ambition to my people…to live in this world and still retain our own society, our own culture, our own beliefs and our own values."

Looking back at his life, he thinks of an old story about the Indians and the white man. "The Indians were on this land and the white people came from across the ocean. They came here in their boats, with their Bible, with their priests and missionaries. And they wanted to translate the Bible into Cree and they didn't know an equivalent word for 'sin'. So they went to the elders and asked the elders, Tell us, what is the equivalent of 'sin' in your language? The Indians didn't have a word for sin…. Our children are our future, and when you shatter those lives, the lives of the children, then you shatter our future…. That's the sin."

CHAPTER NINE

The New Militancy

Louis Stevenson laughs when he thinks of all the trouble he has caused
for the bureaucrats and politicians. A sly grin spreads across his face
as he thinks of the members of Parliament and civil servants he has
outraged and offended. Louis Stevenson just doesn't care about the
rules of etiquette and diplomacy or the bruised feelings of the white
power brokers. He is the most influential Indian leader in Manitoba,
a constant thorn in the side of the federal government, and one of
the most effective native leaders in the country. As he annoys and
embarrasses the guardians of the official process, he brings a ray of
hope and economic rejuvenation to his disadvantaged community. His
abrasive and aggressive leadership style has provoked fierce clashes
with the pillars of white society, but to Louis Stevenson the feuds and
confrontations are just fuel for the fire.

For the past eight years, Stevenson has been the chief of the three-
thousand-member Peguis band in central Manitoba. He is thirty-nine, a
Saulteaux Indian with a broad, gentle face and an innocent demeanour
that conceals a will of iron. A man of apparent contradictions, he is
equally comfortable in a business suit or a ceremonial eagle-feathered
headdress and buckskins. He admits that his favourite television program is *The Cosby Show*, and he loves cooking lasagne or inviting
friends over for a summer barbecue. His secret fantasy is to become a

country and western singer. Yet he spends countless hours in libraries, studying for university sociology courses and reading books on social justice and the struggles of indigenous and minority groups around the world. His favourite book is *Pedagogy of the Oppressed*, the classic treatise by Paulo Freire. Corazon Aquino, the leader of the Filipino revolution, is his personal hero. In his spare time, he pores over the international declarations and covenants that Canada has signed, looking for clauses that might help protect the rights of Canada's aboriginal people.

Since the day of his election as chief of the Peguis band, Stevenson has never stopped dreaming up imaginative new ways to put pressure on the federal authorities. His tactics range from the crude to the sophisticated, but they never fail to get under the skin of the government officials who defend the status quo.

"One time the regional director-general was really mad me," Stevenson laughs. "He was away at a meeting in another part of the province, and we went to his office and had a sit-in when he was gone. He had to come racing home to defuse it. That's why he was upset. He said, "If you ever do that again, I'm not talking to you for 14 days—you or your council or any of your people." It was childish. I said, I don't care if you don't speak to me for 14 days or 140 days, as long as you respond to our problems."

Then there was the controversy in 1987 when Stevenson contacted the South African Embassy in Ottawa and invited the ambassador to visit the Peguis reserve. To some critics, it appeared that Stevenson's invitation was an endorsement of the South African regime. But there was method in his madness. Stevenson knew the national and international media would flock to Peguis to cover such a controversial visit, which would give him the perfect opportunity to display on worldwide television his people's desperate need for government assistance to improve their housing and economic opportunities. Above all, Stevenson knew the ambassador's visit would raise some uncomfortable questions about the parallels between the treatment of Indians in Canada and the treatment of blacks in South Africa.

"The government was neglecting our funding for education and housing at the time, and I just got fed up with it," the chief recalls. "I decided to do something on a larger scale. One of the problems I was experiencing at the time was getting the media to cover the issues

I wanted exposed, nationally and internationally. I couldn't afford to go out and buy the advertising. So by matching a controversial figure with the issues I wanted exposed, it brought the attention I needed."

The bureaucrats and politicians didn't think Stevenson had the right to invite the South African ambassador to Peguis. "I got calls from the United Nations Security Council asking me to cancel the ambassador's visit. I also got calls from members of Parliament in Ottawa saying that I was going to smear Canada's international image. My response was, Who cares?"

What the MPs failed to understand was that Louis Stevenson is not concerned about upholding Canada's global image. Indeed, he wonders how Canada has continued to enjoy a good international image while it has systematically persecuted and neglected its aboriginal people for two hundred years. Besides, the Canadian government could have preserved its relatively untarnished image by ensuring justice for its Indian and Métis people, Stevenson points out. Instead, the country suffered an embarrassment in the world community as a result of the Peguis incident. The South African ambassador's visit to Peguis was covered by newspapers and magazines around the world—in Britain, West Germany, Australia, and South Africa. The Peguis chief found himself quoted in *Der Spiegel*, the *Times* of London, and other foreign publications.

Stevenson has no regrets about his decision to invite the ambassador. He believes it forced the federal government to accelerate its funding for several major projects at Peguis. "I'm satisfied I accomplished what I set out to achieve. There were a few announcements afterwards—a [$1.7 million] treatment centre, a [$5-million] shopping mall. They know now that if they don't take me seriously, I could do something that's going to bring scorn on government officials and embarrassment to Canada…. I've been here for eight years and only recently has there been any response."

The Peguis band has a long tradition of powerful leadership. Its chiefs have been among the greatest in Manitoba's history. The renowned Chief Peguis, for whom the band is named, led his Saulteaux Indian people from northern Ontario to the wilderness of central Manitoba in the 1790s, searching for a good supply of waterfowl and game. Peguis and his followers reached Lake Winnipeg and then travelled south on the Red River, finally settling at a spot on the banks of the river, just south of the lake, where they began hunting. A few years later, in 1812, they watched the arrival of the first white settlers—the Selkirk settlers, who founded the Red River Colony at the present-day site of Winnipeg.

The families of the Scottish settlers came two years later, in the autumn of 1814. With no winter provisions, they trudged south toward the village of Pembina at the U.S. border. They were cold and exhausted when Peguis and his people took pity on them and volunteered to carry their children to Pembina. It was the first of many acts of friendship from Peguis and his people.

For the next six or seven years, the Indians helped the settlers survive the harsh winters, allowing the Scottish men to accompany them as they hunted in the winter. In 1816, after the homes and crops of the settlers were burned to the ground in a battle with the fur-trading North West Company, Chief Peguis gave the homeless victims enough fish and wild rice to keep them from starving. And for many years afterward, he gave the settlers a supply of buffalo meat to carry them through the worst winters. Lord Selkirk described Chief Peguis as "a steady friend to the Settlement ever since its first establishment." In a letter of gratitude, the Scottish nobleman said Chief Peguis "deserves to be treated with favour and distinction."

In 1817, however, the chief was persuaded to sign a treaty with Lord Selkirk, allowing the settlers to gain access to thousands of square kilometres of land along the Red and Assiniboine rivers. In return, the Indians were given a token gift of one hundred pounds of tobacco a year.

The treaty of 1817 marked the beginning of a long history of injustices to the Peguis band. Shortly after it was signed, Chief Peguis tried to make it clear that the treaty did not represent a sale of Indian land. He emphasized that the Indians were simply permitting the settlers to use the land, with further negotiations to come later. But those negotiations never took place. Lord Selkirk died in 1820, and the complaints of the Indians were ignored by his successors.

In the 1850s and 1860s, as the population of the Red River settlement increased, Chief Peguis demanded a resolution to the ownership question. In 1863, in a statement published in a Red River newspaper, the chief said his people had been tricked into signing the treaty of

1817. "Our lands have not been bought, we have not received payment for them," he wrote.

Chief Peguis died in 1864, when he was about ninety years old. By then, he had been given an English name—William King—which signified his position among his people. His sons and descendants, who took the surname Prince, became respected chiefs, war heroes, and prominent political leaders. One of them, Henry Prince, became the next chief of the Peguis band. In 1871, Chief Prince signed a new treaty, which gave the Indians a reserve at St. Peter's parish, north of the Red River settlement, near the present-day town of Selkirk.

The Indians prospered at the St. Peter's reserve, building farms and schools. But soon there was further pressure from white settlers, who had their eyes on the reserve's prime farmland. Just as the townspeople of Sydney had claimed that the presence of the Micmacs was hampering development, the white farmers and businessmen of Selkirk alleged that the Indians were an impediment to progress. Frank Oliver, the federal Cabinet minister responsible for Indian Affairs, complained that the Indian community near the town of Selkirk was "an open sore".

Hector Howell, the chief justice of Manitoba, was appointed to resolve the dispute. Howell became convinced that the Indians of St. Peter's should surrender their land. In a letter to Frank Oliver, he described the Indian reserve as "a pestilence". Then, in 1907, Howell held a series of three meetings with the Peguis band. But at each meeting, the Indians strongly opposed the idea of surrendering their land. "We will have none of your bait," one Indian told Howell. "We will not leave our land." After the third meeting, the Indians declared that they would not meet with Howell again.

After waiting a few months, Howell suggested another tactic. In a private letter to Oliver, he proposed the use of financial promises to influence the Indians. The band members would have to be approached before the beginning of the winter trapping season, Howell said. "This is their hungry time," he wrote in the letter. "This is the period when the present payment of money is a powerful factor with the improvident."

Howell and the government officials arranged to hold a meeting with the Peguis band members on September 23, 1907—giving the Saulteaux just one day's notice, in contravention of the Indian Act.

Many band members, who were away hunting at the time, never learned of the meeting because of the short notice.

The meeting was held in a school house so tiny that it had room for only half of the two hundred Indians who attended. The other half of the Indian group had to stand outside, unable to hear the speakers at the meeting. Even those inside the school house found it difficult to understand the speeches, because of poor translation into Saulteaux. The officials brought a surrender document for the Indians to sign, but instead of reading it all aloud, they described only a few clauses. Many Indians did not realize what they were being asked to do. However, there was still strong opposition to the idea of surrendering the land, so the officials adjourned the meeting until the following day.

It was later discovered that some of the Saulteaux were bribed with cash and whiskey during the night before the meeting resumed. A number of Indians who had previously opposed the surrender were suddenly found to be supporters the next day.

The voting was carried out by dividing the band into a group of supporters and a group of opponents, and then counting the members in each group. Displaying a satchel full of money, the bureaucrats made it clear that the Indians would receive $5,000 immediately if they agreed to surrender their land. And they promised a further $90 to each band member from the proceeds of the sale of the Indian land. Just before the voting began, a federal official shouted: "Who wants $90, let him go over there." He pointed to the group who favoured the surrender. For many band members, this was the only statement they had properly heard or understood in the entire meeting, and it was a decisive factor in shifting a number of votes.

As the Indians divided into two groups, there was a great deal of confusion and milling about, and some were shoved toward the group in favour of surrender. "We were driven around like cattle," one band member recalled later.

Officially, the vote was 107 to 98 in favour of surrender, but some band members doubted that the count was accurate. The group opposed to the surrender seemed to be the largest group, yet the opponents were not permitted to check the count.

Even if the official tally was accurate, the bureaucrats had failed to obtain the consent of a majority of the adult male members of the Peguis band. There were at least 223 adult males in the band, so the surrender had to be approved by a minimum of 112 members, according to the Indian Act. However, the vote was immediately accepted by the federal government, and the surrender was quickly authorized by an order-in-council. The entire reserve was taken away from the Indians, and the band was forced to move to a remote tract of bush and wilderness on the Fisher River, about 150 kilometres north of the St. Peter's reserve. This isolated site is still the home of the Peguis band today.

Angered by the events of 1907, the Indians protested strongly and began filing lawsuits. Eventually the government agreed to appoint a royal commission to investigate the surrender. After a series of public hearings in 1911, the royal commission concluded that the surrender was illegal because the government officials had followed an improper and unfair voting procedure.

However, the whites who had purchased land on the old reserve lobbied the government intensely to have the surrender legalized. The government stalled for time, and then, in 1916, passed special legislation to confirm the legal title of the land purchasers. With the passage of that legislation, the people of Peguis lost their last hope of returning to the St. Peter's reserve.

Life was difficult at the new Peguis reserve on the Fisher River. For years, the Indians worked tirelessly to build houses and clear the brush from their new land, which was so poor that they had to keep oxen instead of horses, because they could not grow enough good-quality hay to keep horses alive. And food had to be rationed because of persistent shortages.

Meanwhile, land speculators made fortunes by buying and selling land at the old St. Peter's reserve. About 85 percent of the reserve was classified as first-class farmland, worth an estimated $100 million today. Yet the land was sold for just $5 an acre, much less than its market value, and the proceeds gave the Indians less than half of the money they had been promised in 1907.

By the middle of the twentieth century, the Peguis band members were dispirited and demoralized, unable to speak their native language and alienated from their cultural traditions. They had been forced to attend a church-run residential school at Portage la Prairie, where they were prohibited from speaking the Saulteaux language. The

Anglican ministers who dominated the reserve had persuaded most band members to abandon their traditional Saulteaux names and accept Scottish names such as Sinclair, McCorrister, Sutherland, and Stevenson.

By this time, few band members bothered to talk about the surrender of 1907. It was a dead issue, a lost war. They knew it was hopeless to protest. Most of the younger band members had never even heard of the events of 1907.

Louis Stevenson was born into this environment on May 19, 1950. His father, a trapper and farmhand, had lost his fluency in Saulteaux after spending his childhood at a residential school. As a result, Louis Stevenson was unable to learn the language of his own people.

He grew up in a crowded two-room log house on the Peguis reserve with nine other children. He remembers the comforting feeling of falling asleep beside a brother or sister under a blanket on a cold winter night.

After finishing Grade 9 at the reserve school, Stevenson was sent to a Presbyterian residential school in the town of Birtle in southwestern Manitoba, about 250 kilometres from his home. "I couldn't tolerate that system," Stevenson says. "You had to work on their farm every day and every weekend, and you had to go to church three times on Sundays. They even told you what colour of clothes to wear—each day of the week. I went there for a couple of months. I couldn't stand it any longer, so I took off."

For two years, he stayed out of school, working occasionally as a manual labourer, picking rocks out of grainfields for a farmer. But most of the time he was unemployed. At the age of seventeen, he had a nervous breakdown.

"The idleness and the effect of unemployment and having nothing in life to look forward to—that's what brought it on. At that age, my mind still had a lot to learn. A person can't remain stationary. You improve or you get worse. The idleness made me depressed, and that's what caused the breakdown. It was almost like living in a dream world. I couldn't differentiate between reality and day dreaming. Alcohol was part of it. There was nothing else to do."

It took months for Stevenson to recover. The doctors at the nearby hospital were unsympathetic. "They didn't understand. They told me to go home and take some aspirin. I recovered on my own, but it left a lot of scars."

Today he realizes he is still motivated by the memories of his troubled youth. He sees his band members struggling with the legacy of discrimination and unemployment, just as he did. "That's where I get my drive," he says.

Two years after Stevenson ran away from Birtle, he returned to school in the town of Fisher Branch, near the Peguis reserve, where he completed Grade 10 and Grade 11. The school's guidance counsellor recommended that Stevenson be sent to a Winnipeg high school for Grade 12. It was the late 1960s, and the government was expanding its new policy of trying to integrate Indian students into white-dominated provincial schools. Stevenson agreed to enroll. "I found out later that the guidance counsellor thought I was a good candidate for integration," he chuckles.

One day the Winnipeg school organized a mini-Folklorama to showcase the cultural backgrounds of its students. It was a pivotal event in Stevenson's life. "I was never so embarrassed, because I knew nothing about myself, the Indian people, and our history. I made a personal commitment never to be caught in that position again."

After graduating from high school, Stevenson entered a training program in the Indian Affairs Department as an assistant to the district superintendent of education. Then he went to a community college in Lethbridge and obtained a diploma in social counselling. For six years, he worked as a counsellor for Indian students in universities and high schools in Winnipeg who needed guidance on classroom problems and future careers.

But it was not until 1980, when he was offered a job as a counsellor at the Peguis school, that he understood the full effects of the poverty on his home reserve. Children were crying because their parents could not afford to buy them proper clothes, or food for lunch. "That sort of thing convinced me…I'd change things on the reserve or I was going to leave."

Stevenson began to stand up at band council meetings, confronting the incumbent chief and asking tough questions about the priorities of the band's leaders. In 1981, he decided to challenge the veteran Peguis chief in the upcoming band council elections. "I figured the only way I could change those conditions was from the top job—the position of chief." He defeated the chief in a landslide, gaining 75 percent of the vote.

Until then, Stevenson had still been an occasional drinker. But he quit drinking as soon as he became chief. "If I hadn't stopped, I wouldn't be able to suggest to other people that they stop using alcohol. I practise what I preach."

One of the new chief's first decisions was to shut down a garment factory on the reserve. Heavily subsidized by the federal government, the factory had been losing money for fourteen years and showed no signs of becoming profitable. "It was just throwing good money after bad," Stevenson says. "Our resources are scarce. We have to make good use of our resources and produce some results." The chief simply informed the Indian Affairs Department that the band would be closing the factory.

For years, the three thousand Indians of Peguis had been spending their money in the nearby towns of Hodgson and Dallas, draining money out of the reserve. Stevenson wanted to tap into this flow of money and create a self-sustaining economy on the reserve. With the help of grants and loans from several federal programs—obtained after the South African ambassador's visit—the band constructed its $5 million shopping centre, anchored by a band-owned IGA supermarket. All of the shopping mall's eight businesses, including a pharmacy, a hardware store, a restaurant, and a clothing boutique, will be owned by band members. Together, they will employ more than fifty people from the reserve.

By halting the drain of money from the community, the shopping mall has helped reduce the band's unemployment rate to about 60 percent—considerably less than the 90 percent jobless rate that is routine on many Manitoba Indian reserves. "All of the jobs we've created are permanent," Stevenson says. "Nobody can take them away. They're not just short-term make-work projects."

But Stevenson isn't satisfied yet. He knows that about $12 million worth of wages and welfare payments are entering the Peguis reserve every year. By establishing the supermarket, the band has managed to retain $1.8 million of that revenue, and the retail stores in the shopping mall have captured another portion of the money, but most of the $12 million is still flowing to merchants outside the community. Stevenson is also hoping to develop forestry, farming, fishing, and other resource industries. "We want to be sure they are viable industries that will survive."

Meanwhile, Stevenson was mobilizing his community to fight the politicians and the bureaucrats. In 1981, when the provincial and federal governments refused to take action to protect Peguis from the annual spring flooding that had plagued the community for a decade, Stevenson ordered the construction of an illegal dam on the Fisher River to hold back the floodwaters. The dam stayed up for two years, until the governments finally agreed to provide compensation and build dozens of houses to replace those that had been flooded. In 1982 the chief led a series of demonstrations in Winnipeg to protest a severe housing shortage at Peguis, and in the spring of 1984 he persuaded six hundred Indian students to boycott the Peguis school for several weeks to protest the underfunding of education on the reserve.

Later in 1984, Stevenson grabbed headlines again. For years, the band had been complaining about a rotting wooden bridge on the reserve. The bridge had been condemned as unsafe, yet a school bus was forced to travel over it every day. Fed up with waiting for the federal or provincial government to replace the hazardous structure, the chief and five of his councillors simply burned it down. "I figured I would send the government a message," Stevenson says.

The chief and his councillors were eventually convicted of mischief and fined $100 each. But the strategy worked. The province built a new bridge—a non-combustible one.

Despite the improvements Stevenson had brought about, the houses on the reserve were still overcrowded and there was a shortage of funds for economic development, education, health services, and recreation. The Peguis band members marched into the regional office of the Indian Affairs Department on Portage Avenue in downtown Winnipeg, and held sit-ins in the offices of the bureaucrats who worked there. From 1984 to 1986, Stevenson and his band members took over the departmental offices a total of six times. In one incident, five hundred Indians occupied the offices for two days.

The owner of the Indian Affairs building became so frustrated that he obtained a court injunction to prohibit the Indians from "picketing, parading, barricading, or congregating" at the entrances of the eighteen-storey building. Stevenson and his supporters were prohibited from "loitering in the hallways" or entering the premises "with megaphones, drums, communications equipment, or any other sound devices, food, beverages [or] sleeping material." And they were prohibited from entering the building "in such numbers as to, in the opinion of the Plaintiff, deprive the tenants of the building from the reasonable use of elevators, washroom facilities, quiet enjoyment and safety."

Several months later, the Peguis band members returned to the building. Twenty police vehicles immediately surrounded them, and fifteen of the Indians were arrested by Winnipeg police. Stevenson and several other chiefs went to court to challenge the injunction, contending that it was a form of "institutionalized racism", since the Winnipeg police were preventing any Indians from entering the building until they had stated the reasons for their visit. Stevenson argued that the Indians were exercising their rights of peaceful assembly. He pointed out that they were not pushing or harming anyone. But the injunction was upheld, and it remains in force today.

Thwarted by the courts, Stevenson adopted a new strategy. He knew the Indian Affairs Department was more likely to respond to the band's needs if public attention was focused on Peguis. The sit-ins and demonstrations had already helped, and more publicity had been generated in 1986 when Stevenson had persuaded the Indian Affairs minister, David Crombie, to visit the Peguis reserve. So in early 1987 Stevenson invited the South African ambassador to visit the reserve.

It was a daring gamble. Stevenson realized that the invitation would be controversial among white liberals in Canada. The ambassador, Glenn Babb, had already criticized Canada for neglecting its native people. Prime Minister Brian Mulroney, on a tour of Africa, had faced similar questions from Canadian reporters who asked him if he was ignoring the problems of indigenous people in his own country. Mulroney had angrily denied that there was any similarity between the living conditions of Canadian Indians and those of South African blacks.

Stevenson was annoyed that the prime minister was touring through Africa while he paid little attention to Canada's aboriginal people. "He seems to be gung-ho about inspecting conditions in other countries," Stevenson said. "He can do that in his own backyard."

The chief admitted that he was hoping to embarrass the federal government. "I have nothing to lose," he told reporters. "If embarrassing them is the only thing that can light a fire under them, then I'll do it."

Stevenson was quickly criticized by several anti-apartheid groups, who said the Glenn Babb invitation was like an invitation to the Ku Klux Klan to inspect the conditions of blacks. Stephen Lewis, the Canadian ambassador to the United Nations, also opposed the planned visit by the South African ambassador. But the Peguis chief refused to back down. He pointed out that the Indians had been trying to catch the attention of the Indian Affairs Department for years. "We did not invite the Ku Klux Klan to inspect the conditions of blacks," Stevenson said. "We did not invite the Nazis to investigate the treatment of Jews. Unfortunately, we invited the Department of Indian Affairs to investigate the conditions of Indians, which I suppose is just as ridiculous."

In mid-February 1987, Stevenson sent a telex to Mulroney, offering to cancel his invitation to Glenn Babb if the prime minister agreed to visit the reserve. "It is a much shorter trip than flying to Africa," Stevenson said. "Surely our prime minister could extend the same consideration to Canadian Indians to investigate our oppression, substandard living conditions, poverty, welfare dependency and unequal education systems."

Mulroney rejected Stevenson's offer. But in the meantime, Stevenson was gaining support from many Canadian observers. Maurice Strong, the Canadian who headed the United Nations Office for Emergency Operations, said he agreed with the actions of the Peguis Indians. "They are, out of sheer frustration and desperation, seeking ways to draw the attention of Canadians to their plight," Strong said. "There's nothing that can prick the Canadian conscience more than to be equating virtuous Canada with evil South Africa."

Even the conservative *Winnipeg Free Press* rallied to the defence of Louis Stevenson. "Canadians should not be proud of the position of most of the native peoples in this country," the newspaper editorialized. "Louis Stevenson, the forceful and politically astute chief of the Peguis reserve, is quite right to use all the means at his disposal to embarrass Canada before the world about the position of his people."

At the heart of the controversy was the question of whether Canada's treatment of its aboriginal people could actually be compared to South Africa's treatment of its black population. Clearly there are differences—but there are also some disturbing parallels. South African blacks are prohibited from voting in national elections. Canadian Indians have the right to vote—but they were prohibited from voting in federal elections until 1960. South African blacks are segregated from whites. Canadian Indians are not officially segregated—but they are governed by a separate law, the Indian Act, which gives the federal government tremendous powers over every Indian who lives on a reserve. Until recently, South African blacks were restricted from moving freely around their own country. Canadian Indians suffered similar restrictions until the 1950's. They were required to obtain a special permit from their Indian agent if they wanted to leave the reserve, and they could be arrested if they left without permission. Some historians believe the notorious South African "pass laws" were actually inspired by the Canadian system for regulating travel by Indians.

Indeed, there is evidence that the South African government had studied Canada's system of Indian administration in the nineteenth and early twentieth centuries. Some historians believe that South African officials may have used the Canadian Indian reserves as a model for the South African policy of apartheid. These interpretations may be more accurate than Canadians like to think: administrators from South Africa have, in fact, visited Canada several times in the past century to examine the country's Indian reserves. As recently as 1962, for example, a South African ambassador made an extensive tour of Indian reserves in western Canada after he told Canadian officials that he wanted to see how the Indians were maintained in their reserves and how they were administered by the federal government. During the first half of the twentieth century, a large number of former "native administrators" from South Africa were hired by Canada's Indian Affairs Department.

Historically, both the Canadian Indians and the South African blacks were pushed aside as their land was taken over by white newcomers. The blacks and the Indians were shunted into designated areas, known as "homelands" in South Africa and "reserves" in Canada. In both countries, these designated areas were often deliberately located on isolated patches of second-rate land, where farming was difficult and economic development was next to impossible.

More recently, South Africa has enforced strict regulations to control the political and economic activities of its black population. Canadian Indians have more freedom, but their political rights were severely curtailed for most of this century. An amendment to the Indian Act in 1927 made it illegal for Canadian Indians to raise money to finance Indian political organizations or to pursue legal claims against the government. For several decades, Indian organizations were harassed and suppressed by the RCMP and by federal bureaucrats. It remained illegal to raise money for Indian organizations until 1951.

Louis Stevenson, who was fully aware of the parallels between Canadian Indians and South African blacks, had carefully chosen his strategy to highlight those similarities. "I've always picked issues that are valid and legitimate—issues that would generate support," he says. "I'm effective because I hit a raw nerve in the government. I guess they're afraid that the truth is being exposed."

On March 10, 1987, Glenn Babb was helicoptered into the Peguis reserve. As Louis Stevenson greeted him, they were mobbed by dozens of reporters and television crews from across Canada and around the world. They made their way to the Peguis community hall, where Stevenson delivered a long speech about the federal government's neglect of its native people. "The Indian people are the poorest of any minority in Canada," Stevenson told the ambassador as several hundred band members listened intently. "Canada's treatment of its aboriginal people is hypocritical and makes a mockery of the image it portrays to the rest of the world." As he spoke, the chief was interrupted by loud applause and chants of "We want jobs" and "We want freedom". The chants by the band members were perfect television material—and were clearly aimed at the cameras.

Stevenson presented Babb with a formal request for $99 million in foreign aid from the South African government. The reporters were given stacks of reports on the problems of the Peguis band. Then the chief gave Babb a two-hour tour of the reserve. He showed the ambassador a twenty-foot trailer that served as the home for an Indian family and a ramshackle one-bedroom house where an Indian couple lived with their five children. The television cameramen swarmed around the broken-down shacks. "It's the first time so much attention has been directed at an Indian reserve in Canada," Stevenson told the reporters.

The event was a complete success. Stevenson received telephone calls from people across Canada who were moved to express their support for the Indian cause. Donations of money flowed into the Peguis band office. The largest newspaper in South Africa ran a front-page story on Babb's visit, comparing the poverty on the Peguis reserve to conditions in the black townships and homelands of South Africa. And shortly afterwards, the Peguis band received the funding it needed from the federal government for its treatment centre and shopping mall.

Stevenson is always searching for new weapons in his battle with the government. "I never allow myself to develop a pattern that the government can predict. If you keep doing the same things, it's going to lose its effect and the government will be prepared for your next move. The government will never admit it, but every time we've had a sit-in or a protest, we've always come away with additional resources. It's embarrassing for the government to have these issues paraded nationally and internationally. By responding to these issues, it's their way of trying to keep us quiet. If you look around the reserve, you can see the development that has been taking place in the past few years. We would never have had all that if we hadn't gone out and done something about it."

In 1988, the chief organized a protest to intercept the Olympic torch as it was being carried through Winnipeg on its way to Calgary. The protest was a symbol of solidarity with the Lubicon Indians of northern Alberta, who were boycotting the Calgary Olympics because of an unresolved dispute with the federal and provincial governments. Municipal officials in Winnipeg were annoyed by the Indian protest. "We offended the mayor," Stevenson laughs. "He said I didn't have very good manners."

Later that year, Stevenson tried another tactic: confronting the premier of Quebec, Robert Bourassa, as he gave a speech in Winnipeg. Bourassa—a strong supporter of the Meech Lake constitutional accord, which describes Quebec as a distinct society—had just finished his talk when Stevenson stood up and peppered the premier with questions. The television crews sprang into action. "If there's any group of people that should be recognized as a distinct society in this country, it's Indian people," Stevenson said later. "Bourassa was saying that the Québécois have been around for two hundred years and they have to preserve their language and their culture. Well, what about us? We've been here for eight thousand years."

Forty years ago, the people of Peguis passively accepted their treatment at the hands of the government. Today, inspired by their chief, they are well organized and militant. They are ready, at a moment's notice, to charter a bus and travel to Winnipeg for protest rallies. In their history classes, students at the Peguis school study a 595-page report on the illegal surrender of the St. Peter's reserve. When the Manitoba aboriginal justice inquiry held a hearing at Peguis, the school children trooped down to the community hall to listen to Stevenson's presentation. And in the spring of 1989, in defiance of the court injunction, the people of Peguis held another sit-in at the offices of the Indian Affairs Department, protesting the federal government's restrictions on the funding of Indian post-secondary education.

"There's a healthy, positive attitude on the reserve now," Stevenson said. "They have a lot more hope for the future. It took a while, but once they knew what they could accomplish, and the good feeling it gave them, that's when things started happening. We've never looked back."

As conditions improve at Peguis, the chief is turning his attention to one of the most difficult problems in aboriginal politics: the task of uniting dozens of separate Indian bands into a single, powerful movement. The Manitoba Indian Brotherhood had split apart in the early 1980s, fragmenting into regional and tribal groups. "The government was taking advantage of us being divided and fragmented," Stevenson says. "The only way to resolve our problems is to show some unity and a collective approach."

The bands finally came back together in 1988, forming a new organization called the Assembly of Manitoba Chiefs, which has become the lobbying agency and political voice for Manitoba's 60,000 Indians. Louis Stevenson was chosen as the first leader of the assembly. Some called him the grand chief, although he preferred not to use such an exalted title.

Despite his tough rhetoric and his militant tactics, Stevenson knows when to put down his weapons and work quietly within the political system. In the 1988 federal election, he endorsed the local Conservative member of Parliament—a signal of his willingness to deliver votes to the Conservatives in return for their approval of grants and loans for the Peguis reserve. It was the Tories, after all, who had buckled under the strong pressure from the Peguis band in 1987 and 1988, and it was the Tories who had approved the treatment centre and the shopping mall. Stevenson knew how to reward the government.

Stevenson's headline-grabbing tactics and his flamboyant style have provoked criticism from a few of Manitoba's Indian chiefs. "I think they're just too chicken to stand up to the system," he says.

Many chiefs, however, have learned from Stevenson's success. "I've noticed that a lot of Indian leaders are using the media a lot more to expose their situations," Stevenson says. "I think that's necessary. It's unfortunate that many Indian people have become conditioned to be ashamed of their problems, so they're not prepared to expose their circumstances. If we don't expose our problems, we're not going to convince society that there are problems to be rectified."

For years, cautious observers have warned Louis Stevenson to beware of a backlash from the politicians and the public. The chief refused to back down, and today he knows he was right. "There's no backlash," Stevenson says. "People have more respect for Indian people who stand up for their rights, who say they've had enough shabby treatment and they demand fair treatment. If our rights are trampled and we do nothing about it, the public will say we deserve what we get. But if you stand up for your issues and demand fair treatment and get results, people say we deserve what we've received because we've fought for it. People come up to me on the street— native people and white people—and they say it's about time someone stood up for Indian people. They have respect for me. They come up and shake my hand."

Stevenson has travelled across the country and met many of the other leaders of the new Indian militancy. "They're breaking the psychological barrier of being conditioned to think that someone else has to decide what is best for us," Stevenson says. "They're more aggressive. They're shrewd politicians. They've studied and learned the system well enough to play the games and select the most effective strategy. You can negotiate and have meetings and write letters, but if that isn't productive you have to cause some kind of crisis to generate a response. You have to create a situation where the government is forced to act. If anybody's going to do anything to improve our situation, it has to be Indian people themselves—if history tells us anything."

Indian activism has always been an annoyance to the federal government, and for most of the twentieth century Ottawa worked hard to suppress it. Every possible tactic, from financial pressure to police intervention, was used to block the development of Indian organizations. It was not until the 1970s that the federal government finally abandoned its suppression of Indian political activism.

One of the earliest aboriginal organizations, the League of Indians of Canada, was founded at the end of the First World War by F. O. Loft, a charismatic Mohawk from the Six Nations reserve in southern Ontario. By 1919, the league was attracting members from Manitoba and Saskatchewan as well as Ontario. "We as Indians, from one end of the Dominion to the other, are sadly strangers to each other," Loft told his supporters. "We have not learned what it is to cooperate and work for each other as we should; the pity of it is greater because our needs, drawbacks, handicaps and troubles are all similar."

Loft wanted Indians to have the right to vote, greater freedom from government supervision, a new system of secular schools, protected hunting rights, and better economic development on their reserves. Although these goals were modest by today's standards, the Indian Affairs Department quickly took steps to suppress the League of Indians and its work. One of the department's main weapons was its control of band funds. The money theoretically belonged to the Indian bands, but it was kept in a federal trust fund, where the department could veto all expenditures. When a number of Indians asked to use their band funds to cover the cost of travelling to league meetings, the department refused to grant permission. Despite these restrictions, however, the League of Indians had gained 8,000 to 9,000 members in western Canada alone by the early 1920s, and its mass rallies were attended by as many as 1,500 Indians.

Departmental officials described Loft as a Bolshevik who was fomenting unrest. Duncan Campbell Scott, the deputy superintendent in the Indian Affairs Department, ordered his officials to curb Loft's activities. Loft was "posing as a friend and champion of the Indian," Scott said. "What he ought to get is a good snub."

In 1921, in an attempt to destroy the League of Indians by eliminating its charismatic leader, the department proposed that Loft be enfranchised. That is, they would give him the right to vote, but at the cost of his Indian status—a process that was authorized by a 1920 amendment to the Indian Act. The department's plan was thwarted when a new Liberal government repealed the compulsory enfranchisement clause in 1922.

According to historian E. B. Titley, the Indian Affairs Department monitored the league with "a vast network of spies, which included missionaries, police, and subservient Indians." These sources "kept the department's agents informed of the agitator's every move." For example, the department arranged for two RCMP officers to patrol a league rally in Alberta in June 1922. To intimidate the Indians, the police officers made themselves highly visible at the rally. At other assemblies, the RCMP planted questioners in the audience to try to undermine the effect of Loft's speeches.

Loft, like Louis Stevenson, soon learned how to use the media. In 1920 alone, he was featured in the Toronto *Sunday World,* the Toronto *Star Weekly* and the Regina *Leader.* "If anything is responsible for the backwardness of the Indians today, it is the domineering, dictating, vetoing method of the Indian department," Loft told the Toronto *Star Weekly.* "The position and treatment of the Indian today is as if he were an imbecile."

By the late 1920s, Loft was hampered by poor health and old age, but he continued to inspire Indian audiences at rallies across the Prairies, where the league was strongest. In 1931, he attempted to organize a legal challenge of provincial game laws, which had severely restricted the hunting and fishing rights of Indians. In response, the Indian Affairs Department asked the RCMP to gather evidence to prosecute Loft for fraud or for violations of the 1927 amendment which prohibited Indians from raising money for court actions. Shortly after the RCMP investigation began, Loft abandoned his political activism.

John Tootoosis, one of the founders of the Indian political movement in Saskatchewan, lived in fear of the RCMP when he tried to organize the province's Indians in the 1920s and 1930s. He travelled by horse or train from reserve to reserve without the special permit that Indians were supposed to obtain before leaving their home reserve. Always one step ahead of the Mounties, he would pass the hat to raise money for the fare to his next destination.

The so-called "pass system" had been established in 1885 as a departmental policy for Prairie reserves at the time of the Riel rebellion. Originally intended to discourage Indians from joining Riel's insurrection, the system soon became a way of forcing Indians to remain on their reserves. The policy stayed in effect until the late 1950's. It was never legalized by federal legislation, but the RCMP were instructed to enforce the policy as if it were law, and Indian agents threatened to cut off all food rations to any Indian who failed to obtain a permit before leaving the reserve.

In 1933 and 1934, John Tootoosis made plans to travel to a number of Prairie reserves to inform the Indians about their treaty rights. He applied for a permit, but the government refused to give him one. He decided to travel without a permit, despite the risk of arrest. In early 1934, as he was passing through Edmonton on his way to the Driftpile reserve in northern Alberta, the RCMP picked him up, questioned him, and then contacted a federal official, who warned Tootoosis to stay away from Driftpile. After a long argument, the Indian activist was finally permitted to travel to Driftpile, but when he arrived he was interrogated and closely watched by a federal Indian agent.

"It would have been so much easier to subside into the quiet, if stagnant, life on the reserve, to be closer to his growing family and to forget the whole struggle," the biographers of John Tootoosis wrote. "But he simply could not sit back and watch the systematic degradation of his people. And so he continued to plod along the long and lonely roads, often cold and hungry, sometimes penniless, poorly clothed against the bitter prairie winters, hounded by police and agents and threatened by the clergy who saw him as the agent of the devil."

In 1935, Tootoosis asked for a dozen copies of the Indian Act to distribute to Indians. The government gave him two copies. "It is not considered necessary to make a wide distribution of the Act," wrote the bureaucrat who had received the request.

Two years later, another federal agent found Tootoosis travelling without a permit in Saskatchewan. In a report to his superiors in Ottawa, the Saskatchewan Inspector of Indian Agencies explained that Tootoosis "has been absent from his reserve since December without permission.... I instructed the Agent at Crooked Lakes to advise Tootoosis to return to his reserve immediately.... Tootoosis was also warned that he should not be absent from his Reserve without the permission of his Indian agent."

In the late 1930s, when the Indian Association of Alberta was recruiting members, federal agents often threatened to have the organizers arrested. And the chief of the Peguis reserve in Manitoba—a great-great-grandson of the original Chief Peguis—was harassed by the RCMP when he tried to recruit support for a North American Indian organization. The chief, Albert Edward Thompson, was arrested on a charge of trespass when he ventured to another reserve to organize a branch of the organization.

Meanwhile, in southern Ontario, the Iroquois people of the Six Nations reserve had been mobilized by their militant leader, Chief Deskeheh. An eloquent orator and a shrewd organizer, Deskeheh had demanded complete sovereignty for his reserve. Like the Indian leaders of today, he adopted a variety of tactics to advance his cause, including the use of international pressure. While his supporters raised funds by organizing lacrosse games and other activities on the reserve, Deskeheh hired lawyers, lobbied the federal government, travelled to London to petition the British government, met foreign diplomats, petitioned the League of Nations, and generated considerable publicity in the foreign media.

The Indian Affairs Department acted ruthlessly to suppress the threat from Deskeheh. A permanent RCMP detachment was established on the Six Nations reserve to maintain order, and the reserve's hereditary council, which gave Deskeheh his power base, was abolished by a federal order-in-council. Colonel C. E. Morgan, a harsh Indian Affairs superintendent who had previously been a colonial administrator in South Africa, arranged for the RCMP to expel the hereditary chiefs from the council hall.

When Deskeheh died in 1925, even his funeral was monitored, and the RCMP interrogated Indians who attended. But protests continued on the Six Nations reserve. Several years later, when the agitation increased, the RCMP hired an Indian informer to spy on political activities on the reserve.

The government often used its Indian agents to harass and suppress activists. The presence of the federal agents enabled the Indian Affairs officials to keep a watch on the reserves and respond quickly to any agitation. In 1943, for example, an agent informed his superiors that Quebec Indian activist Jules Sioui was organizing a national meeting of chiefs from across the country. A senior Indian Affairs official immediately sent letters to every Indian agent in Canada, ordering them to warn all Indians not to attend the meeting. Jules Sioui was "an agitator and trouble-maker with whom the department has had a great deal of difficulty over a considerable period," the official said. "I sincerely hope that none of the Indians of your agency will waste their time and money by travelling to this meeting."

Restrictions on Indian activism began to decrease after the Second World War. In 1946 Tommy Douglas and his newly elected socialist government in Saskatchewan became the first provincial government to finance an Indian organizational meeting. The National Indian Council, formed in 1954, became the official voice of Canadian Indians in the early 1960s.

The greatest catalyst for post-war political activism, however, was the federal government's attempt in 1969 to eliminate all special Indian rights. In its announcement of its new Indian policy, the government argued that the "separate legal status" of Indian people had "kept the Indians apart from and behind other Canadians." By abolishing the concept of aboriginal rights, the government said it would be giving Indians "full and equal participation in the cultural, social, economic and political life of Canada." It proposed to terminate the reserve system, phase out the Indian Affairs Department, and make Indians a provincial responsibility.

Indian leaders were outraged by the federal plan, which would have released Ottawa from all of its traditional obligations to Indians. They saw it as an effort to assimilate Indians into white society. In response to the White Paper of 1969, native organizations began to proliferate. Indian associations became well organized and outspoken, and they forced Ottawa to abandon the 1969 policy. The National Indian Brotherhood, an offshoot of the National Indian Council, became a major organization with a large office in Ottawa and a staff of about fifty people. The Native Council of Canada, formed in 1970, represented the Métis and non-status Indians.

At the same time, Indian leaders were becoming more militant. Several violent clashes and confrontations took place, including a month-long armed occupation of a municipal park in Kenora by Ojibway activists in July 1974 and a battle between hundreds of Indians and riot police on Parliament Hill in September 1974. Shortly afterward, the RCMP described the Indian movement as the single greatest threat to Canada's national security. The federal government, anxious to defuse this threat, funnelled money to moderate native groups such as the National Indian Brotherhood. As more money became available, native groups began to flourish.

The increasing effectiveness of native political organizations became apparent during the lengthy debate over constitutional reform in the late 1970s and early 1980s when sophisticated lobbying and protest campaigns were undertaken by Indian groups from across the country. The "constitutional express" of November 1980 brought more than a thousand native people by train to Ottawa to lobby their members of Parliament. Others petitioned the Queen and launched court actions. A delegation of three hundred chiefs and elders travelled to London to present their case to British politicians. An estimated $4.5 million was spent to fund the Indian lobby in London. At one point in 1981, several premiers persuaded Ottawa to withdraw aboriginal rights from the proposed constitution, but an angry response from Indian leaders helped to ensure the reinstatement of the clause. The final result was a constitutional amendment that explicitly recognized "the existing aboriginal and treaty rights" of Canada's native people—a major achievement for the native political movement, although most Indian leaders feel the amendment is still too weak.

Today, the major national Indian and Métis organizations have articulate leaders, multi-million-dollar budgets, large numbers of employees, teams of high-powered lawyers and constitutional experts, economic analysts, and media advisers. They have quick access to many of the top bureaucrats and politicians on Parliament Hill. It is a remarkable shift from the situation that existed a few decades ago. "I can remember sitting outside ministers' offices for days at a time because they simply wouldn't see you," says Smokey Bruyere, a veteran leader of the Native Council of Canada. "We don't have to do that kind of thing any more."

Some observers, however, suggest that the federal government has developed a more subtle method of controlling Indian activism. By funding native organizations directly, Ottawa may have co-opted or moderated the most militant of the native leaders. The organizations have become, to a certain extent, creatures of government. "Because the bureaucracies within native organizations are similar to those in government, both can now interact in an orderly, legitimate fashion," University of Calgary sociologist James Frideres has noted. "In addition, the government funding of most native organizations makes them more vulnerable to government control."

Some of the most powerful and imaginative strategies have been adopted by individual bands and regional groups of Indians. The Cree Indians of the James Bay region of Quebec, for example, used a court action to force the federal and provincial governments to negotiate an adequate compensation package to counterbalance the effects of flooding caused by the James Bay hydro project. The Quebec Cree gained full Non-Government Organization (NGO) observer status at the United Nations, allowing them to travel to Geneva to make formal submissions to the United Nations Human Rights Commission. Saskatchewan Métis activist Jim Sinclair has won an audience with the Pope on three separate occasions in the past five years, helping to pave the way for the Pope's sympathetic statements on aboriginal rights in recent years. British Columbia Indian bands have obtained court injunctions to halt mining and logging operations on land they have laid claim to. The Haida Indians of the Queen Charlotte Islands have issued travel permits to tourists to assert their authority on the islands, and they are planning to issue passports to their band members as a symbol of their independence.

A growing number of Indian chiefs are armed with degrees from universities or law schools. They could have stayed in the cities and earned comfortable salaries, but instead they have returned to their isolated reserves to prepare a better future for their home communities. "This is our way of giving something back to the community," Louis Stevenson says. "Once you get into the mainstream, you become aware of the difference in lifestyles and opportunities. You become concerned about your people and your family members who are still back on the reserve. You realize that the reserve is never going to advance itself if all the educated and experienced people keep going out of the reserve."

Most Indian bands are no longer reluctant to use confrontational tactics to protect their land from the damaging effects of industry. In 1985, for example, the Haida Indians blockaded logging roads that were being built in their ancestral homelands on the Queen Charlotte Islands. Their strategy helped force the federal and provincial governments to stop the logging and create a national park on the islands.

In 1988, the Cree people of Lubicon Lake blockaded roads in their traditional territory to halt oil extraction and force a settlement of their long-ignored land claim. The Bear Island Ojibway of northern Ontario have also blockaded logging roads to put pressure on the provincial government to resolve a land claim. And the Innu of Labrador have camped on a runway at Goose Bay airport to protest low-level military flights over their land.

Are confrontational tactics always successful? Certainly they have helped Indian bands at Lubicon Lake, the Queen Charlotte Islands, and Peguis. According to scholars of Indian politics, high-profile public confrontation is one of the most effective strategies for pushing the Indian Affairs Department into action. Richard Ponting, a sociologist at the University of Calgary, has conducted extensive research on native politics. His interviews with senior officials in the Department of Indian Affairs have confirmed that the department tends to respond to Indian bands that succeed in capturing the attention of the media and the politicians. For example, if Opposition politicians are rising in Question Period and demanding to know why the government is mistreating a particular band, regional bureaucrats will often feel pressure from their superiors in Ottawa to increase the band's budget, Ponting says.

Bernard Ominayak admits he never realized what he was up against. He was a Grade 10 dropout, the son of a Cree trapper who lived in a remote log cabin in northern Alberta. Until he was elected chief of the Lubicon Lake band in 1978 at the age of twenty-eight, he had never conducted business with a government official.

Ominayak, a modest man with a soft voice who wears a black baseball cap wherever he goes, had a simple faith in the Canadian system of government when he entered his first meetings with provincial and federal officials. The federal government had made a promise to the Cree people of Lubicon Lake. The elders remembered it—a promise that they would be given a reserve and treaty benefits, just like the other Indians in the province. Ominayak and his people assumed it would be easy enough to draw this promise to the attention of the federal government.

"We believed in justice," he recalls. "We never stole, we never took anything from anyone else. Being brought up that way, we thought we would just have to prove who we were and it would go smoothly. We believed that a wrong would be corrected."

His political education began at those early meetings. "It shocked me when it first happened. I don't think I'll ever get used to it— watching someone sitting across the table from you, telling a straight lie. That's something I don't think I'll ever understand."

In 1940, the federal government had promised to establish a reserve for the people of Lubicon Lake. Now, in the early 1980s, the officials were denying that they had any obligation to the Lubicon Cree. In the meantime, bulldozers and oil exploration crews were roaring through the bush, destroying Cree traplines and scaring away the moose that the Indians had always hunted.

Ominayak had been chosen chief in 1978 because he was one of the brightest and most articulate of the young band members. By 1982, he was facing an almost impossible task: trying to negotiate an agreement for a reserve while his band members saw their way of life disappearing each day. "Everything was happening at the same time," he remembers. "It came at us full-force. You turn one way and there's something there. You turn the other way and there's something else there. It was never-ending."

He knew there could be a violent outburst at any time. "There were some close calls. Some of the trappers were ready to go and hang the bulldozer operators. I had to call meetings to cool them down. I told them, you can't win that way. They'll put you in jail and throw away the key."

The chief persuaded his people to follow a non-violent strategy and channelled his anger into a relentless campaign of court actions, demonstrations, boycotts, lobbying, blockades, media campaigns, and political pressure. Whenever one tactic faltered, he switched to another, having learned that a combination of tactics was the most effective way to keep the pressure on the bureaucrats and politicians. "We move from one thing to another, to try to keep the government off balance."

Ominayak's faith in the justice system soon disappeared. When the Cree went to court, they found themselves facing judges who had previously acted as lawyers for the oil companies. As their court case dragged on, their traplines continued to be bulldozed every day. And so Ominayak learned another lesson: having justice on your side is not enough. "Politics gets into everything—even the courts," he says.

The chief developed some of his most effective techniques by watching the Indian Affairs Department. He saw the department hiring Indians and sending them into native communities as the official representatives of the federal government, thus creating splits and confrontations between Indian groups. So he decided to turn the tables on the department by hiring white consultants who were experts on media relations and lobbying. White advisers were now fighting the white bureaucrats. "We've got to fight fire with fire," the chief says bluntly.

Ominayak learned that television was the most powerful weapon of politics. When he organized a boycott of the Calgary Olympics and when he blockaded the roads that led to the oilfields, he knew that television crews would be sending out his message and helping him build support across the country.

In one of his shrewdest moves, Ominayak decided to retain the services of Fred Lennarson, a former Chicago management consultant who was a specialist in media relations and political strategy. Lennarson helped the Lubicon turn to a new source of assistance: the people of Europe.

Ominayak travelled twice to Europe to gain international support for his cause. In 1983 he won the support of the World Council of Churches, which has provided an annual grant to the Lubicon Indians ever since. Ominayak and Lennarson also persuaded a number of European museums to boycott a cultural exhibit at the Calgary Olympics to protest the plight of the Cree. Eventually they built a network of support from twenty-three organizations in nine foreign countries. Petitions from cities like Bonn and Berlin arrive regularly at the prime minister's office in Ottawa, urging support for the Lubicon band.

Lennarson remembers the first time the Lubicon leaders were invited to Europe to address a congress on aboriginal rights and to drum up support for their cause. "They looked at a globe and they saw the Atlantic Ocean and they weren't quite sure if they were up to this business." But the strategy has succeeded in putting international pressure on Canada. "The activity in Europe has an impact on the Canadian government. The Lubicon have been very creative tactically, and that has caught the attention of the media. These are very politically literate people. They have good relationships with book publishing companies and the governments and the visual media."

Ominayak's biggest triumph came in 1988 when he sat down with Alberta Premier Donald Getty and reached an agreement on the exact size and location of the reserve to be set aside from provincial land for the people of Lubicon Lake. The agreement followed months of intense work, including the five-day blockade of a road into the oilfields that ended in the arrest of fifteen band members. The deal represented a dramatic shift in the official position of the provincial government.

Lennarson marvels at Ominayak's achievements. "He's a true Canadian historical figure. This is a guy who didn't do business in English until 1980, who didn't even know what a government was. It would be like you or I plunked down in China and trying to come to grips with a huge country."

However, the final step would be the hardest. The agreement with the Alberta government had to be followed by an agreement with Ottawa, to ensure the provision of basic community services and economic development programs at the new reserve. The Cree also wanted compensation for the years of damage to their land and the loss of millions of dollars of oil revenue that should have been theirs. By the spring of 1989, the Lubicon and the federal government were deadlocked. The fate of the reserve was still uncertain.

Ominayak, like Louis Stevenson and other native leaders, has also made efforts to bring Canada's aboriginal people together in a united movement. He came up with the idea of a mutual defence treaty to ensure that Indians supported each other in confrontations with governments. In the summer of 1989, the Lubicon chief and eight other Canadian Indian chiefs signed a NATO-style defence pact, requiring its signatories to cooperate in political battles and to send reinforcements whenever requested by bands in confrontations with federal and provincial authorities.

Ominayak acknowledges that the struggle has become a grinding marathon. Sometimes he is weary. His burdens are greater than those of most political leaders. He is much more than just a chief to his people. Everyone in the band looks to him to solve their problems. As one of the few band members who is proficient in written English, he is regularly called upon to help decipher manuals and repair broken appliances. During one round of tense negotiations with the government, Ominayak was frequently called away to help with broken furnaces and similar problems in his community.

Whenever he feels the stresses and strains of the political wars, he returns to the bush to hunt and trap. "It does me a lot of good to go out and stay out even for one night," he says.

And always he talks to the elders. The old trappers are the ones who think of the future of the Lubicon Cree. They encourage Ominayak to keep fighting. The chief knows how they saw their way of life destroyed by the oil exploration. "We had it one day, and then the next day it was gone. It hurts me in a lot of ways when I see our older people who can't do anything now. They have so much experience in their way of life. The knowledge is there, but it can't be used any more because of the damage that has been done. It's sad to see."

In the summer of 1985, the Indian movement seemed to be facing one of its bleakest moments. A deep split had emerged within the Assembly of First Nations. Indian groups from the Atlantic provinces and the Prairies had abandoned the organization, and it was crippled by a $3.6 million deficit. The RCMP was investigating the possible misuse of assembly funds, and the federal government was cutting back its funding. The national unity of Canada's aboriginal people seemed to be collapsing.

It was a difficult beginning for Georges Erasmus, the new leader of the Assembly of First Nations. He was thirty-six years old, a curly-haired Dene from the Northwest Territories, and he had just defeated David Ahenakew of Saskatchewan to become the national chief of the assembly. His victory had provoked the walkout by the Prairie groups, who favoured Ahenakew.

Outsiders may have doubted that anyone could restore the unity and credibility of the national Indian movement. But if they did, they underestimated Georges Erasmus. Throughout his career, many people have underestimated Georges Erasmus.

His reputation is that of a conciliator, an efficient administrator with a prodigious memory for facts and numbers. Yet he can be a fiery speaker and a tireless leader who inspires others to follow. He shocked the nation with a powerful speech in Edmonton in the spring of 1988. "Canada, we have something to say to you," Erasmus said. "We have a warning for you. We want to let you know that you are playing with fire…. If you do not deal with this generation of leaders and seek peaceful solutions, then we cannot promise that you are going to like the kind of violent political action that we can just about guarantee the next generation is going to bring to you."

By 1988, Erasmus had already transformed the Assembly of First Nations. He had eliminated the deficit and the financial trouble. He had brought back the bands from Alberta and the Atlantic provinces, and he was on the verge of completing the assembly's reunification by reaching an agreement with the Saskatchewan Indians.

The Assembly of First Nations is the political voice of Canada's 450,000 status Indians. Its lineage can be traced back to the formation in 1954 of the National Indian Council, a body which originally represented both status and non-status Indians. The council split apart in 1968, and a new group, the National Indian Brotherhood, became the voice of status Indians, while the Canadian Métis Society (later the Native Council of Canada) represented non-status Indians.

Galvanized by the controversial White Paper of 1969, the National Indian Brotherhood remained at the forefront of the Indian movement for more than a decade. In the early 1980s, however, as regional and tribal Indian associations in each province were gaining new strength, the leaders of the NIB decided that the organization should become an association of chiefs, rather than an alliance of bands. The new organization was called the Assembly of First Nations. With an annual budget of about $4 million today, the Assembly has remained an active lobbying force on Parliament Hill and is still a cornerstone of the Canadian Indian movement.

It was into this movement that Georges Erasmus arrived in 1985. Born in Fort Rae in the Northwest Territories, he spent much of his childhood accompanying his parents on hunting and fishing trips. Even before he could handle a net, his father would take Georges along in the canoe to keep him company as he fished. He grew up speaking Dogrib, one of two Dene languages spoken in his family.

His father had spent several unhappy years at a residential school and was determined not to subject Georges to the same experience. So the family moved to Yellowknife, where Georges could go to an integrated school. As a teenager, he became a student activist in the native movement and read everything he could find about the liberation movements under colonial regimes in Africa, Latin America, and Asia. He studied Marx, Mao, the Cuban revolutionaries, and the leaders of the black civil rights movement in the southern United States. "I read everything I could get my hands on," he remembers. And he began to see similarities between the Dene and oppressed groups in the Third World.

After graduating from high school, he became active with the Indian Brotherhood of the Northwest Territories, and in 1976 he was elected president of the brotherhood (which later became known as the Dene Nation). It was a time of ferment for the Dene people. Land claims were a major issue in the north, and Thomas Berger was holding his inquiry into the proposed Mackenzie Valley pipeline. Erasmus fought the pipeline and helped to block it. He was also a key figure in the early land claims negotiations of the Dene Nation.

In 1983, he was elected a vice-chief of the Assembly of First Nations, and two years later he became the national chief. The awards soon followed—the Order of Canada in 1987 and an honorary doctorate from Queen's University in 1989. The principal of Queen's University praised Erasmus for producing "a miracle of re-creation" by bringing the regional groups back into the Assembly.

Constitutional negotiations, including a failed bid for a national accord on aboriginal self-government, were the focal point of his first three-year term in office. But it was his passionate speech in Edmonton on May 31, 1988—the day of his re-election to a second term as national chief—that caught the attention of the Canadian public. His speech warned Canadians that the current generation of Indian leaders "may be the last generation of leaders that are prepared to sit down and peacefully negotiate [their] concerns with you."

Erasmus urged the chiefs of the assembly to become much more aggressive. He spoke of the "warrior societies" emerging at several reserves in Ontario and Quebec. Then he delivered a blunt message to the country. "We say, Canada, time is running out. Our people are not going to sit on the sidelines for much longer. We are not going to accept second-class education systems. We are not going to accept sub-standard housing. We are not going to continue to accept a situation where we know this land is ours and we virtually have to beg to add an inch to our reserves. We are not going to stand for that any longer. We are tired of filling your jails and giving employment to your people to watch us there. We do not like being shot down on your streets.... We say, Canada, deal with us today because our militant leaders are already born."

The speech captured the national spotlight for several days, but from the federal government there was only a stony silence. Bill McKnight, the Indian Affairs minister at the time, made no response. "He just ignored me completely," Erasmus says. "I honestly don't know what he thought about it. I don't think he was paying attention—he couldn't care less. If it's going to happen to future generations, so what, he'll be long gone."

Erasmus has noticed a distinct hardening of federal attitudes toward aboriginal issues in recent years. That, in turn, has led to a mounting frustration among ordinary Indians on the reserves. Some of the most intense native protests in recent times have been spontaneous eruptions from the rank-and-file of the Indian movement.

In the spring of 1989, for example, a group of Indian students in Thunder Bay began a hunger strike to protest the new federal restrictions on Indian post-secondary education. It was a spontaneous action—national Indian leaders had never even suggested it. In fact, the national leaders had suggested the traditonal tactics of sit-ins and demonstrations. But once the hunger strike had begun, the Assembly of First Nations decided to fly the students into Ottawa. As each day of the strike went by, the determined young students became the focus of more attention from television crews and opposition politicians. Soon the pressure on the federal government was almost unbearable.

"It was very effective," Erasmus says. "It was something the government wasn't ready for. It was a new arrow in our quiver. They had never seen it, and they didn't know how to deal with it. They were really under tremendous strain for a long time. There's going to be many other actions like that. By the year 2000, there will be actions that we haven't even thought of yet."

Erasmus remembers how he was perceived as "a long-haired young radical" when he was protesting the Mackenzie Valley pipeline in the 1970s. "That kind of activity nowadays seems pretty mild. With every passing generation, it takes more to catch the attention of the government. Right now, we're leading fairly peaceful, non-violent protests. We may find that, in ten or fifteen years, people like Louis Stevenson and I were not very radical at all. There isn't going to be the patience among our people."

There has been remarkable progress in the native movement in the past decade, Erasmus says. "We now have over 15,000 native students involved in post-secondary education every year, and there's going to be far more than that. In ten years, we'll have professionally trained native people in every walk of life across this country. We'll have a whole new generation, far better trained."

The signs of a quiet revolution are already emerging. "This crop of leaders is not mystified by Ottawa," Erasmus says. "We know exactly how it operates. We could be ministers in government. We could hire deputies, we could run that show, we could take over the $3 billion that Canada spends on Indians annually. All of that nonsense about the Great White Father is long gone. It's a puff of wind from another time. On any day, any issue, any argument, we can hold our own with any premier or prime minister. The generation before me could not have predicted what we're doing now. Virtually every major political leader in this country has to deal with native people. They have to talk to people like myself. And there's far more control in our communities now. There's far more money under Indian control than ever before. The concept of Indian government is an accepted fact—we're just debating what kind of government. It's going to go ahead. We're going to leave a foundation, and it's from there that we're going to launch the next generation."

Epilogue: The Fifth Generation

When the Indian chiefs of the Canadian Prairies signed their treaties in the 1870s, they were starving and demoralized. Their way of life was already disappearing under the pressures of white settlement, disease, and alcohol. But as they signed the documents that surrendered their land to the white man, they looked into the future. In treaty after treaty, they talked about their descendants. They spoke of their "children's children's children's children's children." This vision, which became known as the fifth-generation prophecy, has been widely interpreted to mean that the fifth generation would witness the rebirth of the Indian people. The chiefs were looking toward a day when their people would again have strength and a renewed confidence and pride in their identity.

Five generations have passed since the prophecy of the Prairie chiefs. Today, as the chiefs foresaw, a new era has arrived for native people. Tough-minded leaders like Georges Erasmus and Louis Stevenson have become masters of the game of negotiations and political strategy. They have mobilized their people and asserted their rights in the courts, on the city streets, and on the traplines and lakes. Bernard Ominayak, the soft-spoken chief of the Lubicon Lake band in Alberta, has stubbornly fought for the land his people were promised a half-century ago. Ruby Dunstan, the indefatigable leader of the Lytton band in British Columbia, has helped Indians recover from the terrors of the residential school system. Oscar Lathlin, the man who controls one of the largest shopping malls in northern Manitoba, is carving out a new economic future for the Cree of his band in The Pas.

At the same time, there has been a resurgence of aboriginal culture. Indian and Métis people are reviving their language, their customs, their spiritual beliefs, and their traditional methods of teaching and healing.

On the Nelson House reserve in northern Manitoba, eighty-seven-year-old Nazer Linklater is a medicine man, a traditional Indian healer whose remedies are wrapped in small plastic bundles and hidden in a moose-hide pouch. In a potful of water, he boils dried herbs, roots, muskeg grass, and other plants for his patients to drink. Sometimes he just talks to a suffering band member. "He's a mixture of a psychiatrist, a priest, and a doctor," says Joan MacPhee, a federal nurse at Nelson House.

For many years, the activities of medicine men were suppressed or discouraged by the federal Indian agents and white clergymen who regarded the traditional healers as superstitious heathens. Even today, some medicine men are still secretive because of their memories of the persecution. Sometimes they keep their identities hidden from white officials on the reserves.

Most of the traditional Indian healers, however, are no longer afraid to use their skills openly on the reserves. White doctors and nurses are admitting something that they never would have acknowledged before: medicine men can be as effective as non-native physicians. Many northern nurses are regularly sending their patients to medicine men. The federal Health and Welfare Department, tacitly recognizing the powers of the traditional healers, now voluntarily pays the airfare and travel expenses of Indians who need to visit medicine men at other reserves. A growing number of medicine men and native healers are being hired by hospitals and health centres to work with native patients. And a federal report in 1984 concluded that some of the practices of the traditional healers are "superior to those of modern medicine."

The suppression of medicine men was just one example of the federal government's relentless campaign to stamp out aboriginal culture in the nineteenth century and the first half of the twentieth century.

Many traditional Indian dances and ceremonies—recognized as a vital element in the native cultural and spiritual identity—were outlawed as a result of amendments to the Indian Act in 1884 and 1895. Sun dances, thirst dances, potlatches, and other native ceremonies were raided and shut down by vigilant police officers. The complete assimilation of Indian people was the government's official strategy, and no vestiges of the old way of life were permitted to remain.

In January 1904, an Indian elder from Alberta was found dancing in a traditional Indian ceremony. Although he was more than ninety years old, feeble, and almost blind, he was charged and sentenced to two months of hard labour in prison. The Indian Affairs Department eventually agreed to free the elder because of his age and poor health. But dozens of other Indians were less fortunate. They were fined or jailed for as long as four months for the same crime. The restrictions on Indian dances were tightened again in 1914 and 1918 with new amendments to the Indian Act which made it easier for the government to obtain convictions for spiritual misbehaviour. In 1921, the RCMP raided a potlatch on Vancouver Island, arresting dozens of Indians and confiscating masks and other spiritual objects. Forty-five of the Indians were jailed.

Yet the Indians refused to abandon their culture. Dances and spiritual ceremonies were still held, in defiance of the government. Finally, in 1951, the Indian dances and potlatches were legalized.

Today, the evidence of a cultural revival can be seen across Canada. Native culture is being taught at Indian-controlled schools and even in some provincial schools. Elders are becoming part-time school teachers, passing on their wisdom to the children, while sacred pipe ceremonies and sweat lodges are the cornerstone of daily life at native-controlled colleges and adult education programs. Indian languages are being revived and strengthened by schools on Indian reserves and by institutions such as the Saskatchewan Indian Federated College and the Manitoba Association for Native Languages. Pre-school children in Winnipeg are attending an Ojibway immersion nursery.

Native spirituality has become the focal point of successful new programs to rehabilitate native prisoners and to overcome alcoholism among Indian and Métis people. At the Brokenhead reserve in southern Manitoba, where thirty-three children were orphaned after an alcohol-linked car crash in 1969, band members are now learning about their

Ojibway roots as part of a mental health program developed by the band in cooperation with the Canadian Mental Health Association. School classes and workshops have helped the community regain pride in its culture.

Native leaders are also beginning to recover some of the thousands of spiritual artifacts that were removed from Indian communities in the nineteenth and early twentieth centuries. In British Columbia, for example, an estimated 300,000 totem poles, masks, and other Indian artifacts were purchased or simply stolen by private collectors and international museums. In recent years, native leaders have begun campaigning for the repatriation of the artifacts, which still have a strong symbolic and spiritual significance for native communities.

Native people have fought to get recognition for their culture and spirituality within mainstream churches as well. In 1988, sweetgrass burned in a ritual fire as the United Church established the All Native Circle Conference—a group within the church that will be fully controlled by aboriginal people. The church asked for forgiveness for its suppression of native culture in the past.

The native heritage is an increasingly visible presence in Canadian arts and literature, through the work of talented native people such as composer John Kim Bell, playwright Tomson Highway, and architect Douglas Cardinal. They have helped educate Canadians by translating aboriginal culture into the universal language of the arts—without compromising their own cultural integrity. In his design for the Canadian Museum of Civilization, for example, Douglas Cardinal created a building whose flowing, curved walls evoke a landscape shaped by wind and water.

Until recently, any Indian woman who married a white man automatically lost her Indian status. But native women have lobbied successfully for federal legislation to help these women regain their legal status as Indians. After the legislation was approved in 1985, Indian status was restored to tens of thousands of native women. "It's a wonderful experience when we discover what it is to be Indian," said Mary Davis, a Winnipeg woman who lost her Indian status when she married a white man in 1960 and finally regained it in 1988. "I wanted to tell everyone, 'I am an Indian.' "

For most of the past one hundred years, the Indian reserve system was an effective tool for suppressing native aspirations in Canada. Ironically, however, the reserves have helped preserve native culture. Although the isolation of many of these communities has led to economic difficulties, it has also allowed Indians to resist the forces of assimilation. Now, as native activism has begun to remove the political shackles from Indian land, the reserves can provide a territorial base for self-government in schools, courts, child welfare, social services, policing, and economic development.

Some of these programs are already being successfully administered by Indian bands on their own reserves. "We are a capable people," says Chief David Perley of the Tobique Indian reserve in northern New Brunswick. "We are not children who have to be controlled, guided, and directed by the federal officials. Let us take control of our own life."

One of the greatest obstacles to aboriginal self-government, however, is strong political resistance from provincial governments, especially in western Canada. Existing aboriginal rights were entrenched in the constitutional amendments of 1982, but since then the forward momentum has stalled. At a series of constitutional conferences ending in March 1987, the premiers refused to guarantee the right of aboriginal self-government. They said the concept was too vague, too undefined.

Yet just a few weeks later, those same premiers agreed to the Meech Lake constitutional accord, which gave some remarkably vague and undefined powers to Quebec. The accord gave Quebec the power to "preserve and promote" its "distinct" linguistic characteristics. There was no definition of what exactly this meant. Politicians across Canada later admitted they were uncertain of what powers were contained in the distinct-society clause. The premiers were willing to give these indefinite powers to Quebec, but they complained about the vagueness of the aboriginal proposal.

The Meech Lake accord declares that a "fundamental characteristic" of Canada is the presence of English-speaking and French-speaking people in different regions of the country. In effect, the accord identifies Quebec as the foremost "distinct society" within Canada. It implicitly accepts the old notion of Canada's "two founding races"—the English and the French—and completely ignores the fact that aboriginal people lived in Canada for thousands of years before the "founding races" arrived.

Other government actions in recent years have signalled an increasing neglect of native issues. Confidential government strategy papers have recommended that Ottawa restrain its spending on native people by halting the creation of new reserves and bands, cutting back on the construction of Indian schools, reducing funding for aboriginal groups, refusing to expand social services, and transferring federal Indian responsibilities to the provinces.

In the international arena, federal officials have done their best to weaken any attempt by United Nations agencies to study Indian treaties and the rights of indigenous people. Officials clashed openly with Canadian Indian leaders who tried to persuade the United Nations Human Rights Commission to launch a broad study of treaty rights. The federal officials insisted on an amendment to dilute the study by requiring it to take into account "the socio-economic realities of states and the inviolability of their sovereignty and territorial integrity."

Crippled by government apathy and political resistance, progress on aboriginal rights is stagnating. Improvements in native health and housing and economic development are painfully slow. Frustrations are mounting among native people across the country. Warrior societies have been organized on several of the largest Indian reserves in Ontario and Quebec. A prominent Indian leader in British Columbia urged his people to "confront the military apparatus of this country" if necessary. "You have to be prepared for war," he said.

Canada continues to face international criticism for its neglect of its aboriginal people. At the United Nations, delegates from the Soviet Union and other countries have cited cases of abuse of native people in Canada. "The moments when I was most embarrassed in the human rights field was when our treatment of native people in Canada was thrown at us," says Stephen Lewis, the former Canadian ambassador to the United Nations. He describes the native rights issue as the "Achilles' heel" of Canada's performance on the international scene.

The attitudes of government officials cannot be divorced from those of society as a whole. The politicians who ignore native issues are reflecting the views of voters and taxpayers. Opinion polls suggest that Canadians know little about Indian and Métis people. Indeed, almost one-quarter of those surveyed in a 1986 poll had no idea what the term "aboriginal" referred to. More than half of those polled were completely unaware that aboriginal rights are protected in the constitution. And the level of support for native people had dropped from 1976 to 1986. Richard Ponting, the University of Calgary professor who directed the poll, concluded that aboriginal people remain "a comparatively unknown people" to most Canadians. The gulf between natives and non-natives has created "a modern-day two solitudes," Ponting says.

Aboriginal people continue to face more hostility than any other ethnic group in Canada. The Canadian Human Rights Commission, in its annual report issued in the spring of 1989, concluded that discrimination against native people is at the top of the list of human rights abuses in Canada today. "The situation faced by Canada's native peoples is, in many ways, a national tragedy," the commission reported. "The grand promise of equality of opportunity that forms the central purpose of the Canadian Human Rights Act stands in stark contrast to the conditions in which many native people live."

Racial slurs against Indians and Métis are still common today—even among politicians, public officials, broadcasters, newspaper columnists, and others who would never dream of making such comments against other ethnic goups. One member of Parliament, for example, described Indians who seek federal assistance as "mentally deficient." He was re-elected and continues to stand by his contention that Indians should "take [their] part of North America and bog off." Another MP made similar comments in 1988. "I think that all the Indians should be all sent to Labrador, to all go live together and have peace and leave us in peace," the MP said. And a senator remarked that the government could solve Indian problems more easily "if they just did what they did in Newfoundland and shot them all."

Meanwhile, a radio broadcaster in Niagara Falls described Indians as "slovenly, lazy bums" whose ancestral dress is "childish and immature." Another broadcaster in Vancouver made racial slurs against Indians in 1985. When he apologized for the comments, his radio phone-in show was flooded with calls from people who said he should never have apologized. A newspaper columnist in Winnipeg referred to Indians as "redskins" and declared that "the average Canadian Indian is a drunk, a wastrel, an idlemonger, a person who is only too happy to live on a government cheque, an in-breeder, a parasite...." A columnist in Vancouver accused Indians of "whining and cadging." And a magazine columnist in Alberta said that Indian culture is "uniquely deplorable."

None of this is intended to deny that progress has been made in educating non-native Canadians about aboriginal rights and other native issues. There is certainly greater tolerance than there was a few decades ago. Yet the racism persists. It is a constant reminder of the attitudes that played such a crucial role in white society's suppression of native culture.

The title of this book alludes not only to the loss of aboriginal land. It also refers to the social attitudes and government policies that aimed to assimilate native people, leaving them dispossessed of their culture, their language, their children, and their power of self-determination.

The cultural revival among aboriginal people is just one step toward regaining what has been lost. Self-government is the other key to the future of native people. When they are permitted to gain influence over the central institutions in their communities—the schools, the justice system, the child welfare system—Indian and Métis people have already demonstrated that they can repair the damage caused by centuries of racism and neglect.

Even at the Shamattawa reserve in the wilderness of northeastern Manitoba, the first steps toward self-government are helping to launch the long process of healing. By the middle of 1988, a series of reforms was quietly transforming the community. The ancient crank telephones at the Shamattawa band office were replaced by modern direct-dial phones—but that improvement was soon overtaken by more profound changes. Sam Miles, the bright and energetic son of Judah Miles, became chief of the Shamattawa band. The new federal school at Shamattawa was beginning to improve the quality of life in the community. For the first time, the children had a gymnasium and a skating rink—an alternative to gas sniffing and crime. And in September 1988, the people of Shamattawa took control of the school.

Their first decision was to recruit a greater number of Indian teachers who could speak Cree. They hired a full-time native culture instructor and established a board of directors from the community to run the school. They created a fund to pay for student trips, camping, and outdoor education.

The results soon became obvious. As more and more children flocked to school each morning, the attendance rate increased from 60 percent to 82 percent by 1988. In the last six months of 1988, the RCMP reported that the youth crime rate declined by 79 percent. The number of gasoline sniffers dropped dramatically.

For many years, the bureaucrats in Winnipeg had doubted that Shamattawa could administer its own $2 million education program. "The Department of Indian Affairs thought I was crazy," Sam Miles says. "We fought for seventeen years to get this school. Now we finally own something we can be proud of. The kids like coming to school. They like their teachers. And the children can see that we're running our own school. The kids respect it now, because this is their classroom now and it's controlled by them. We proved to everybody that we are capable."

Shamattawa became suffused with a curious combination of Christianity and traditional native spirituality. Many of the people—including Sam Miles—became born-again Christians. At the same time, they often travelled outside Shamattawa to attend pow-wows. "I don't think the Bible says you can't go to a pow-wow," Sam Miles muses. "Without guidance from the Great Spirit, you cannot do anything."

The gasoline plague has fallen into decline, but it has not disappeared. There is still a core of children who continue to sniff gas. Others have switched to plastic wood, nail polish, and hairspray—often obtained by mail order. "The police can do nothing," says Sam Miles. "It will never go away. If there's a family of ten and maybe three or four of them are sniffing, then if they really try hard, maybe two or three of them will quit. But there will always be one left."

Although the youth crime rate has been reduced, the rate of crime among adults has remained high. In the last six months of 1988, the adult crime rate increased by 4.9 percent. A few days before Christmas, two Shamattawa residents died from the effects of drinking gas-line antifreeze. Ten others from Shamattawa were sent to hospital as a result of the same incident. They had found the antifreeze in a plastic bottle on the reserve and thought it was vodka.

In the spring of 1989, Manitoba's aboriginal justice inquiry came to Shamattawa. Murray Sinclair and A. C. Hamilton—the two judges heading the inquiry—sat behind a wooden table in the school gymnasium and listened to Sam Miles as he talked about the problems of a justice system imposed on Shamattawa from outside the community. He recalled the court officials who had refused to hold trials in Shamattawa because they objected to the absence of modern toilets in the drop-in centre where court cases are heard. He described the plight of band members who were stranded in Thompson for weeks because they could not afford the cost of airfare to return to Shamattawa after their court cases had ended. The Indians had been forced to use their welfare money to survive in Thompson while their children sat at home in Shamattawa without money to buy food.

Later, in a conversation at the end of the day, Sam Miles gave a glimpse of his vision of the future. He spoke of the need for training programs to help his people become police officers, alcohol and drug counsellors, and social workers. He wants a treatment centre on the reserve, so that Shamattawa's youths can remain in the community when they need help. He dreams of a native-run court system, a locally controlled police force, and perhaps a tourist lodge for economic development. "The community has to run its own affairs," Sam Miles says. "We have to be given the opportunity to do that."

When the opportunity comes, they will be ready. Across Canada, a generation of native leaders has begun blazing a path toward an era of self-government and economic revitalization. There are chiefs and visionaries like Sam Miles at every reserve in the country.

"Aboriginal people are not without hope, for we are strong peoples," says Judge Murray Sinclair. "We have overcome seemingly insurmountable obstacles in our long and painful histories, because our creator has given us the tools necessary for our survival. We must not be shy to use them. We must no longer feel the shame and fear that our grandmothers and grandfathers felt about what we are and where we have come from. We must look to ourselves for our own guarantees, for we are the only ones that we can trust to ensure that our needs are met."

Postscript

When I completed this book a year ago, the warning signs were everywhere. The anger and frustration of Canada's aboriginal people was dangerously close to the boiling point. There were bitter protests by Indians who had seen their friends and relatives killed by police bullets or jailed by a discriminatory justice system. There were hunger strikes and sit-ins by native students whose dreams had been crushed by Ottawa's budget cuts. There were highway barricades and tense confrontations between Indian bands and the oil companies and loggers whose relentless activities were destroying the traditional economy of hunting and fishing. Across the country, from Lubicon Lake to James Bay, from Labrador to Temagami, the pent-up rage of aboriginal people was obvious to anyone who looked.

Canada's elected officials chose to ignore those warning signs. In the spring and summer of 1990, they finally paid the price for their neglect. And the price was steep: the demise of the Meech Lake Accord and the death of a police officer in Oka, Que. Because of their failure to understand the anger of aboriginal people, Canada's political leaders were left with a disintegrating nation.

Much of the anger could be traced back to 1987. That was when Canada's first ministers refused to entrench the simple notion of aboriginal self-government in the Canadian Constitution. Just a few weeks later, those same first ministers drafted the Meech Lake Accord, giving Quebec the kind of recognition that was consistently denied to aboriginal people. Meech Lake was the official perpetuation of the myth of "two founding races." It defined Canada as a duality— English and French—and it ignored the people who had lived in Canada for thousands of years before the arrival of the Europeans.

Aboriginal people fought vigorously against the Meech Lake Accord. The politicians gave them a polite hearing—and then the natives were disregarded. For three years, their concerns were treated as a trivial matter. In early June of 1990, when Canada's first ministers held a marathon negotiating session in Ottawa to settle the Meech Lake question, it was again the aboriginal people who were forced to wait outside on the street. They were kept in the dark, locked out of the private negotiations, while their rights were bartered by eleven white men who saw aboriginal issues as just another bargaining chip.

When a deal was struck, it was the aboriginal people who were told to wait for a future bargaining round. The politicians assumed, once again, that the anger in Indian country could be safely ignored. This time, they were wrong.

The supporters of Meech Lake failed to understand the growing strength of the Indian movement. Aboriginal leaders were determined, intelligent, sophisticated, and resourceful. On June 12, just three days after the constitutional deal in Ottawa, dozens of Indian chiefs from across Manitoba travelled to Winnipeg to formulate a plan. They mapped out a nine-point strategy to kill Meech Lake.

At first, few people took them seriously. But soon it was clear that the chiefs had adopted a brilliant strategy, exploiting Manitoba's legislative rules and the shortage of time before the June 23 deadline. They hired a procedural expert to determine the best tactics for blocking Meech Lake in the legislature. They recruited thousands of natives to form a time-consuming parade of speakers at the public hearings that Manitoba was legally required to hold. They hired lawyers to prepare a possible court challenge. And in the most crucial move of all, they persuaded Elijah Harper to spearhead their attack on Meech Lake.

Elijah Harper was the former chief of Red Sucker Lake, an impoverished Ojibway-Cree community in northeastern Manitoba. A quiet but eloquent man who wears his jet-black hair in a long braid, Harper had been the MLA for the vast northern riding of Rupertsland since 1981. Like most aboriginal people, he had nothing to lose in the

Meech Lake debate. The threats of separatism in Quebec and inst-ability in the money markets—the pressure tactics that had worked so effectively against every other opponent of Meech Lake—were irrelevant to aboriginal people on reserves where the unemployment rate was 90 per cent. They knew their conditions could not possibly get any worse. It was the anger of these aboriginal communities that fueled Elijah Harper's decision to fight the Meech Lake Accord.

The top federal officials in Ottawa were baffled by the Manitoba chiefs. For a while, they assumed that the chiefs were simply trying to extract a few concessions from the government. They assumed that the aboriginal leaders would succumb to the pressure-cooker negotiating tactics that had eventually defeated the dissident premiers at the Ottawa bargaining sessions. But the Manitoba chiefs were seeking something more profound: a deep and fundamental shift in Canadian power relationships, forcing the country's political leaders to stop ignoring Indian people.

I remember the frustration and bewilderment on the face of Sena-tor Lowell Murray after his failed efforts to persuade the Manitoba chiefs to accept Meech Lake. He had hoped to establish a negotiating session with the chiefs, allowing him to recreate the same pressure-packed conditions that led to the constitutional deal in Ottawa on June 9. The chiefs, however, had anticipated the federal strategy. After pleading with the chiefs for an hour, Lowell Murray was politely ushered out of the meeting room. For once, the tables were turned. The federal officials were impotent and the aboriginal people held all the power.

The chiefs showed Canadians that power could be exercised in a principled way. By rejecting an offer of minor concessions from the federal government, they proved that their opposition to Meech Lake could not be bought off by short-term rewards. "We're going to put ethics into the political process," a native lawyer said.

All of the actions of the Manitoba chiefs were formulated in a traditional system of consensus-building and collective decision-making. It was a unique form of democracy, with roots that stretched back for thousands of years. Nobody could impose any decision on the chiefs. Each issue was discussed collectively, with the debate moving around the table until each chief had said as much as he wanted to say. The discussion continued until a consensus emerged. The chiefs continually consulted their elders and the ordinary people in their communities to ensure that their decisions were broadly supported. It was a method that could serve as a model for democracy in Canada.

The successful battle against Meech Lake transformed Elijah Harper into a national hero. It generated a tremendous outpouring of public support for the Indian cause. The Manitoba chiefs received as many as 600 telephone calls of support per day from non-native Canadians. And the battle achieved something else: it united Indians from across Canada, pulling them together in an alliance to rally around Elijah Harper. By killing Meech Lake, the aboriginal leaders had put themselves in a much stronger position. They had proven themselves to be powerful, united, tenacious, and increasingly capable of winning public support.

On the evening of June 23, when Meech Lake officially died, more than 200 aboriginal people gathered on the grounds of the Manitoba Legislature to hold a candlelight vigil. It was a solemn and moving ceremony. Elders prayed in the Ojibway language. The Indians sang a Cree song of thanksgiving, and they gathered in a circle to hold their candles silently aloft under the dark Prairie sky. "We're here to celebrate the rebirth of our people and the death of Meech Lake," said Phil Fontaine, the calm and dignified leader of the Manitoba Assembly of Chiefs. "It's never going to be the same. There's been a change in the consciousness of the Canadian people. We have a hopeful future now, a bright future."

In the tradition of the aboriginal people, anyone is allowed to speak when the people are gathered in a circle. One of those who stepped forward to speak was Sydney Garrioch, chief of the Cross Lake Band in northern Manitoba. "Next time, we will not be forgotten," he told the gathering. "We went through a hardship, but we never hesitated. We were proud of what we were doing."

The growing unity and strength of Canada's aboriginal people was demonstrated again in the summer of 1990, when the Quebec police attacked a Mohawk barricade in the peaceful town of Oka. The barricade was intended to prevent the expansion of a golf course onto the ancestral land of the Mohawks. Across the country, thousands of Indians rallied to the defence of the Mohawks. At the nearby Kahnawake reserve, Mohawks blocked the Mercier bridge, cutting off a major artery to Montreal. In native communities throughout Ontario and Quebec, aboriginal people organized convoys of food and emergency supplies for the Mohawks. In western Canada and northern Ontario, Indian bands established their own blockades of highways and railway lines to show their support for the Mohawks and to press for a resolution of their own longstanding grievances.

Federal officials and Quebec politicians were quick to accuse the Mohawks of being ''criminals'' and ''terrorists.'' The Quebec police refused to allow food to be delivered to the Mohawks—even after the food blockade was condemned by human rights groups. The residents of Chateauguay, unable to tolerate a delay in their commuting to Montreal, went on wild riots and burned the Mohawks in effigy. Media commentators, obsessed by the masks and semi-automatic weapons of the Mohawk warriors, talked incessantly of the need for law and order. But almost everyone ignored the basic underlying issue: Canada's failure to resolve the legitimate land claims of aboriginal people.

For decades, the Mohawks of Kanesatake (the native community near Oka) had been crowded onto tiny parcels of land. Convinced that they had been cheated of their rightful land, the people of Kanesatake had tried to follow the official rules to resolve their grievance. They filed a land claim in 1975, but it was rejected by the federal government almost immediately. They filed another land claim in 1977. This time the government delayed its decision for nine years— and then it again rejected the claim. Only after the violence at Oka in 1990 did the government finally take concrete steps to provide the land that the Mohawks so desperately needed.

The delays were typical of Ottawa's handling of land claims across the country. For many Indian bands, justice was almost impossible to obtain. Federal officials have privately admitted that hundreds of Indian bands have a morally valid claim to a larger land base. Virtually every band in the country has suffered the loss of reserve land as a result of railway expropriations, highway construction, urban encroachment, or the simple theft of their land by early settlers. Yet despite the acknowledged legitimacy of their claims, it can take a decade or longer to resolve a single case.

The government has adopted a rigid and legalistic set of criteria to determine whether a claim should be accepted. Claims are often rejected for technical reasons, even if they are morally legitimate. The federal budget for specific land claims has been steadily reduced (after taking inflation into account). Of the 578 specific land claims that have been filed in the past two decades, only 44 have been resolved to the satisfaction of the Indian bands. At the current slow pace, it will take another 40 years to clear the backlog of land claims.

"It seems that the only time real progress is made in claims negotiations is when there is pressure of some kind... when there is court action or when development is being held up," said Murray Coolican, the former head of a federal task force which reviewed Ottawa's policy on comprehensive land claims.

In 1985, the Coolican task force had recommended a broader and fairer set of criteria for determining whether Indian claims should be accepted. But the government rejected the recommendation. By stifling the legitimate claims of the aboriginal people, Ottawa made it almost inevitable that communities such as Kanesatake would eventually respond with violence. "You close off the channels of peaceful and legal negotiation... and you provoke violence," said University of Toronto professor Peter Russell, a member of the Coolican task force. He said the government's handling of Indian land claims was "a classic recipe" for violence.

The death of Meech Lake and the violent confrontation at Oka were just a foreshadowing of the potential consequences of the anger in Canada's aboriginal community. Ultimately, the frustration and rage of the aboriginal people is the result of centuries of persecution by Canada's official institutions. They have been patient for hundreds of years. As their unity and their determination grows stronger, they will begin to turn their attention to the injustices of recent history. They will seek compensation for the evils of residential schools and the destructive effects of hydro flooding. They will refuse to accept the slum housing and the lack of running water on their reserves. They will demand reforms to the child welfare system and the justice system. And if Canada continues to ignore the warning signs, the anger of the aboriginal people will be felt again.

In the hot days of August, in that eventful summer of 1990, a visitor from South Africa came to a remote Indian reserve in northwestern Ontario. The visitor was Archbishop Desmond Tutu, the anti-apartheid leader who has fought injustice in South Africa for decades. In his eloquent words to the Ojibway people of the Osnaburgh reserve, he remarked on the similarities between Canada's treatment of its aboriginal people and South Africa's treatment of its black majority. "When your nation lives a lie, God cannot allow that lie to prevail," he told the Ojibway band. "Because your cause is just, it will prevail. One day, you will be free in the way you want to be free."

When he toured the Osnaburgh Reserve, Tutu saw the same squalor and deprivation that he had seen in the townships and ghettos of South Africa. He saw flimsy shacks of wood and plastic with two or three families crowded into them. He saw the lack of running water and the diseases that resulted from the absence of basic sanitation. The people of Osnaburgh are forced to live "as if they were dirt," he said. "It distresses me. How is it possible anywhere?"

It was extraordinary that the Ojibways could still remain human under those living conditions, Tutu said. Yet the Osnaburgh Reserve is typical of hundreds of Indian reserves across Canada. The aboriginal people of Canada, like the blacks of South Africa, have always been ignored and neglected by the official insitutions of their society. It is a peculiar state of invisibility. "You are there and yet you are not there," Tutu told the Ojibways.

Today, the invisibility of Canada's aboriginal people is finally beginning to end. In this country, as in South Africa, a growing number of the indigenous people are turning to radical and militant tactics. For many, it has become the only way to gain the attention of the government. And the strategy is beginning to succeed. "Even when people have been oppressed and stood upon for years, one day they will stand up and enjoy their freedom," the South African bishop told the people of Osnaburgh. And then he led the Ojibways in a familiar chant—a chant from South Africa. The bishop and the Indians shouted it together: "We will be free."

Geoffrey York
Ottawa
September 1990

Acknowledgements

I am grateful to the *Globe and Mail* for its continuing interest in native issues and its willingness to give me the time and resources to track down native-related stories in many regions of the country.

I am indebted to Brian Maracle for his help at several stages of my research. His comments on the first draft of the manuscript were invaluable.

I would like to thank Malcolm Lester, Louise Dennys, Catherine Yolles, and Kathryn Dean for their support and editorial assistance in this project.

Lisa Patterson and Francis Johnston have allowed me to quote from their university theses, and I appreciate their help.

I would also like to thank Sandro Contenta, Brian Preston, David Johnston of Peter Livingston Associates, and especially Maria Bohuslawsky.

A Note on Sources

Most of the research for this book was conducted in personal interviews with hundreds of native people at about forty reserves and Métis communities across the country. Evidence given at provincial and federal inquiries constituted another major source. Historical information came from studies, interviews, theses, academic journals, and government records. The research was supplemented by information from newspaper and magazine articles. Following is a summary of the key written sources for each chapter.

Chapter 1 — Shamattawa: The Gasoline Plague

Among the international studies on gasoline sniffing are Fred Beauvais, E. R. Oetting, and R. W. Edwards, "Trends in the Use of Inhalants among American Indian Adolescents," *White Cloud Journal* (1985) 3, no. 4: 3-11; Arthur Kaufman, "Gasoline Sniffing among Children in a Pueblo Indian Village," *Pediatrics* (1973) 51: 1060-64; B. Nurcombe et al., "A Hunger for Stimuli: The Psychosocial Background of Petrol Inhalation," *British Journal of Medical Psychology* (1970) 43: 367-74; Martyn Gay et al., "Drug Abuse Monitoring: A Survey of Solvent Abuse in the County of Avon," *Human Toxicology* (1982) 1; 257-63; David Skuse et al., "A Review of Solvent Abusers and Their Management by a Child Psychiatric Out-patient Service," *Human Toxicology*

(1982) 1: 321-29; and Joyce M. Watson, "Solvent Abuse by Children and Young Adults: A Review," *British Journal of Addiction* (1980) 75: 27-36.

The major study of gas sniffing in northern Manitoba was prepared by Bob Moore Native Consultants and submitted to Manitoba Keewatinowi Okimakanak Inc. of Thompson, Manitoba, in 1986. Other useful studies include Gordon Barnes, "Northern Sniff: The Epidemiology of Drug Use among Indian, White and Métis Adolescents," Final report to Health and Welfare Canada, 1980; and Gary Remington and Brian Hoffman, "Gas Sniffing as a Form of Substance Abuse," *Canadian Journal of Psychiatry* (1984) 29: 31-35.

Chapter 2 — From Lytton to Sabaskong Bay: Fighting for the Schools

John Kelly's thesis on the takeover of the Sabaskong school, submitted to the University of Manitoba for his master's degree, was a valuable source on the Sabaskong experience.

Much of the historical information about Indian residential schools came from E. Brian Titley, *A Narrow Vision: Duncan Campbell Scott and the Administration of Indian Affairs in Canada* (Vancouver: University of British Columbia Press, 1986); Robin Fisher, *Contact and Conflict: Indian-European Relations in British Columbia, 1774-1890* (Vancouver: University of British Columbia Press, 1977): Jane Willis, *Geniesh: An Indian Girlhood* (Toronto: New Press, 1973); Jean Barman et al., *Indian Education in Canada, Vol. 1* (Vancouver: University of British Columbia Press, 1986); Basil Johnston, *Indian School Days* (Toronto: Key Porter, 1988); Celia Haig-Brown, *Resistance and Renewal: Surviving the Indian Residential School* (Vancouver: Tillacum Library, 1988); Eric Robinson and Henry Bird Quinney, *The Infested Blanket: Canada's Constitution—Genocide of Indian Nations* (Winnipeg: Queenston House, 1985); Anastasia Shkilnyk, *A Poison Stronger Than Love: The Destruction of an Ojibwa Community* (New Haven: Yale University Press, 1985); and Ronald Wright, "Beyond Words," *Saturday Night*, April 1988, pp. 38-46.

Information on sexual abuse in native communities came from "B.C. Natives Criticize White Men's Laws as Inappropriate," *The National*, Canadian Bar Association, May 1988.

Annual reports of the Department of Indian Affairs from 1904 to 1916 were a major source of information on the residential school at Lytton, B.C.

The judge's ruling in the Derek Clarke case is Judge William Blair, *Proceedings at Sentencing*, Provincial Court of British Columbia, April 20, 1988.

For current issues, sources include Barbara Burnaby, *Language and Education among Canadian Native Peoples* (Toronto: Ontario Institute for Studies in Education, 1982); *Recent Developments in Native Education* (Toronto: Canadian Education Association, 1983); David R. Hughes and Evelyn Kallen, *The Anatomy of Racism: Canadian Dimensions* (Montreal: Harvest House, 1974); Jean Barman et al., *Indian Education in Canada, Vol. 2* (Vancouver: University of British Columbia Press, 1987); G. McDiarmid and D. Pratt, *Teaching Prejudice* (Toronto: Ontario Institute for Studies in Education, 1971); *Indian Control of Indian Education* (Ottawa: National Indian Brotherhood, 1972); *Edmonton Journal*, June 20, 1984, p. A1, and June 26, 1984, pp. A1 and A6; and *Globe and Mail*, May 23, 1983, p. 4, and May 25, 1983, p. 4.

Chapter 3 — Inside the Reserves

Analysis of the Indian Act and the reserve system is based partly on the *Report of the Special Committee on Indian Self-Government in Canada* (Ottawa: Queen's Printer, 1983); Thalassa Research Associates, "The Economic Foundation of Indian Self-Government," Victoria, 1983; Donald Purich, *Our Land: Native Rights in Canada* (Toronto: James Lorimer, 1986); Edward Ahenakew, *Voices of the Plains Crees* (Toronto: McClelland and Stewart, 1973).

The history of the Micmacs is drawn from L. F. S. Upton, *Micmacs and Colonists: Indian-White Relations in the Maritimes*, 1713-1867 (Vancouver: University of British Columbia Press, 1979); Virginia Miller, "The Micmac: A Maritime Woodland Group," in *Native Peoples: The Canadian Experience*, ed. R. Bruce Morrison and C. Roderick Wilson (Toronto: McClelland and Stewart, 1986); and Fred Wien, *Rebuilding the Economic Base of Indian Communities: The Micmac in Nova Scotia* (Montreal: Institute for Research on Public Policy, 1986).

Much of the historical information on the Membertou reserve came from the files of the Union of Nova Scotia Indians, from records kept by Helen Martin of Membertou, and from *Micmac News*, January 1975, p. 5.

The best source on the centralization episode is Lisa Patterson, "Indian Affairs and the Nova Scotia Centralization Policy," M.A. thesis, Dalhousie University, 1985. Further information is found in Fred Wien, *Rebuilding the Economic Base of Indian Communities* (Montreal: Institute for Research on Public Policy, 1986); and in various documents in the files of the Union of Nova Scotia Indians.

A good overview of Indian living conditions is given in *Indian Conditions: A Survey* (Ottawa: Department of Indian Affairs, 1980). Other sources include James Frideres, *Native People in Canada: Contemporary Conflicts* (Toronto: Prentice-Hall, 1983); and J. Rick Ponting, ed., *Arduous Journey: Canadian Indians and Decolonization* (Toronto: McClelland and Stewart, 1986).

Sources on housing conditions include *Indian Housing and Living Conditions* (Ottawa: Assembly of First Nations, 1987); Ekos Research Associates, *Evaluation of the On-Reserve Housing Program* (Ottawa: Assembly of First Nations, 1985); Stewart Clatworthy et al., *Overview of Housing Conditions of Registered Indians in Canada* (Ottawa: Department of Indian Affairs, 1987); the Manitoba Association for Rights and Liberties, "*Asserting Native Rights in the Housing Maze*," paper presented to Workshop Conference on Native Rights, Winnipeg, 1981; and Manitoba Association for Rights and Liberties, "Update on Racial Discrimination in Housing," paper presented to Human Rights Advocacy Housing Conference, Winnipeg, February 19-20, 1988; "Special Report on Natives in Saskatoon," *Saskatoon Star-Phoenix*, October 7, 1986.

Studies on native health conditions include T. Kue Young, "The Canadian North and the Third World: Is the Analogy Appropriate?" *Canadian Journal of Public Health* (1983) 74: 239-41; Donald A. Enarson et al., "Incidence of Active Tuberculosis in the Native Population of Canada," *Canadian Medical Association Journal* (1986) 134: 1149-52; T. Kue Young, "Epidemiology of Tuberculosis in Remote Native Communities," *Canadian Family Physician* (January 1982) 28: 67-74; T. Kue Young, "The Health of Indians in Northwestern Ontario:

A Historical Perspective," in *Health and Canadian Society: Sociological Perspectives*, 2nd ed., ed. David Coburn et al. (Toronto: Fitzhenry & Whiteside, 1987); Diana Ralph, "Faulty Prescription for Northern Native People," Faculty of Social Work, University of Regina, 1984; *Indian Mental Health Research Formulation* (Winnipeg: First Nations Confederacy, 1985); *Issues for Health Promotion in Family and Child Health: A Source Book* (Ottawa: Department of Health and Welfare, 1985); Brian Postl et al., *Report of the Subcommittee on Indian Health Care* (Winnipeg: Manitoba Health Services Review Committee, 1985); T. Kue Young, "The Decline and Persistence of Tuberculosis in a Canadian Indian Population," *Canadian Journal of Public Health* (1988) 79: 302-6; and an unpublished report on health conditions by Union of Nova Scotia Indians (1980).

The analysis of economic development is based partly on Paul Driben and Robert Trudeau, *When Freedom Is Lost: The Dark Side of the Relationship between Government and the Fort Hope Band* (Toronto: University of Toronto Press, 1983); Fred Wien, *Rebuilding the Economic Base of Indian Communities: The Micmac in Nova Scotia* (Montreal: Institute for Research on Public Policy, 1986); Thalassa Research Associates, "The Economic Foundation of Indian Self-Government," Victoria, 1983; and *Globe and Mail*, October 24, 1987, p. B1.

Chapter 4 — Hobbema: Oil and Suicide

Historical information on Hobbema is from A. Bert Reynolds, *Siding 16: An Early History of Wetaskiwin to 1930* (Wetaskiwin: Wetaskiwin Times Ltd. and Bulletin Commercial Printers Ltd., 1975).

A valuable source on Alberta's oil-rich Indian bands is Dion Resource Consulting Services Ltd., "Indian Lands: Social Impact of Petroleum Activity," Edmonton, 1984.

Among the sources on Indian suicides are the Department of Health and Welfare, *Suicide in Canada* (Report of the Task Force on Suicide in Canada, 1987); J. A. Ward and Joseph Fox, "A Suicide Epidemic on an Indian Reserve," *Canadian Psychiatric Association Journal* (1977) 22; 423-26; and Thomas R. Thompson, "Childhood and Adolescent Suicide in Manitoba: A Demographic Study," *Canadian Journal of Psychiatry* (May 1987) 32: 264-69.

The classic work on suicide is Emile Durkheim, *Suicide: A Study in Sociology* (Toronto: Collier-Macmillan Canada, 1951). It was originally published in 1897 under the title *Le Suicide*.

Chapter 5 — Defence of the North: The Native Economy and Land Claims

The best description of the relationship between hydro dams and native communities is found in James Waldram, *As Long as the Rivers Run* (Winnipeg: University of Manitoba Press, 1988). Another important source is E. E. Hobbs & Associates, "The Grand Rapids Hydro Development and the Devastation of the Cree," Final report, 1986.

Published sources on Wollaston Lake include Miles Goldstick, *Wollaston: People Resisting Genocide* (Montreal: Black Rose Books, 1987); and Damas and Smith Ltd., "Wollaston Lake: Community Planning Study," Toronto, 1981; and Deloitte Haskins and Sells, "Economic Development Strategic Plan," Report for the Visions North Community Futures Committee, Saskatoon, 1988.

Thomas Berger's pipeline report was published under the title *Northern Frontier, Northern Homeland* (Ottawa: Department of Supply and Services, 1977). Another useful source is Hugh Brody, *Maps and Dreams: Indians and the British Columbia Frontier* (Vancouver: Douglas and McIntyre, 1981). See also *Report of the Special Committee on Indian Self-Government in Canada* (Ottawa: Queen's Printer, 1983); Thomas Berger, "Introduction to the Revised Edition," in Thomas Berger, *Northern Frontier, Northern Homeland* (Vancouver: Douglas and McIntyre, 1988); Michael Asch, *Home and Native Land: Aboriginal Rights and the Canadian Constitution* (Toronto: Methuen, 1984).

Sources for other communities include Anastasia Shkilnyk, *A Poison Stronger Than Love: The Destruction of an Ojibwa Community* (New Haven: Yale University Press, 1985); Jacques Frenette, *The History of the Chibougamau Crees* (Chibougamau, Quebec: Cree Indian Centre of Chibougamau, 1985); John Goddard, "Forked Tongues," *Saturday Night*, February 1988, pp. 38-45; and *Globe and Mail*, March 31, 1986, p. A1.

Much of the information on international cases was drawn from the newsletters and publications of the World Council of Indigenous

Peoples, including World Council of Indigenous Peoples, "Transnational Corporations and Their Effect on the Resources and Lands of Indigenous Peoples," paper presented to International Conference on Indigenous Peoples and the Land, September 1981.

Sources on Indian land claims include Donald Purich, *Our Land: Native Rights in Canada* (Toronto: James Lorimer, 1986); James Frideres, *Native People in Canada: Contemporary Conflicts* (Toronto: Prentice-Hall, 1983); and Carolyn Swayze, *Hard Choices: A Life of Tom Berger* (Vancouver: Douglas and McIntyre, 1987).

Chapter 6 — Foreign Justice: Native People and the Law

Submissions to the Manitoba aboriginal justice inquiry and the Donald Marshall inquiry in Nova Scotia were important sources of information for this chapter.

Other sources include Michael Jackson, "Locking Up Natives in Canada: A Report of the Canadian Bar Association Committee on Imprisonment and Release," 1988; Don McCaskill, "Native People and the Justice System," in *As Long as the Sun Shines and Water Flows: A Reader in Canadian Native Studies*, ed. Ian A. L. Getty and Antoine S. Lussier (Vancouver: University of British Columbia, 1983); G. S. Clark and Associates Ltd., *Natives in the Criminal Justice System in New Brunswick* (Ottawa: Department of Justice, 1987); Curt Griffiths et al., *Criminal Justice in Canada* (Toronto: Butterworths, 1980); John Hylton, "The Native Offender in Saskatchewan," *Canadian Journal of Criminology* (1982) 24: 121-31; Paul Havemann et al., *Law and Order for Canada's Indigenous People* (Regina: Prairie Justice Research, University of Regina, 1985); J. Rick Ponting, "Institution-Building in an Indian Community: A Case Study of Kahnawake," in *Arduous Journey: Canadian Indians and Decolonization*, ed. J. Rick Ponting (Toronto: McClelland and Stewart, 1986); James Harding, "Unemployment, Racial Discrimination and Public Drunkenness in Regina," Faculty of Social Work, University of Regina, 1980; *Ottawa Citizen*, April 18, 1989; Judge John Enns, "Report by Provincial Judge on Inquest," May 26, 1988; and *Winnipeg Free Press*, September 18, 1987, p. 1.

The case of Helen Betty Osborne is described in Lisa Priest, *Conspiracy of Silence* (Toronto: McClelland and Stewart, 1989). Racial attitudes in The Pas are described in Heather Robertson, *Reservations are for Indians* (Toronto: James Lorimer, 1970). The classic book on the Donald Marshall case is Michael Harris, *Justice Denied: The Law versus Donald Marshall* (Toronto: Macmillan, 1986).

Chapter 7 — Alkali Lake: Resisting Alcohol

Two of the best descriptions of the history of Alkali Lake are Francis Johnson, "We Made Our Lives Good: The Struggle and the Success of the People of Alkali Lake against Their Alcohol Problem, 1950-86," M. Ed. thesis, University of British Columbia, 1986; and Elizabeth Mary Furniss, "A Sobriety Movement among the Shuswap Indians of Alkali Lake," M.A. thesis, University of British Columbia, 1987.

Among the key sources for the early history of Indian alcohol consumption are Georgia Green Fooks, *Fort Whoop-up* (Lethbridge, Alberta: Historical Society of Alberta, 1983); Peter C. Newman, *Caesars of the Wilderness* (Toronto: Penguin Books, 1987); and R. C. Dailey, "The Role of Alcohol among North American Indian Tribes as Reported in *The Jesuit Relations*," in Mark Nagler, ed., *Perspectives on the North American Indians* (Toronto: McClelland and Stewart, 1972).

Information on current alcohol problems came from *Alcohol and Drug Abuse among Treaty Indians in Saskatchewan* (Regina: Federation of Saskatchewan Indian Nations, 1984; Whitehead Research Consultants, "Assessment of National Needs through Regional Needs Assessment Studies: National Native Alcohol and Drug Abuse Program," London, Ontario, 1985; Lynn Bennion et al., "Alcohol Metabolism in American Indians and Whites," *New England Journal of Medicine* (1976) 294: 9-13; Heather Evans, *O'Chiese Information Package: Guidelines for Community Sobriety* (Edmonton: Nechi Institute, 1987); Maggie Hodgson, *Indian Communities Develop Futuristic Addictions Treatment and Health Approach* (Edmonton: Nechi Institute, 1987); Bob Moore Native Consultants, Report to Manitoba Keewatinowi Okimakanak, 1987; *An Evaluation of the Operations and Funding of the Native Alcoholism Foundation of Manitoba* (Winnipeg: Yellowquill Inc., 1986); Paul Driben and Robert Trudeau, *When Freedom Is Lost: The Dark Side of the Relationship between Government and the Fort Hope Band* (Toronto: University of Toronto Press, 1983); Nancy Wigston, "Nanabush in the City," *Books in Canada* (March 1989), p. 8; Anastasia Shkilnyk, *A Poison Stronger Than Love:*

The Destruction of an Ojibwa Community (New Haven: Yale University Press, 1985); Hugh Brody, *Maps and Dreams: Indians and the British Columbia Frontier* (Vancouver: Douglas and McIntyre, 1981); D. Fenna et al., "Ethanol Metabolism in Various Racial Groups," *Canadian Medical Association Journal* (September 4, 1971) 105: 472-75; Lillian Dyck, "Are North American Indians Biochemically More Susceptible to the Effects of Alcohol?" *Native Studies Review* (1986) 2, no 2: 85-95; *Globe and Mail*, July 4, 1988, p. 8; and "National Native Alcohol and Drug Abuse Program," Discussion Paper (Ottawa, 1982).

Chapter 8 — From Manitoba to Massachusetts: The Lost Generation

The various reports of the Kimelman inquiry (Review Committee on Indian and Métis Adoptions and Placements) from 1983 to 1985 are a major source for this chapter. Other valuable sources are Patrick Johnston, *Native Children and the Child Welfare System* (Ottawa: Canadian Council on Social Development, 1983); reports and records by Dakota Ojibway Child and Family Services and the Manitoba Métis Federation; Manitoba Community Services Department, "Summary of Findings and Recommendations of the Review into the Repatriation of a Fourteen Year Old Girl ('Amy') to a Northern Manitoba Reserve," June 1987; *Winnipeg Free Press*, February 6, 1988; *Globe and Mail*, October 2, 1984, p. 1; National Film Board, *Richard Cardinal: Cry from a Diary of a Métis Child*, 1986; and *Winnipeg Free Press*, March 4, 1982, p. 1, and March 18, 1987, p. 1.

The best description of the Cameron Kerley case is found in Ray Aboud, "A Death in Kansas," *Saturday Night*, April 1986, pp. 28-39. The story of Laurence Boucher is drawn from a National Film Board documentary, *Poundmaker's Lodge: A Healing Place* (1987).

Chapter 9 — The New Militancy

The history of the Peguis reserve was drawn from Albert Edward Thompson, *Chief Peguis and His Descendants* (Winnipeg: Peguis Publishers, 1973); Tyler, Wright and Daniel Ltd., "The Illegal Surrender of St. Peter's Reserve," a report prepared for the Treaty and Aboriginal Rights Research Centre of Manitoba, Winnipeg, 1979; and *Chief Peguis* (Winnipeg: Manitoba Historic Resources Branch, 1982).

Historical information on Indian politics came from Jean Goodwill and Norma Sluman, *John Tootoosis* (Winnipeg: Pemmican Publications, 1984); E. Brian Titley, *A Narrow Vision* (Vancouver: University of British Columbia Press, 1986); Donald Purich, *Our Land: Native Rights in Canada* (Toronto: James Lorimer, 1986); and Ron Bourgeault, "The South African Connection," *Canadian Dimension*, January 1988, pp. 6-10.

Among the sources on contemporary Indian activism are James Frideres, *Native People in Canada: Contemporary Conflicts* (Toronto: Prentice-Hall, 1983); J. Rick Ponting, ed., *Arduous Journey: Canadian Indians and Decolonization* (Toronto: McClelland and Stewart, 1986); Noel Dyck, ed., *Indigenous Peoples and the Nation-State: Fourth World Politics in Canada, Australia and Norway* (St. John's: Memorial University Institute of Social and Economic Research, 1985); John Goddard, "Forked Tongues," *Saturday Night*, February 1988, pp. 38-45; and Alan Saunders, "A Native Perspective: An Interview with Georges Erasmus," *Canadian Business Review*, Summer 1989.

Epilogue: The Fifth Generation

Historical information on the suppression of native culture is drawn from E. Brian Titley, *A Narrow Vision* (Vancouver: University of British Columbia Press, 1986); and Dara Culhane Speck, *An Error in Judgement: The Politics of Medical Care in an Indian-White Community* (Vancouver: Talonbooks, 1987).

Of the many publications on aboriginal rights, one of the best is Michael Asch, *Home and Native Land: Aboriginal Rights and the Canadian Constitution* (Toronto: Methuen, 1984).

Other sources include *Globe and Mail*, April 7, 1989, p. A8; January 13, 1988, p. A9; and March 25, 1987, p. A1; Canadian Press, Moncton, N.B., February 13, 1989; *Inner City Voice*, Winnipeg, June 1988, February 1988, and December 1988; *Western Report*, November 28, 1988, p. 20; and Judge Murray Sinclair, "Speaking Notes for a Speech to the Annual General Assembly of the Native Council of Canada," May 24, 1989.

*

For permission to reprint excerpts in this text, acknowledgement is made as follows:

Durkheim, Emile, *Suicide*, trans. J. Spaulding and G. Simpson, © 1951 by The Free Press, to the publisher.

Johnston, Patrick, *Native Children and the Child Welfare System* (Ottawa, 1983), to the Canadian Council on Social Development.

Nurcombe, B., G.N. Bianchi, J. Money and J.E.Cawte, "A hunger for stimuli: the psychosocial background of petrol inhalation," in *British Journal of Medical Psychology* (1970) 43: 367-74, to the British Psychology Society.

Patterson, Lisa, "Indian Affairs and the Nova Scotia Centralization Policy," unpublished M.A. thesis, Dalhousie University, 1985, to the author.

Poundmaker's Lodge: A Healing Place, directed by Alanis Obomsawin, to the National Film Board of Canada.

The Report of the Mackenzie Valley Pipeline Inquiry (Ottawa, 1977), to the Minister of Supply and Services Canada.